SYSTEMATIC GUIDE
TO
FLOWERING PLANTS OF THE WORLD

SYSTEMATIC
GUIDE TO
FLOWERING
PLANTS
OF THE WORLD

By

S. A. MANNING, F.L.S.

Illustrated by Mina Smith

LONDON
MUSEUM PRESS LIMITED

First published in Great Britain by Museum Press Limited
26 Old Brompton Road, London, S.W.7
1965

Printed in Great Britain by
Butler and Tanner Limited, Frome and London
R.3473

To the memory of my mother
VIOLET MANNING (1898–1962)
who loved plants

Preface

THE author received much help in preparing this book. He is grateful to numerous authors whose works were scanned for facts. He is no less grateful to the Director of the Royal Botanic Gardens, Kew, who kindly allowed him to visit the library, where he was given every assistance by the librarian and his staff.

In recording his gratitude, he must add that any mistakes are his.

S. A. MANNING

Introduction and General Notes

THERE are up to a quarter of a million known species of flowering plants, according to some authorities. Clearly it is not possible to deal in a book of this size with more than a representative cross-section of them. However, there are in this book, arranged systematically under orders and families, details of nearly 400 species, including many that are common in the wild, often grown in parks and gardens, or well-known because they have some economic value.

Information about the species selected is recorded in the form of notes under distinct headings. This may have led to what has been called a "clinical approach," but at least it has enabled more to be included in the limited space.

Many people find flowering plants a source of pleasure, but become confused immediately botanical terms are used. With such readers in mind, botanical jargon has been avoided as far as possible. In places this may have resulted in over-simplification or the neglect of details considered vital by specialists.

Wherever possible, established English or popular names have been included, but some plants appear to be without them. If such omissions do nothing more, they serve to remind us of the great value of describing plants and giving them scientific or Latin names in accordance with the International Code of Botanical Nomenclature, which is generally accepted throughout the world and revised periodically at international congresses.

SPECIES: The species is the basic unit in classification. By a species we mean a group of individual plants which differ from one another in some respects but share in common certain permanent characteristics. Each species has a scientific or Latin name. In most technical works this is followed by the name (or a recognized abbreviation of it) of the botanist who described and named the species.

The scientific name of a species is in two parts. Thus, the meadow buttercup is *Ranunculus acris*. The second word is known as the trivial name or specific epithet. The first word is the generic name, indicating in this case that the species belongs to the genus *Ranunculus*.

GENERA: Each genus (plural, genera) comprises a distinct group of species. It may contain several hundreds of species. For example, in addition to the meadow buttercup, the genus *Ranunculus* includes the creeping buttercup, *Ranunculus repens*, the bulbous buttercup, *Ranunculus bulbosus*, and about 300 other species, each with the generic name *Ranunculus*.

Many genera consist of single species which do not closely resemble

the members of other such groups and therefore cannot be accommo-
dated in them.

FAMILIES: Genera that appear to be related to one another are grouped
into families. The genus *Ranunculus* belongs to the family *Ranunculaceae* whose popular name is the Buttercup Family. Among other
members of this family are the genera *Anemone* and *Clematis*, each of
which includes beautiful species familiar to gardeners.

ORDERS: Related families are grouped together to form larger units
called orders. The family *Ranunculaceae* is placed in the order *Ranales*
together with *Paeoniaceae* (Paeony Family), *Helleboraceae* (Hellebore
Family), *Nymphaeaceae* (Water-Lily Family) and three families not
represented in this book.

LARGER UNITS: As will be evident from the following pages, orders
in their turn may be grouped into even bigger units.

ARRANGEMENT OF THIS BOOK: The sequence of orders and families in
this book is based on that proposed by the distinguished Kew botanist
Dr. John Hutchinson, F.R.S., who enumerates 111 orders and 411
families in his *The Families of Flowering Plants* (Oxford University
Press, 2 volumes, second edition, 1959).

In this *Guide* there are details of plants belonging to 106 of these
orders and to 191 of the families. Included in appropriate places are
short notes on five orders not represented by species.

Readers who need detailed information on the general characters of
orders and families are referred to Dr. Hutchinson's lucid and readable
work. To discover facts about individual species belonging to families
excluded from the present book it will be necessary to consult various
botanical books and papers.

PHYLOGENETIC CLASSIFICATION: Dr. Hutchinson's system of classification is a phylogenetic one, families being arranged according to their
probable phylogeny or evolutionary history. In each of the two divi-
sions of the Dicotyledons and also in the Monocotyledons the most
primitive families are placed first and the most advanced last. Thus the
Division *Lignosae* of the Dicotyledons begins with the primitive *Mag-
noliaceae* whose sepals, petals and numerous carpels and stamens are free
or separate to their bases. In the more advanced *Verbenales*, with which
the Division *Lignosae* ends, flowers have united sepals, united petals,
carpels joined to form single ovaries, and few stamens.

A WORD OF WARNING: One must always remember that systems of
plant classification cannot remain static. Changes must be expected
when the discovery of fresh facts makes them necessary. Also it is important to remember that these systems are man-made and that
taxonomists (classifiers) are blessed with varying degrees of know-
ledge, skill and experience. What one man may regard as one species
another may split into two or more species, and so on.

ON USING THIS BOOK: This book provides the student of botany with a cross-section of the world's flowering plants. Many of the species included as examples were selected because of their economic value. Others that were chosen are common in the wild or in gardens in parts of the world where this book is likely to be used. Most students should, therefore, be able to secure specimens of many of the plants mentioned here.

These specimens should be thoroughly examined for characters listed in this book and other features of interest that may have been omitted here through lack of space. Plants of different families and genera should be compared in detail, notes and drawings being made to illustrate both the resemblances and distinctions that are observed. No expensive and elaborate equipment will be needed. Much can be done with the help of an ordinary hand-lens, a sharp razor-blade or penknife, and a darning needle or a needle mounted in a wooden handle.

Having made a careful examination of any plant which is treated in detail here, the student should note its position in the classification list that follows these introductory notes. The names of many genera which are not represented by species in this book have been added to the classification list to give students a rather wider view of flowering plants. With the help of the index, one can, for example, discover the position in the classification list of such familiar garden plants as Geum, Erica, Delphinium and Anemone. For these or any other plants that interest him, the student can make his own notes on similar lines to those adopted here.

The simple diagrams and glossary at the end of this book may prove useful to those who have had no special botanical training. Such readers who use this book to help themselves to learn something more of flowering plants and their classification will not regret the effort involved. For once one becomes interested in plants, it is difficult not to remain fascinated by their remarkable diversity.

CLASSIFICATION

(Names of genera are followed by the scientific names of species mentioned in the text.)

Helianthus (*Helianthus annuus*), Rudbeckia (*Rudbeckia hirta*), Dahlia, Coreopsis, Cosmos, Zinnia, Tagetes, Gaillardia, Tussilago, Petasites, Doronicum, Senecio (*Senecio jacobaea*), Calendula, Filago, Inula, Solidago (*Solidago canadensis*), Aster (*Aster novae-angliae*), Erigeron, Bellis, Achillea, Artemisia, Gazania, Chrysanthemum, Arctium, Carduus, Cirsium, Centaurea, Cichorium (*Cichorium intybus*), Tragopogon, Lactuca (*Lactuca virosa*), Sonchus, Hieracium (*Hieracium pilosella*), Taraxacum (*Taraxacum officinale*), etc.

Atropa (*Atropa bella-donna*), Solanum (*Solanum nigrum, S. tuberosum, S. melongena*), Capsicum (*Capsicum frutescens*), Lycopersicum (*Lycopersicum esculentum*), Hyoscyamus (*Hyoscyamus niger*), Nicotiana, Petunia, Schizanthus, etc.

Convolvulus (*Convolvulus arvensis*), Calystegia (*Calystegia soldanella*), Ipomoea (*Ipomoea batatas*), etc.

Verbascum (*Verbascum thapsus*), Antirrhinum, Linaria (*Linaria vulgaris*), Scrophularia (*Scrophularia nodosa*), Mimulus, Digitalis (*Digitalis purpurea*), Pentstemon (*Pentstemon digitalis*), Veronica, Calceolaria, Nemesia, etc.

Orobanche (*Orobanche rapum-genistae, O. californica, O. ludoviciana, O. tuberosa*), Lathraea, etc.

Pinguicula (*Pinguicula vulgaris*), Utricularia, etc.

Geranium (*Geranium robertianum*), Erodium (*Erodium moschatum, E. cicutarium*), Pelargonium (*Pelargonium myrrhifolium, P. graveolens, P. odoratissimum, P. capitatum, P. roseum*), etc.

Oxalis (*Oxalis acetosella*), etc.

Tropaeolum (*Tropaeolum majus*).

Impatiens (*Impatiens capensis*), etc.

Phlox (*Phlox divaricata*), Gilia (*Gilia aggregata*), Polemonium, etc.

Phylum ANGIOSPERMAE

Seed-bearing plants with ovules enclosed in ovary. Transference of pollen-grains from stamen to stigma mainly by insects. Fertilization effected by means of pollen-tubes growing down to ovules.

Subphylum DICOTYLEDONES

Embryo with 2 seed-leaves (cotyledons). Leaves usually net-veined (rarely parallel-veined). Vascular bundles of stem usually arranged in a ring. Flowers with parts usually in fives or fours.

Division LIGNOSAE

Woody plants and herbs derived from woody ancestors.

Order MAGNOLIALES

Family *MAGNOLIACEAE*

SOUTHERN MAGNOLIA (*Magnolia grandiflora*)

General characters: Evergreen tree up to 80′ high. Leaves alternate, egg-shaped, up to 10″ long, leathery, glossy. Stipules soon falling. Flowers creamy white, fragrant, up to 10″ across, solitary at ends of branches. Sepals 3, petal-like, free. Petals thick, concave, 4–5″ long, free. Stamens numerous, free. Carpels free, spirally arranged, 1-celled with 2 ovules in each.

Habitat: Coastal sand-dunes, sandy bottoms.

Pollination: By insects.

Fruit: Each carpel becomes a 1–2-seeded pod which splits to release red seeds that dangle on long threads for a time.

Seeds: Large. With copious endosperm. Embryo minute.

Vegetative reproduction: Propagated by layering.

Range: S.E. U.S.A. Cultivated in Europe.

Uses: Timber used for Venetian blinds, panelling, wood wool, cores for veneering. Bark used medicinally as stimulant tonic and diaphoretic. Flowers are useful source of nectar for honey bees in U.S.A.

Special comments: The State Flower of both Mississippi and Louisiana.

Southern Magnolia (*Magnolia grandiflora*)

Poor Man's Banana (*Asimina triloba*)

Order ANNONALES

Family *ANNONACEAE*

Poor Man's Banana (*Asimina triloba*)

General characters: Deciduous shrub or small tree up to 30' high. Leaves alternate, reverse-egg-shaped, up to 1' long, glossy. Flowers dark purplish-brown, nodding, solitary on short thick stalks. Sepals 3. Petals 6, in 2 sets. Stamens numerous. Carpels 3–15. Ovules numerous, in 2 rows.

Habitat: Alluvial soil along streams.

Fruit: A berry. Large (to 5" long), pulpy, bottle-shaped. Edible, but contains many seeds. Known as papaw or pawpaw in U.S.A., but must not be confused with tropical papaw (*Carica papaya*).

Seeds: Large, flat. Endosperm copious, wrinkled. Embryo minute.

Vegetative reproduction: By suckers from roots. Difficult to graft. Cuttings root only with great care.

Range: Eastern N. America.

Uses: Edible fruit. Inner bark from branches used by fishermen to string fish.

Special comments: Specimens have reached 100 years. Some have borne fruit for at least 60 years.

Order LAURALES

Family *LAURACEAE*

Avocado Pear (*Persea americana*)

General characters: Evergreen tree up to 100' high. Bark thick, fleshy. Leaves alternate, leathery, broadly egg-shaped to almost lance-shaped, pointed. Flowers small, greenish-yellow, numerous, in compact groups at ends of younger branches. Perianth segments 6. Stamens 9, free. Ovary of 1 carpel, 1-celled, with 1 ovule.

Habitat: Native to rain forests, but now cultivated throughout tropics.

Pollination: Cross-pollination by bees. Most cultivated varieties appear to be self-fertile.

Fruit: A berry. 1-seeded. Different varieties show wide range in shape (rounded, egg-shaped, pear-shaped) and colour (yellowish, green, reddish, dark purple). Skin thin or thick and tough. Flesh light-coloured, rich in protein, oil (5–25%), minerals (including calcium, phosphorus, iron) and vitamins (9, including A, B_1, B_2, C, E). Low in

carbohydrates, but 93% of oil entirely digestible. Fruit eaten raw. Flavour rich, buttery, somewhat nut-like.

Seeds: Large, oval-shaped. Seed-coat thin. Without endosperm. Cotyledons thick, fleshy. Source of non-drying pleasant-flavoured oil used in cosmetics and as salad dressing. Said to be dispersed by terrestrial mammals (cats and jaguars fond of fruits).

Vegetative reproduction: Propagated by budding or grafting. Mexican varieties used as hardy rootstocks for better types.

Range: Originated Mexico and Central America. Grown throughout tropics. Of economic importance in California and Florida (limited areas), Brazil, S. Africa, Hawaii, tropical Australia.

Uses: Fruit (meat substitute in Mexico and Central America). Avocado oil.

Special comments: Numerous varieties (mostly of recent development) cultivated. Varieties grouped·into 3 races: Mexican (fruits thin-skinned, small), West Indian (fruits with leathery skin, less hardy than others), and Guatemalan (fruits with thick woody skin). Various hybrids produced between races.

Order **DILLENIALES**

Family *DILLENIACEAE*

HONDA-PARA (SINHALESE) (*Dillenia indica*)

General characters: Round-headed tree up to 25' high. Bark papery, cinnamon brown. Leaves alternate, oblong-lance-shaped, 10–12" long, pointed, margins toothed, with stout stalk. Flowers white, 6–7" across, on stout stalks. Sepals 5, thick, fleshy, persistent, becoming enlarged and enclosing ripe carpels. Petals 5, rounded. Stamens very numerous, persistent. Carpels free, 15–20. Ovules numerous. Styles white, spreading.

Habitat: Low country by stream sides. Planted in gardens.

Fruit: Fruiting carpels enclosed in thick persistent sepals, forming a large green apple-like "fruit" 5–6" across.

Seeds: Numerous. Flattened, with hairy margin. With copious fleshy endosperm. Dispersed by elephants, which eat the fruit, and by water.

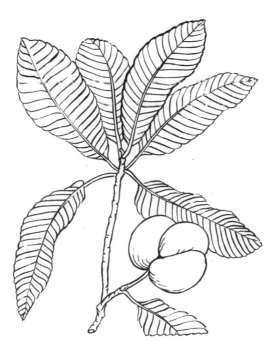

Range: India. Ceylon. Malay Peninsula and Islands.

Uses: Timber used for window frames, gun stocks, beams. Fruit used as soap (gives lather with water).

Order **CORIARIALES**

Family *CORIARIACEAE*

REDOUL (*Coriaria myrtifolia*)

General characters: Deciduous shrub 4–6′ high. Stems erect, 4-angled. Leaves opposite, egg-shaped, 1–2½″ long, pointed, glaucous green. Flowers small, greenish, in short racemes. Sepals 5. Petals 5, persistent, becoming thick, juicy, black and shining and enclosing the fruit. Stamens 10, free. Carpels 5, free. Ovule solitary in carpel.

Habitat: Open places. Often colonizes waste land.

Fruit: A pseudo-drupe. Eaten by blackbirds in Italy.

Seeds: Flattened. With thin endosperm.

Vegetative reproduction: Propagated by cuttings.

Range: Mediterranean region. Cultivated in Europe.

Uses: Bark and leaves used for tanning. Leaves yield black dye and are used for making ink.

Special comments: Leaves and fruits poisonous, affecting people and various animals (including goats).

Order **ROSALES**

Family *ROSACEAE*

European Red Raspberry (*Rubus idaeus*)

General characters: Deciduous prickly shrub. Stems ("canes") woody, 3–5' high, flowering and fruiting the second season. Leaves alternate, pinnate with 3–5 leaflets, with soft felt of white hairs beneath. Stipules thread-like, 2 attached to leaf-stalk. Flowers small, white, drooping, normally bisexual. Sepals 5. Petals 5. Stamens numerous. Carpels free, numerous, 2 ovules in each.

Habitat: Woods, heaths, railway embankments. Thrives where fires have been. Several forms in cultivation.

Pollination: Cross-pollination by insects. Self-pollination also occurs.

Fruit: An aggregate of numerous 1-seeded druplets. Red or amber. Juicy when ripe. Honey bees puncture skin and collect juice. Remains of fruit found in debris of Swiss lake dwellings.

Seeds: Without endosperm. Small, pitted. Dispersed by birds that eat fruit. Seeds from jam that had been boiled germinated in moist soil.

Vegetative reproduction: By root suckers.

Range: Europe (including Britain). Asia.

Uses: Fruit eaten raw. Also used in jams, pastries, beverages. Dried leaves used medicinally (contain fragarine, which acts on pelvic muscles of mother, making childbirth easier). Source of pollen and nectar to bees (high-quality honey).

Special comments: Forma *obtusifolius* is sex variant with unisexual male flowers. Its sepals and leaflets are blunt. Female and neuter variants also known.

N. American Raspberries

Several N. American species of *Rubus* are known as raspberries. American Red Raspberry (*Rubus strigosus*) closely related to European Red Raspberry and regarded as variety of it by some botanists. Grown for fruit in U.S.A. and Canada. Purple Flowering Raspberry (*Rubus odoratus*), native of eastern N. America, has almost inedible fruit, but is cultivated for large and beautiful rose-purple flowers.

Silverweed (*Potentilla anserina*)

General characters: Perennial herb. Silky and silvery-white all over. Leaves spreading horizontally from base of stem, pinnate, 7–12 pairs main leaflets alternating with smaller pairs of leaflets. Flowers yellow, solitary on long slender stems from rootstock or leaf-axils of runners. Petals 5. Sepals 5. Epicalyx of 5 bracts. Stamens about 20. Carpels numerous.

Habitat: Damp places, meadows, roadsides, dunes, waste places.

Pollination: Cross-pollination by insects. Self-pollination may occur when flowers close at night or in dull weather.

Fruit: Dry. Consists of 12–50 achenes inserted on receptacle.

Seeds: Average weight of achene: 0·0008 gm. Dispersed in mud, by rain-wash, rivers (achenes said to float for 15 months) and geese (which are fond of plant).

Vegetative reproduction: By long runners that root. 10 runners on some plants. Runner may grow 3′ a year.

Range: Europe (including Britain). N. & S. America. Asia. Australia. New Zealand.

Uses: Sometimes visited by bees for nectar. Source of Herba Anserinae (used for various complaints). Once grown for edible roots.

DOG ROSE (*Rosa canina*)

General characters: Prickly shrub, 3–9'. Stems arching. Leaves pinnate (2–3 pairs leaflets) with large 2-lobed stipule joined to stalk. Flowers often in clusters of 3, sweet-scented, 1½–2" across. Petals 5, pink or white. Sepals 5, falling before fruit ripens. Stamens numerous. Carpels numerous, 1 ovule in each.

Habitat: Woods, hedgerows, thickets. Occasionally in tops of pollard willows.

Pollination: Cross-pollination by insects or self-pollination.

Fruit: Of many hairy achenes enclosed in smooth red fleshy receptacle (known as "hip").

Seeds: Average weight of achene: 0·017 gm. Dispersed by birds.

Range: Europe (including Britain). N. America. Asia. N. Africa.

Uses: Rose-hips rich in vitamin C and used to make anti-scorbutic syrup. N. American growers recommend cultivation of *Rosa rugosa* whose large succulent hips contain high percentage of natural ascorbic acid (sometimes 25 times vitamin C content of citrus juices).

Special comments: A very variable species. Many varieties and forms described.

Order **LEGUMINALES**

Family *MIMOSACEAE*

AUSTRALIAN BLACKWOOD (*Acacia melanoxylon*)

General characters: Evergreen tree up to 80' high. Leaves 5–6" long, reduced to reverse-lance-shaped phyllodes (leaf-like stalks) with 3–5 longitudinal veins. Flowers small, pale yellow, fragrant, in 30–50-flowered globular heads about ½" across. Calyx tubular, 5-toothed. Petals 5, united into a tube. Stamens numerous, free, short. Ovary superior, 1-celled.

Habitat: Moist forest areas and ravines.

Fruit: A many-seeded oblong flat pod which is twisted or waved, narrow, 3–5" long.

Seeds: Black. Without endosperm.

Range: Australia. S. Africa.

Uses: Timber used for furniture, gun stocks, railway carriages, high-class joinery, cabinet work, panelling.

Family *PAPILIONACEAE*

TREE LUPIN (*Lupinus arboreus*)

General characters: Shrub up to 10' high. Leaves alternate, long-stalked, of 7–11 reverse-lance-shaped leaflets palmately arranged.

Stipules narrow, 2 at base of leaf-stalk. Flowers papilionate (butterfly-like), yellow or white (sometimes with bluish tinge), in showy racemes at top of shoots, fragrant. Calyx deeply 2-lipped. Petals 5, consisting of standard (encloses other petals in bud), 2 lateral petals or wings and 2 lower petals (keel). Stamens 10, all united. Ovary of 1 carpel.

Habitat: Dryish sandy places. Waste places.

Pollination: By insects.

Fruit: A hairy flattened 8–12-seeded pod opening on both sides (legume), the 2 valves separating and twisting spirally so that seeds are expelled.

Seeds: Without endosperm.

Vegetative reproduction: Propagated by cuttings.

Range: Native of California. Cultivated in Europe.

Uses: No information (certain other lupins grown and ploughed in as green manure, soil being enriched by nitrates produced by nitrogen-fixing bacteria living in swellings upon roots).

Special comments: At least 300 species of lupins (lupines in U.S.A.), most N. American natives. Blue-flowered *Lupinus havardii*, Bluebonnet, State Flower of Texas, often covers acres of prairie country.

White Clover (*Trifolium repens*)

General characters: Creeping perennial herb. Stems spreading, rooting at nodes. Leaves long-stalked, of 3 rounded leaflets. Stipules joined to leaf-stalk, oblong, with short points. Flowers papilionate, white or pinkish, in long-stalked globular heads. Calyx tubular, 5-lobed. Petals 5 (standard, 2 wings, 2 keel-petals). Stamens 10, 1 free, 9 united in sheath. Ovary of 1 carpel.

Habitat: Pastures. Grassy places. Likes clayey soils.

Pollination: Cross-pollination by bees.

Fruit: A small 3–6-seeded pod.

Seeds: Globose. Average weight: 0·000642 gm. Natural dormancy shown by 5–15% (sometimes more) of seeds. Some of these "hard" seeds may remain dormant for more than 20 years. Dispersed by wind, birds (attached to feet and plumage), such mammals as horse, cow, yak and deer (seeds passing through them in excreta).

Vegetative reproduction: By prostrate rooting stems.

Range: Europe (including Britain). Asia. N. Africa. Introduced in various parts of Old and New World.

Uses: An important pasture plant and hay crop. A valuable bee plant, white clover honey being the honey *par excellence*. Plant even thrives on industrial slag heaps, enabling good quality honey to be produced there.

Special comments: Many improved strains or varieties cultivated. Will overspread and kill certain tufted plants.

Purple Milk Vetch (*Astragalus danicus*)

General characters: Low slender perennial herb. Leaves alternate, pinnate with up to 15 pairs small leaflets and odd end leaflet. Stipules large, joined in lower half. Flowers papilionate, bluish-purple, in long-stalked racemes from leaf-axils. Calyx tubular, 5-toothed, covered with white and blackish hairs. Petals 5 (standard, 2 wings, 2 keel-petals). Stamens 10, 1 free, 9 united in sheath. Ovary of 1 carpel.

Habitat: Short turf on chalky soils. Coastal sand-dunes.

Pollination: Cross-pollination by bees.

Fruit: Small 2-valved hairy pod containing 2–7 seeds.

Seeds: Smooth, kidney-shaped.

Range: Europe (including Britain). N. America.

Uses: No information.

Special comments: Several American species of *Astragalus* known as Loco-weed. Some accumulate Selenium from soil to level toxic to livestock.

TUFTED VETCH (*Vicia cracca*)

General characters: Scrambling perennial herb. Stems annual, slender, sometimes 5′ high or more. Leaves pinnate, with 6–12 pairs narrow leaflets, common leaf-stalk ending in branched tendril. Stipules small, pointed. Flowers papilionate, bluish-purple, drooping, in crowded 1-sided racemes on long stalks from leaf-axils. Calyx shortly tubular, 5-toothed. Petals 5 (standard, 2 wings, 2 keel-petals). Stamens 10, 1 free, 9 united in sheath. Ovary of 1 carpel.

Habitat: Hedges and grassy places.

Pollination: Cross-pollination by bees.

Fruit: A flat smooth pod, $\frac{1}{2}$–1″ long, opening in 2 valves, containing 2–6 seeds.

Seeds: Dark brown. Weight: 0·012–0·015 gm.

Range: Europe (including Britain). N. America. Asia.

Uses: Sometimes grown as hay crop and fodder for cattle. (Cobalt, element important in rumen digestion, may reach 24 parts per million of dry weight of Tufted Vetch. Only about 0·15 p.p.m. in fodder grasses.)

Order **CUNONIALES**
Family *PHILADELPHACEAE*
MOCK ORANGE (*Philadelphus coronarius*)

General characters: Deciduous shrub 8–10′ high. Buds closely protected by leaf-bases. Leaves egg-shaped, 2–4″ long, margins with distant teeth. Flowers creamy white, very fragrant, 1–1½″ across, in racemes at ends of branches. Calyx-tube united to ovary, 4-lobed. Petals 4, contorted in bud. Stamens numerous. Ovary inferior, usually 4-celled. Ovules numerous (placentation axile).

Habitat: Sunny places, often on poor soils.

Pollination: By insects.

Fruit: A dry 4-celled capsule with numerous seeds.

Seeds: Small. With copious fleshy endosperm.

Vegetative reproduction: Propagated by cuttings.

Range: Native of S.E. Europe. Planted in Britain and N. America and sometimes escaping from gardens.

Uses: A strong-growing garden shrub. Gives a good display even on poor soils.

Special comments: A cultivated form has young leaves bright yellow (becoming greenish-yellow).

Family *GROSSULARIACEAE*

BLACK CURRANT (*Ribes nigrum*)

General characters: Deciduous shrub up to 6′ high. Leaves alternate, 3–5-lobed, dotted with brownish glands, strongly scented. Flowers small, bell-shaped, in nodding 5–10-flowered racemes on young wood. Calyx-tube united to ovary, 4–5-lobed. Petals 4–5, whitish, much shorter than sepals. Stamens 4–5. Ovary inferior, 1-celled. Ovules numerous (placentation parietal).

Habitat: Woods, hedges, boggy thickets. Sometimes in tops of pollard willows.

Pollination: Cross-pollination by bees, but often self-pollinated.

Fruit: A black globose juicy berry. Rich in vitamin C.

Seeds: With copious fleshy endosperm. Dispersed by birds.

Vegetative reproduction: Usually propagated from cuttings.

Range: Europe (including Britain). Asia.

Uses: A good bee plant, yielding nectar and pollen fairly early in season (honey bees will even open older flower buds with their jaws). Cultivated varieties grown for fruit which are eaten raw, bottled, made into jam, a liqueur called Cassis, and syrup. Dried leaves sometimes added to Indian tea.

Special comments: Black currant is alternate host to white pine blister rust. American states where white pine important prohibit planting of black currants. U.S. Dept. of Agriculture discourages planting anywhere in country, even where not unlawful.

Order **STYRACALES**

Family *STYRACACEAE*

Snowdrop Tree (*Halesia carolina*)

General characters: Deciduous tree up to 45' high. Leaves alternate, egg-shaped, pointed, minutely and distantly toothed, 2–6″ long, downy beneath with star-shaped hairs. Flowers white, bell-shaped, drooping in clusters. Calyx-tube united to ovary, 4–5-toothed. Petals 4–5, partially united. Stamens 8–10. Ovary inferior, 4-celled, with about 4 ovules in each cavity (placentation axile).

Habitat: In woods and along streams.

Pollination: By insects.

Fruit: Dry, pear-shaped, 4-winged longitudinally, tipped with style and minute calyx-teeth. Floats for about 4 days. Mainly wind-dispersed.

Seeds: With copious endosperm.
Vegetative reproduction: Propagated by layering.
Range: S.E. United States. Cultivated in Europe.
Uses: A beautiful garden subject in spring. Flowers worked by honey bees.

Order **ARALIALES**

Family *CORNACEAE*

RED-OSIER DOGWOOD (*Cornus stolonifera*)

General characters: Deciduous shrub up to 15′ high. Bark of young shoots bright reddish-purple. Leaves opposite, egg-shaped or oval, pointed, 1–5″ long, on slender stalks. Flowers small, white, in flat-topped cymes 1–2″ across. Calyx-tube minutely 4-toothed. Petals 4, free. Stamens 4. Ovary inferior, 2-celled, with 1 ovule in each cell.
Habitat: Moist soil along streams and in swamps.
Pollination: Cross-pollination by insects.
Fruit: A white or whitish globose drupe containing a 2-celled 2-seeded stone.
Seeds: With endosperm.

Vegetative reproduction: By suckering from prostrate and under-ground stems.

Range: Eastern N. America. Cultivated in Europe.

Uses: Inner bark used by American Indians for smoking. *Cornus stolonifera* var. *flaviramea* cultivated for beauty of yellow shoots in winter.

Special comments: Also called *Thelycrania sericea* in some Floras.

Family *ARALIACEAE*

Ivy (*Hedera helix*)

General characters: Evergreen woody climber, climbing to tops of trees and buildings or creeping along ground. Stems with adhesive roots, becoming thick. Leaves alternate, smooth, leathery, stalked. Leaves of creeping and climbing stems with 3–5 triangular lobes, but those of flowering branches less lobed or without lobes. Flowers small, yellowish-green, in subglobose umbels, appearing only on shoots in sun. Calyx short, with 5 small teeth. Petals 5, free. Stamens 5, free. Ovary inferior, 5-celled, 1 ovule in each cell.

Habitat: Woods, hedges, walls, tops of pollard willows. Thrives in shady places.

Pollination: Cross-pollination by flies and wasps. Self-pollination believed to be ineffective.

Fruit: A smooth black berry-like drupe containing 2–5 seeds. Eaten by blackbirds, thrushes, wood pigeons and blackcaps.

Seeds: With abundant endosperm. Embryo small. Average weight: 0·0259 gm. Dispersed by birds.

Range: Europe (including Britain). Asia Minor.

Uses: Flowers last important source of nectar (very concentrated) and pollen to bees (September). Wood can be substituted for Box-wood in engraving. Many varieties of Ivy grown for attractive foliage.

Special comments: Not, as commonly believed, a parasite. Adhesive roots ("suckers") merely assist plant in climbing. Can affect trees (as when branches break under its weight). Walls sometimes damaged by Ivy roots and stems. Has remarkable compressing power which has caused damage to leaden water-pipes and newly developed secondary tissues of trees.

Family *CAPRIFOLIACEAE*

GUELDER ROSE (*Viburnum opulus*)

General characters: Deciduous shrub or very small tree, 6–15′ high. Leaves opposite, divided into 3 (rarely 5) toothed and pointed lobes. Stipules awl-shaped. Flowers white, fragrant, in clusters up to 3″

across. Inner flowers of cluster fertile. Outer ones larger but sterile. Calyx united to ovary, minutely 5-toothed. Corolla funnel-shaped, 5-lobed. Stamens 5, inserted on corolla-tube. Ovary inferior, 1-celled, with 1 ovule.

Habitat: Woods, hedges, often in damp places. Sometimes in tops of pollard willows (seeds probably taken there by birds).

Pollination: Self-pollination or cross-pollination by bees and other insects.

Fruit: A small 1-seeded subglobose red drupe.

Seeds: Seed-coat bony. Average weight ("stones"): 0·046 gm. With fleshy endosperm.

Vegetative reproduction: Propagated by cuttings.

Range: Europe (including Britain). N. America. Algeria. Asia.

Uses: Fruit recommended as substitute for cranberries (hence American name "Cranberry Tree"). Dried bark used medicinally (antispasmodic). Cultivated for beauty of flowers, fruit and rich crimson autumn leaf colour.

Special comments: "Snowball Tree," form of Guelder Rose with all flowers sterile (var. *roseum*), is well-known garden shrub.

HONEYSUCKLE (*Lonicera periclymenum*)

General characters: Deciduous climbing shrub reaching 20′. Sometimes trails over low hedges. Leaves opposite, egg-shaped. Flowers

fragrant, in heads at end of shoots. Newly opened flowers white within, but becoming yellow after pollination and later a darker brownish colour. Calyx joined to ovary, 5-toothed, glandular. Corolla tubular (tube long), 2-lipped, upper lip 4-lobed, lower of 1 lobe. Stamens 5, inserted on corolla-tube. Ovary inferior, 2-celled. Ovules numerous, axile.

Habitat: Woods, hedges, thickets.

Pollination: Cross-pollination by hawk-moths and other insects.

Fruit: A red globose berry. Fruit in crowded clusters.

Seeds: Average weight: 0·004536 gm. Dispersed by birds which eat fruits. Accelerated germination after passing through birds (Kerner's experiments).

Range: Europe (including Britain). Morocco.

Uses: See *Special comments.*

Special comments: Sometimes damages stems of young trees, encircling and constricting them and causing corkscrew-like contortions. Ornamental walking-sticks made from these curious stems.

Order **HAMAMELIDALES**

Family *HAMAMELIDACEAE*

WITCH HAZEL (*Hamamelis virginiana*)

General characters: Deciduous shrub or small tree up to 25′ high. Leaves alternate, reverse-egg-shaped or broadly oval, unequal-sided and slightly heart-shaped at base, coarsely round-toothed, 2–5″ long, with star-shaped hairs on both sides (at least on young leaves). Flowers bright yellow, clustered in leaf-axils, appearing in late summer or autumn when leaves are falling. Calyx 4-parted. Petals 4, strap-shaped. Stamens 4. Ovary 2-celled, 1 ovule in each cell.

Habitat: Moist woods and along streams.

Fruit: A beaked woody 2-celled capsule. Eventually bursts elastically.

Seeds: Large, oblong, with shiny seed-coat. With thin fleshy endosperm. As fruit dries seeds are shot out "with great violence" to distance of 4–17′ (one botanist records 40′).

Vegetative reproduction: Propagated by layering. Sometimes by rooted suckers.

Range: Eastern N. America. Cultivated in Europe.

Uses: Bark and leaves used medicinally.

Family *PLATANACEAE*

BUTTON-WOOD OR PLANE-TREE (*Platanus occidentalis*)

General characters: Large deciduous tree up to 130′ high. Outer bark peeling off in large thin flakes. Leaves alternate, almost circular in outline or wider than long, 4–9″ across, palmately 3–5-lobed, with lobes usually sharply toothed. Base of leaf-stalks hollowed, enclosing buds. Stipules thin, dry, soon falling. Flowers green, very small, in dense globular heads, unisexual but both sexes on same tree. Male heads with numerous anthers. Female heads with numerous carpels. Ovary narrow, 1-celled, with ovule solitary (rarely 2).

Habitat: Along streams and in wet woods.

Pollination: Wind-pollination.

Fruit: Fruiting head of numerous narrow 1-seeded nutlets with long hairs at base. Heads long-stalked, about 1″ across, usually solitary, hanging on tree during winter, nutlets eventually being dispersed by wind.

Seeds: With thin endosperm.

Range: N. America (where often called Sycamore, name reserved for *Acer pseudoplatanus* in Europe).

Uses: Wood used for boxes, crates, furniture, butcher's blocks (hard, difficult to split, weight about 35 lb. per cu. ft.).

ORIENTAL PLANE (*Platanus orientalis*)

Also called Lacewood. Native of Near East. Leaves deeply lobed, lobes longer than broad. One fruiting head at end each stalk. Wood hard, tough, used for wood pulp and inlay work.

LONDON PLANE (*Platanus* × *hybrida*)

Hybrid between *P. occidentalis* and *P. orientalis*, London Plane originated about 1700. Leaves shallowly lobed, lobes being coarsely toothed

and longer than broad. Usually several fruiting heads on one stalk. Hardy and thrives under London's smoke conditions, leaves remaining fresh green during summer.

Order **SALICALES**

Family *SALICACEAE*

WHITE WILLOW (*Salix alba*)

General characters: Deciduous tree up to 90′ high. Branches ascending, forming narrow crown. Bark greyish, deeply fissured, not peeling readily. Young twigs silky, but older ones smooth. Leaves alternate,

lance-shaped, 2–4" long, finely toothed, white silky hairs pressed close to both surfaces. Stipules small, soon falling. Flowers small, appearing with leaves, without perianth, grouped in catkins, unisexual (sexes on different trees). Male flower with 2 nectaries and 2 stamens in axil of yellowish scale. Female flower with 1 nectary and 1-celled ovary (ovules numerous) in axil of scale.

Habitat: Along rivers and streams, marshes, damp woods.

Pollination: By insects.

Fruit: A conical capsule opening in 2 valves.

Seeds: Without endosperm. Minute, with tuft of long white silky hairs. Dispersed by wind and water. Fruiting catkins often float down rivers before capsules open, seeds being distributed when they drift on mud, dry out and capsules open. Seeds of some Willows can germinate only within one week of being shed.

Vegetative reproduction: Branches and twigs break off, fall on damp ground and readily root. Stems used as posts or pea-sticks will root (hence saying "As easy to strike as a Willow").

Range: Europe (including Britain). N. America. Asia. N. Africa.

Uses: Visited by honey bees for nectar and pollen. Bark contains tannin and salicylates, used medicinally and for tanning. Twigs used for basketry and garden furniture. Timber yields high-class medicinal charcoal. Best cricket bats made from wood of Cricket-bat Willow (*Salix coerulea*), treated by some botanists as variety of *Salix alba*.

Special comments: Willows hybridize very readily.

Order **LEITNERIALES**

Family *LEITNERIACEAE*

CORKWOOD (*Leitneria floridana*)

General characters: Deciduous shrub or small tree up to 20' high. Bark smooth, grey. Leaves alternate, egg- or lance-shaped, apex pointed or rounded, bright green, firm, 3–6" long. Flowers small, unisexual, sexes on different plants, in erect catkin-like spikes. Male flower without perianth, of 3–12 stamens inserted on a bract. Female flower in a bract, with small perianth whose parts are joined at base, superior 1-celled ovary and 1 ovule.

Habitat: In swamps.

Fruit: A flattened oblong drupe.

Seeds: With thin fleshy endosperm.

Range: S.E. United States.

Uses: Wood used for floats of fishing nets (soft, very light, $12\frac{1}{2}$ lb. per cu. ft.).

Order **MYRICALES**
Family *MYRICACEAE*
SWEET GALE (*Myrica gale*)

General characters: Deciduous shrub, usually 2–3′ high. Stems reddish-brown to purplish, with scattered yellowish glands. Leaves alternate, 1–2″ long, inversely lance-shaped, produced after flowering, grey-green, dotted with resinous glands and aromatic when bruised. Flowers small, in catkin-like spikes, sexes usually on separate plants (which may change sex from year to year). Male flower of a bract and about 4 stamens. Female flower of a bract, 2 small bracteoles and a 1-celled ovary with 1 ovule.

Habitat: Boggy acid soils: bogs, wet heaths, fens.

Pollination: Wind-pollinated.

Fruit: A very small dry 1-seeded nut. Gland-dotted. Enclosed in 2 floral scales. Floats for 14–15 months. Dispersed by wind and water.

Seeds: Without endosperm.

Vegetative reproduction: By suckers.

Range: Europe (including Britain). N. America.

Uses: Leaves used medicinally (aromatic and astringent). Formerly

used to make flea-proof beds, yellow dye, and faggots (fuel), to repel
moths, and flavour beer or ale.

Order **BALANOPSIDALES**

Family *BALANOPSIDACEAE*

Balanops australiana

General characters: Small evergreen tree. Branchlets angular. Leaves
alternate, leathery, oblong or reverse-egg-shaped, 3–4″ long, 1–1½″
across. Flowers unisexual (sexes on different trees), without sepals or
petals. Males in catkins, each flower with several stamens and a small
bracteole. Female flower solitary within involucre of overlapping
bracts, with an imperfectly 2-celled ovary (2 ovules in each cell) and
2 styles parted almost to base.

Fruit: An ovoid drupe within persistent·bracts. Pale brown. ½″ or
more long. 2-celled or 1-celled by obliteration of placenta. Pyrenes 2
or 1 by abortion, 1-seeded.

Seeds: Egg-shaped. Seed-coat brown. With some endosperm.

Range: Queensland.

Uses: No information.

Order FAGALES

Family *BETULACEAE*

SILVER BIRCH (*Betula pendula*)

General characters: Deciduous tree up to 75' high. Bark silvery-white, smooth, peeling. Base of trunk dark, fissured. Smaller branches pendulous. Twigs brown, shining, without hairs but with small scattered warts (glands). Leaves alternate, triangular with wedge-shaped base, long-pointed, sharply toothed, without hairs but young leaves with glands on upper surface. Flowers small, in 3s in axils of bracts, each such group with 2 bracteoles. Groups of flowers arranged in unisexual catkins (both sexes on same tree). Male catkins drooping, females erect. Male flowers with 2 stamens, females with 2-celled ovary (each cell with 1 ovule).

Habitat: Woods. Colonizes heathland, woodland clearings, etc. Prefers light soil.

Pollination: Wind-pollinated.

Fruit: A 1-seeded flattened nutlet. Winged, crowned by persistent styles. Average weight: 0·00017 gm. ("Betula alba L."). Fruiting catkin breaks up when fruit ripe. Fruit dispersed by wind, rain-wash, animals (seeds in excreta). Probably also water-borne (fruit of "Betula alba" said to float 2–3 months).

Seeds: Without endosperm. 25% viable.

Range: Europe (including Britain). Asia Minor. Morocco.

Uses: Twigs used for besoms, forest fire-fighting beaters, clarifying vinegar (bundles of twigs placed in bottom of vats), punishing offenders (birch twigs flown specially from England to Australia for birching of prisoner, 1962). Bark used for tanning leather (Russian leather). Timber used for plywood, furniture, toys, pegs. Oil from bark and wood used medicinally in lotions or ointments.

Special comments: B. *pendula* and B. *pubescens*, a very variable species more tolerant of cold and wet conditions, formerly regarded as one species and called "Betula alba L."

Family *FAGACEAE*

BEECH (*Fagus sylvatica*)

General characters: Deciduous tree 100' or more high, with clean trunk of 50–60' when grown under forest conditions. Crown broad, dense. Bark smooth, grey. Winter buds spindle-shaped, with reddish-brown scales. Leaves alternate, 1½–3" long, egg-shaped to elliptic, pointed, slightly toothed. Young leaves soft and silky, but older ones

smooth except for hairs on veins and in their axils. Flowers small, unisexual, both sexes on same tree. Males in many-flowered, long-stalked,
tassel-like heads. Perianth of male 4–6-lobed. Females usually in pairs
on short erect stalks, with scaly involucre at base. Males with 8–16
stamens. Females with a 3-celled ovary (2 ovules in each cell).

Habitat: Woods on chalk and soft limestone and well-drained loamy
soil.

Pollination: Wind-pollinated.

Fruit: A brown sharply 3-angular 1-seeded nut. Groups of 2–3 nuts
in a brown bristly woody cupule. Average weight: 0·225 gm. Fruits
heavily in "mast years" about once every 5–7 years. Edible. Eaten by
pigs, field mice, grey squirrels, wood pigeons, pheasants, rooks and
jays (often buried by last two and squirrels). Some fruit dispersed by
wind.

Seeds: Without endosperm. Cotyledons fleshy. Germination epigeal.

Range: Europe (including Britain).

Uses: Timber used for furniture, cabinet-making, domestic wood-
ware (e.g. brush backs), toys, flooring, piano wrest-planks (fine quality
Beech). Provides good firewood. Seeds yield oil. Honey bees sometimes collect pollen freely. Makes good hedge, standing close trimming
and retention of dead brown leaves in winter adds to shelter value.

Special comments: Largely because they cast deep shade, few plants
grow under Beeches. In dense beechwoods saprophytes (e.g. bird's nest

orchid) and mycorrhizal plants (e.g. tway-blade) may be only herbs. Mycorrhizas ("fungus-roots") occur on Beeches. Several varieties in cultivation, including "Copper Beech" (colouring matter, anthocyanin, in cell-sap).

PEDUNCULATE OAK (*Quercus robur*)

General characters: Large deciduous tree, 80' or more. Open crown. Bark fissured, brownish-grey. Leaves alternate, reverse-egg-shaped, deeply and irregularly lobed, with reflexed auricles ("ears") at base, 2-4" long, on very short stalk. Flowers small, unisexual but sexes on same tree. Males in loose many-flowered pendulous catkins surrounded by small lobed perianth, each flower with 6-8 stamens. Females grouped in short stiff spikes, each flower surrounded by bracts and scales and with a 3-celled ovary (2 ovules in each cell, though normally only 1 of the 6 ovules matures).

Habitat: Woods, hedges, on clays, loams, damper acid sands, alluvium.

Pollination: Wind-pollinated.

Fruit: A large nut whose lower half is enclosed in cup-like cupule. Solitary or clustered on long smooth slender stalk. Fresh mature acorn pale fawn with olive-green longitudinal stripes. Acorn normally 1-seeded, but 2-seeded ones frequent and acorns with 4 or 6 seeds have been recorded. Mean fresh weight of ripe acorn: 3·5 gm. (Oxford district).

Seeds: Without endosperm. Cotyledons fleshy. Germination hypogeal. Seed production erratic (in S. England heavy seed-crops only once in 6 or 7 years, moderate crops every 3 or 4 years, many years when very few seed produced). Many acorns eaten by grey squirrels, voles, mice, deer, rooks, jays, wood pigeons, certain of these creatures burying some seed and thus aiding seed dispersal.

Range: Europe (including Britain).

Uses: Timber, one of most useful hardwoods in world, used for furniture, heavy construction, gates, posts, joinery. Acorns fed to pigs and used as coffee substitute. Bark used for tanning.

Special comments: Mycorrhizas normally present. Galls of several species of gall-wasp found on leaves, stems, roots, catkins. Ages given to old trees often inaccurate, but one old specimen in Switzerland found to be at least 930 years old (by ring counts).

SESSILE OAK (*Quercus petraea*)

Similar to *Q. robur* but leaves shallowly and regularly lobed, hairy beneath, without "ears" at base, leaf-stalk fairly long. Acorns uniform dark brown (no stripes), without stalk or borne on short stout hairy stalk. Tree with dense crown.

AMERICAN RED OAK (*Quercus borealis* var. *maxima*)

Native of N. America. Leaves turn dark red in autumn. Now naturalized in parts of Europe. In Britain a useful tree for very heavy clays and base-deficient acid soils. Seed-bearing begins at early age (fertile seed from 22-year-old trees at Oxford). Hardly affected by several insects that eat leaves and acorns of certain other Oaks.

Family *CORYLACEAE*

HAZEL (*Corylus avellana*)

General characters: Deciduous shrub or small much-branched tree up to 20′. Bark smooth, brown, peeling in thin strips. Young shoots clothed with reddish gland-tipped hairs. Leaves alternate, nearly rounded, shortly pointed, sharply and doubly toothed. Flowers small, unisexual but sexes on same plant. Males numerous in long pendulous "lamb's-tail" catkins. Females in short bud-like clusters, with protruding red stigmas. Male flower solitary in axil of bract, with 2 bracteoles joined to bract, and about 4 stamens. Female flowers in pairs in axil of bract, with bracteoles, minute lobed perianth, and inferior 2-celled ovary (each cell with 1 ovule).

Habitat: Woods and hedges. Basic, neutral and moderately acid soils.

Pollination: Wind-pollinated.

Fruit: A large 1-seeded nut surrounded by a lobed leafy involucre. Nuts in clusters of 1–4, brown with hard woody shell. Average weight fruits: 1·08 gm., kernels: 0·801 gm. Dispersed by squirrels, jays, rooks and nutcrackers, all of which store nuts underground. According to Darwin, sinks when fresh but floats 90 days after long drying.

Seeds: Edible. Without endosperm. Cotyledons large, fleshy.

Vegetative reproduction: By root suckers. In cultivation propagated by grafting or by layering.

Range: Europe (including Britain). Asia Minor.

Uses: Male flowers provide early pollen for honey bees. Nuts eaten raw or in confectionery. Nuts source of clear yellow oil used in food, soap, perfumes. Wood is source of charcoal for gunpowder. Stems made into baskets, hoops, hurdles, walking-sticks. Twigs make peasticks. Forked hazel rods used in water divining.

Special comments: Widely cultivated for nuts and stems. Hazel coppice (from French *couper*, to cut) cut every 7–10 years, yielding large numbers sticks, rods, etc. Of considerable importance when England's wealth and trade based on sheep and wool (sheep hurdles, fencing). Hazel charcoal in Neolithic and Late Iron Age deposits from Maiden Castle, Dorset.

Order JUGLANDALES

Family *JUGLANDACEAE*

WALNUT (*Juglans regia*)

General characters: Deciduous tree up to 100′ high. Crown large, spreading. Bark grey, smooth at first, fissured in old trees. Main branches twisted. Branchlets with chambered pith. Leaves alternate, fragrant when bruised, pinnate with 3–4 pairs reverse-egg-shaped or elliptic leaflets. Flowers unisexual but both sexes on same tree. Each individual flower in axil of a bract, with bracteoles and minute lobed perianth. Males in drooping catkins, each flower with 8–40 stamens. Females in erect 1–few-flowered spikes, each flower with inferior 1-celled ovary (1 ovule).

Habitat: Woods, parks, gardens.

Pollination: Wind-pollinated.

Fruit: A large globular drupe. Green fleshy husk encloses 2-valved wrinkled stone containing large crumpled seed-leaves (cotyledons). Young fruit rich in vitamin C. Buried (stored) by both red and grey squirrels, also rooks.

Seeds: Without endosperm. Cotyledons edible, containing 15% protein, 16% carbohydrate, high percentage oil.

Vegetative reproduction: Propagated by grafting.

Range: Europe (including Britain). Asia. N. America.

Uses: Young fruits pickled in vinegar. Edible "nuts." Oil from cotyledons used in food, soap, paint. Wood in great demand for veneered furniture, gun stocks, ornamental tableware. Strong brown dye from roots, leaves and husk of fruit used as hair dye and floor stain. In California honey bees work male flowers for pollen.

Special comments: Several varieties in cultivation. Crath Carpathian walnuts, new varieties developed within last 20 years, have borne fruit after exposure to temperature of 30 degrees below zero and they are free of insect pests and disease.

PECAN (*Carya olivaeformis*)

General characters: Large slender deciduous tree up to 170′ high. Bark roughened. Leaves alternate, pinnate with 5–7 pairs leaflets and odd one at end. Leaflets sickle-shaped, toothed, pointed, oblong-lance-shaped. Flowers are unisexual, sexes on same tree, without petals. Long drooping catkins containing male flowers borne in 3s. Calyx of male flower joined to bract, 3-lobed. Stamens 3–10. Female flowers 2–6 together on a terminal stalk; calyx 4-toothed, ovary 1-celled, ovule 1.

Habitat: Moist soil, especially along streams.

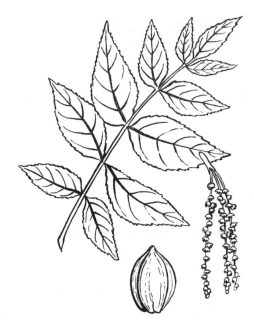

Pollination: Wind-pollinated.

Fruit: An oblong-cylindric drupe 1½–2½″ long. Outer husk thin, separating into 4 valves. Nut smooth, oblong, thin-shelled, pointed.

Seeds: Large, solitary, edible. Sweet and delicious. Without endosperm. Cotyledons corrugated, very oily.

Range: E. and S. United States, into Mexico.

Uses: Nuts eaten raw, salted, in cakes and confectionery. Wood sometimes used for agricultural implements, wagons, fuel.

Special comments: Grown commercially as nut tree in southern United States. Several varieties in cultivation, including paper-shelled or thin-shelled ones.

Order CASUARINALES

Family *CASUARINACEAE*

CASSOWARY TREE (*Casuarina equisetifolia*)

General characters: Evergreen tree up to 140′ high. Leaves reduced to scales. Branches jointed, drooping. Branchlets needle-like, scaly, greenish. Flowers without sepals or petals, unisexual. Male flowers in spikes, each with 1 stamen and 4 small bracts. Female flowers in spherical heads, each with superior 1-celled ovary with 2 ovules.

Habitat: Sandy coasts, but planted to 2,500 ft.
Pollination: Wind-pollinated.
Fruit: Nuts in a globular or oblong woody cone-like head.
Seeds: Winged. Without endosperm.
Range: Australia. Burma. Malaya. Pacific Islands. Planted in India and Ceylon.
Uses: Valuable for reclaiming sand-dunes as permits other vegetation to grow beneath it. Timber used for shingles, gates, fencing. Planted for fuel and coppiced at 10–20 years.

Order **URTICALES**

Family *ULMACEAE*

WYCH ELM (*Ulmus glabra*)

General characters: Deciduous tree up to 130′ or more. Round-headed. Twigs with coarse short hairs at first, but smooth and grey later. Leaves alternate, varying in shape but apparently in a regular manner. Clapham, Tutin and Warburg (*Flora of the British Isles*, 2nd edition, 1962) recognize two subspecies: Ssp. *montana*, with narrow leaves, northern and western in its distribution, and Ssp. *glabra*, leaves broader and sometimes almost rounded, southern distribution. Leaves rough above, hairy below, long-pointed at apex, sharply toothed, base unequal and long side forming ear-like projection (well developed in Ssp. *glabra*, less so in Ssp. *montana*). Flowers small, appearing before leaves, clustered, bisexual. Perianth bell-shaped, 4–5-lobed. Stamens 4–5. Ovary superior, 1-celled, 1 ovule.

Habitat: Woods and hedges, but seems to prefer valley bottoms and stream-sides.

Pollination: Wind-pollinated. Failing this, automatic self-pollination.

Fruit: A samara. Seed in centre of thin dry flattened wing. Average weight: 0·0138 gm. Dispersed by wind.

Seeds: Without endosperm.

Vegetative reproduction: By suckers, but apparently very rarely.

Range: Europe (including Britain). Asia. N. Africa.

Uses: Timber used for coffin boards, packing cases, wharf piling (durable under water), wheelbarrows, panelling, bent shafts. Bees sometimes collect Elm pollen, but more so in California (from introduced European trees) than in Britain.

HACKBERRY (*Celtis occidentalis*)

General characters: Deciduous tree or shrub up to 125' high. Bark becoming dark and rough. Leaves alternate, egg-shaped, sometimes

almost lance-shaped, sharply toothed, pointed, thin, unequal at base, $1\frac{1}{2}$-4″ long. Flowers small, greenish, without petals, unisexual, both sexes on same tree (apparently bisexual flowers sometimes occur). Calyx small. Male flowers clustered, with few stamens. Female flower usually solitary, with superior, 1-celled ovary, 1 ovule.

Habitat: Dry soil.

Pollination: Wind-pollinated.

Fruit: A globose drupe. Purple, black or orange. Sometimes edible. Eaten by birds.

Seeds: Without endosperm. Dispersed by birds.

Range: N. America. Cultivated in Europe.

Uses: Fruit sometimes eaten. Wood used for cheap furniture, posts, fuel.

Family *CANNABIACEAE*

HOP (*Humulus lupulus*)

General characters: Climbing perennial herb whose annual stems climb by twisting in clockwise direction. Leaves opposite, 4–6″ long, deeply heart-shaped at base, larger ones deeply 3–5-lobed, sharply toothed, rough. Stipules 2. Flowers without petals, unisexual, sexes on different plants. Male flowers small, yellowish-green, with 5 sepals, 5 stamens, arranged in loose much-branched panicles. Female flowers in small cone-like heads, each yellowish-green bract of "cone" with 2–3 tiny stalkless flowers, each with minute calyx and 1-celled ovary, 1 ovule.

Habitat: Hedges, thickets, open woods. Sometimes in tops of pollard willows. Also cultivated.

Pollination: Wind-pollinated.

Fruit: An achene. Fruits concealed by green or yellow scales of fruiting "cone." Scales and fruits with resinous glands. Ripe fruiting "cones" are the hops of commerce.

Seeds: With fleshy endosperm. Dispersed by wind when ripe "cones" of wild hops break up.

Range: Europe (including Britain). N. & S. America. Asia. Australia.

Uses: Bitter substance of fruiting "cone" used in flavouring beer. Dried fruiting "cone" used medicinally as bitter tonic, sedative, hypnotic (contains lupuline, humuline, cerotic acid, resins). Young shoots eaten like asparagus in Belgium, plants being forced December–February for this purpose.

Special comments: Widely cultivated. In Britain about 20,000 acres grown, Kent producing about two-thirds of crop. Fruiting "cones" dried in oast houses. Hop also grown for screening and ornamental purposes in gardens.

Family *MORACEAE*

BREADFRUIT (*Artocarpus communis*)

General characters: Much-branched tree up to 60′ high. Bark smooth. With milky juice (latex). Leaves alternate, large, thick, shiny, on long thick stalks. Stipules 2, large, soon falling. Flowers small, unisexual, both sexes on same tree. Males in dense yellow pseudo-catkins 6–12″ long, each flower with a 2- or 4-lobed perianth and 1 stamen. Females embedded in fleshy receptacle, many together, each with tubular perianth and small ovary.

Habitat: Wet coastal plains and elsewhere on well-drained soils.

Pollination: Wind-pollinated.

Fruit: A fleshy multiple fruit 4–8″ in diameter develops from each collection of female flowers. Thick brownish-yellow warty rind surrounds yellowish fibrous flesh. Eaten by people, bats and birds.

Seeds: Some cultivated forms are seedless.

Vegetative reproduction: Shoots develop from roots, especially when they are damaged. Propagated by root cuttings.

Range: Widely cultivated in tropics.

Uses: Fruit cooked and eaten, being staple food in some parts. (Contains carbohydrate, calcium, vitamins A, B and C.) Seeds of one variety cooked and eaten.

Family *URTICACEAE*

STINGING NETTLE (*Urtica dioica*)

General characters: Coarse perennial herb 2–4′ high. With stinging hairs. Leaves opposite, stalked, lower ones egg-shaped, upper becoming lance-shaped, coarsely toothed. Flowers small, green, unisexual, sexes usually on separate plants, clustered in branched spikes in leaf-axils. Perianth 4-lobed. Stamens 4. Ovary 1-celled, 1 ovule.

Habitat: Neglected gardens, farmyards, etc. Woods, hedges, grassland, rubbish heaps. Sometimes on walls and in tops of pollard willows and other trees. On almost all soil types (not waterlogged soils and rarely on acid peats).

Pollination: Normally wind-pollinated. Insects may pollinate some flowers. About 6,000 pollen-grains per flower and nearly 45,000,000 pollen-grains produced by shoot bearing 24 groups of flowers.

Fruit: A tiny achene enclosed in hispid perianth. Dispersed by wind, adhesion to clothing, fur and feathers, and in excreta of animals (cattle, fallow deer and magpie in Sweden).

Seeds: Oval. Yellowish-grey. Average weight about 0·00016 gm. Germination normally not less than 70%.

Vegetative reproduction: By means of rhizomes.

Range: Widespread in temperate regions, extending into hot areas.

Uses: Leaves yield chlorophyll for use in tonics and other medicines. During Second World War dark green dye for camouflage extracted from nettles (over 90 tons gathered in Britain, 1942). Young nettle-tops boiled and eaten as vegetable. Stems yield tough fibre from which nettle-flax was spun for household linen. Stems have also been used for paper-making. Nettle hay is useful source of protein for rabbits and goats. Dexter cattle eat young nettles.

Special comments: Contains copper (may be over 20 parts per million of dry weight), iron (about 300 p.p.m.).

Order **BIXALES**

Family *BIXACEAE*

ANNATTO TREE (*Bixa orellana*)

General characters: Evergreen tree or shrub. Leaves alternate, heart-shaped, pointed, smooth, 4–8″ long. Stipules minute. Flowers white or pink, in panicles at ends shoots, 2–3″ across. Sepals 5, falling. Petals 5, large, free, falling. Stamens numerous. Ovary superior, 1-celled, with

numerous ovules (placentation parietal). Style slender, curved. Stigma notched.

Habitat: Forests.

Pollination: By insects.

Fruit: A 2-valved capsule covered with long weak bristles.

Seeds: Numerous. Seed-coat red, pulpy. With fleshy endosperm.

Range: Tropical America. Cultivated throughout India and other parts of tropics.

Uses: Pulp surrounding seeds source of dye used for colouring confectionery.

Family *CISTACEAE*

GUM CISTUS (*Cistus ladaniferus*)

General characters: Erect evergreen shrub 3–5′ high. Branches clammy with shining resin. Leaves opposite, sticky, long and narrow, $1\frac{1}{2}$–4″ long, smooth above, covered beneath with dense greyish-white felt, nearly stalkless. Flowers 3–4″ across, solitary at end of side twigs. Sepals 3, large, covered with yellowish scales. Petals 5, crimped at margin, white with blood-red blotch at base. Stamens numerous. Ovary superior, 1-celled, ovules numerous.

Habitat: Dry sunny places.

Pollination: By insects.

Fruit: A 10-valved capsule opening from top downwards.

Seeds: With endosperm.

Vegetative reproduction: Propagated by cuttings.

Range: S. Europe. N. Africa. Sometimes cultivated in Europe.

Uses: Source of labdanum, fragrant gum used for perfumes, soap, cosmetics.

ROCK ROSE (*Helianthemum chamaecistus*)

General characters: Evergreen prostrate dwarf shrub up to 1′ high. Stem short, woody, much-branched. Leaves opposite, up to 1″ long, oblong or oval, green above, white beneath and densely covered with short branched hairs, shortly stalked. Stipules lance-shaped. Flowers in 1–12-flowered cyme at end of shoot, usually one out at a time, unopened flower buds at top. Sepals 5, 3 inner larger with prominent veins, 2 outer small and narrow. Petals 5, lasting 2–3 days only, normally yellow, though forms with cream, orange or white flowers occur. Stamens numerous. Ovary superior, 1-celled, with parietal placentation.

Habitat: Short well-drained chalk and limestone grassland. Dry Agrostis-Festuca grasslands. Prefers S. to S.W. facing slopes.

Pollination: Cross-pollination by insects which visit flowers for pollen (no nectar present). Failing this, automatic self-pollination when

flowers close at night or during wet weather. Stamens sensitive, few seconds after stimulation they spread and lie close to petals, returning to original erect position within 1–2 minutes. This movement probably helps transfer pollen to insect-visitor's body.

Fruit: An ovoid capsule opening in 3 valves.

Seeds: With endosperm. Hard-coated. About 10–20 per capsule, normal wild plant producing 500 or more. Abundant seed produced every year. Weight about 0·0012 gm. Ants may assist dispersal. Fungus present on seed-coat necessary for germination of seeds.

Vegetative reproduction: By layering of branches when old plants are disturbed.

Range: Europe (including Britain). Asia Minor.

Uses: No information. (*Helianthemum canadense* of N. America contains essential oil and bitter principle. Dried and used medicinally as tonic and astringent.)

Special comments: Mycorrhizal fungus on roots.

Family *FLACOURTIACEAE*

WILD PEACH (*Kiggelaria africana*)

General characters: Tree up to 30′ high. Bark smooth. Branches ascending. Young leaves and stems covered with white or brownish star-shaped hairs. Leaves alternate, elliptical or oblong, deeply toothed, hairy below, shortly stalked. Stipules short, narrow. Flowers small, greenish-yellow, in dense clusters in leaf-axils, unisexual, sexes on different trees. Sepals 5. Petals 5, free, each with scale inside base. Male flowers with 10 stamens. Females with superior, 1-celled ovary, numerous ovules.

Habitat: Ravines and sheltered slopes.
Fruit: A dry hairy spherical greenish-yellow capsule.
Seeds: With fleshy endosperm. Black, shiny, enclosed in red or orange oily coat. Dispersed by birds which eat oily coat.
Range: S. Africa.
Uses: Wood used for furniture.

Order **THYMELAEALES**

Family *AQUILARIACEAE*

Aquilaria agallocha

General characters: Large evergreen tree. Leaves alternate, lance-shaped. Flowers in umbellules in leaf-axils and at ends shoots. Perianth bell-shaped, 5-lobed, lobes broad and spreading. Scales on perianth-throat 5, densely hairy, joined below in a short ring. Stamens 10. Ovary superior, perfectly or imperfectly 2-celled, each cell with 1 ovule. Style obsolete. Stigma large.

Habitat: Forests.
Fruit: A flattened capsule.
Seeds: With endosperm. Egg-shaped, with long tail.
Range: India. China. Malaysia.
Uses: Fragrant wood used as incense and joss sticks. Essential oil used in perfumery obtained by distillation of wood.

Family *PENAEACEAE*

Penaea mucronata

General characters: Dense much-branched shrublet $\frac{1}{2}$–$1\frac{1}{2}'$ high. Younger branches 4-angled. Leaves opposite, evergreen, small, stalkless, broadly heart-shaped, pointed. Stipules minute. Flowers dull yellow or reddish, in short racemes with sharply pointed winged bracts. Perianth tubular, 4-lobed, lobes erect and pointed. Stamens 4, inserted at throat of perianth-tube, with short filaments. Ovary superior, 4-celled, 2 ovules in each cell. Style a 4-winged column, stigma 4-lobed.

Habitat: Mountains, sandy plains.
Fruit: A capsule enclosed in persistent perianth.
Seeds: Without endosperm.
Range: S. Africa.
Uses: Source of gum substance.

Family *THYMELAEACEAE*

MEZEREON (*Daphne mezereum*)

General characters: Deciduous shrub up to 4' high. Branches erect, few. Leaves alternate, narrow-oblong, pointed, smooth. Flowers appearing early in year before leaves, sweet-scented, purple (rarely white), in small clusters along preceding year's shoot. Petals none. Sepals 4, petal-like. Stamens 8, in 2 rows of 4, inserted in upper part of tubular receptacle ("calyx-tube"). Ovary superior, 1-celled, 1 ovule.

Habitat: Woods on calcareous soils.

Pollination: Cross-pollination by Lepidoptera and long-tongued bees. Information on self-pollination confusing (one authority says "probably often selfed," another "self-pollination rarely occurs").

Fruit: A round red drupe. Eaten by birds (including lesser white-throat, blackbird), which may help disperse seeds. Greenfinches strip bushes of unripe fruit, crushing unhardened stone to eat seed.

Seeds: With little endosperm. Average weight: 0·069 gm.

Vegetative reproduction: Sometimes propagated from cuttings.

Range: Europe (including Britain). N. America. Asia Minor. N. Africa.

Family *NYCTAGINACEAE*

PARAPARA (*Pisonia brunoniana*)

General characters: Shrub or tree 12–35′ high. Wood soft, brittle. Leaves usually opposite, oblong or elliptic-oblong, stalked, up to 15″ long. Flowers small, greenish, with 2–3 small bracts at base, numerous in much-branched cymes at end shoots. Perianth funnel-shaped, shortly 5-toothed at top. Stamens 6–8. Ovary superior, 1-celled, 1 ovule. Style simple, slender. Stigma small.

Habitat: Seashores and islands.

Fruit: 1-seeded. A utricle enclosed in persistent base of perianth-tube. Length about 1″. Fruits are so sticky that small birds (e.g. white-eyes, fantails) often found firmly glued to them (hence name "Bird-killing Tree").

Seeds: With scanty endosperm. Oblong, grooved. Dispersed by large birds to whose feathers fruits become attached.

Range: Australia. New Zealand. Pacific Islands.

Uses: Leaves used medicinally (diuretic).

Order **PROTEALES**

Family *PROTEACEAE*

SUGAR-BUSH (*Protea mellifera*)

General characters: Spreading evergreen shrub up to 9' high. Leaves alternate, leathery, stalkless, oblong-lance-shaped, 3-4½" long. Flowers in stalked heads (about 3" across) surrounded by involucre of conspicuous sticky scales. Perianth creamy white, of 4 segments (3 united, 1 free), segments shortly awned at apex. Stamens 4. Ovary 1-celled, 1-2 ovules. Style simple.

Habitat: Mountain slopes, sandy plains.

Pollination: By insects. (In Australia nectar-feeding honey mice pollinate species of *Protea.*)

Fruit: A thick-walled achene.

Seeds: Without endosperm.

Range: S. Africa.

Uses: Nectar made into medicinal syrup.

SILVER TREE (*Leucadendron argenteum*)

General characters: Evergreen tree up to 30' high. Leaves alternate, lance-shaped, silvery-grey, densely clothed with soft silky hairs, up to 5" long. Flowers fragrant, unisexual, sexes on different trees. Perianth segments 4, united towards base. Male flowers numerous, yellowish, conspicuous, in globose heads 1-1½" across. Female flowers inconspicuous, in globose heads. Stamens 4. Ovary 1-celled. Style simple, persistent.

Habitat: Lower slopes of hills and mountains.

Pollination: By insects.

Fruit: A dry 1-seeded flattened nut. Black, hairy, about ½" across. Fruits in woody cone-like heads. Dispersed by wind, withered perianth being caught by tip of style and acting as "parachute."

Seeds: Without endosperm.

Range: S. Africa (Cape Peninsula).

Uses: Wood used for boxes. Leaves sold as curios (book-marks, mats).

SILKY OAK (*Grevillea robusta*)

General characters: Medium-sized to large tree. Bark dark-coloured, somewhat furrowed. Leaves alternate, pinnate, much divided and somewhat fern-like, 6-12" long. Flowers orange-yellow, in branched inflorescences consisting of several racemes. Individual flowers up to ¾" long. Perianth of 4 narrow segments. Stamens 4. Ovary 1-celled.

Habitat: Brush or rain forests, usually near coast. Much planted elsewhere.

Pollination: By insects.
Fruit: A boat-shaped follicle about ¾″ long.
Seeds: Without endosperm. Winged.
Range: Australia. Planted in Ceylon and other countries.
Uses: Timber used for cabinet work, indoor fittings, coach building. Planted for shade, shelter and ornamental purposes.
Special comments: A rapid grower.

NEEDLEWOOD (*Hakea leucoptera*)

General characters: Small tree or shrub 6–10′ high. Leaves alternate, cylindrical, needle-like, 1½–3″ long. Flowers white, small, in short racemes in leaf-axils. Perianth falling, petal-like, shortly tubular with 4 segments. Stamens 4, inserted on perianth segments. Ovary superior, stalked, 1-celled, with 1 or several ovules. Style curved.
Habitat: Dry sandy ridges, poorer soils (but also on better soils).
Pollination: By insects.
Fruit: A woody capsule opening in 2 valves. Often 2-seeded.
Seeds: Without endosperm. Flattened. Ending in broad yellowish-white wing.
Range: Australia.
Uses: Famine food for animals. Pipes made from rootstock. Timber sometimes used for small fancy turnery. Water obtained from fleshy roots.
Special comments: Also commonly known as Pine Bush.

Order **PITTOSPORALES**

Family *PITTOSPORACEAE*

KARO (*Pittosporum crassifolium*)

General characters: Evergreen shrub or small tree up to 30′ high. Branches close together, erect or parallel. Leaves alternate, 2–3″ long, narrowly reverse-egg-shaped, shortly stalked, leathery, dark green and shining above, undersurface covered with dense short white or buff woolly hairs, margins recurved. Flowers dark purple, unisexual, 1–10 in umbels at end of branches. Sepals 5, overlapping. Petals 5, tip rolled backwards. Stamens 5. Ovary superior, incompletely 2–4-celled, ovules numerous. Style simple, short.
Habitat: Island shores and coastal regions.

Fruit: A large 3–4-valved globose capsule with thick woody valves.
Seeds: With endosperm. Numerous. Immersed in sticky fluid.
Range: New Zealand. Cultivated elsewhere and sometimes naturalized.
Uses: Whitish wood used for inlay work.

Family *BYBLIDACEAE*

Byblis liniflora

General characters: Branching straggling herb up to 6″ high. Usually sticky with glandular hairs. Leaves alternate, thread-like, 1–2″ long. Flowers violet, solitary on slender stalks from leaf-axils. Sepals 5, free, lance-shaped, small. Petals 5, broad, united in a ring at base. Stamens 5. Ovary superior, 2-celled, several ovules in each cell. Style simple.
Habitat: Swamps.
Fruit: A 2-celled somewhat flattened capsule opening in 2 valves.
Seeds: Oblong, with endosperm.
Range: Western Australia (tropical north).

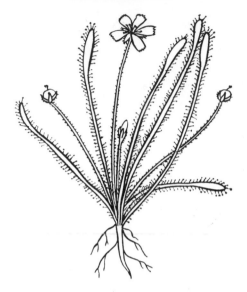

Uses: No information.

Special comments: Byblis gigantea, Rainbow plant, occurs in sandy places in W. Australia. Flowers purple-red, up to 2″ broad. Plant erect, up to 2′ high. *Byblis* species (2 only) trap small insects by means of sticky hairs.

Order **CAPPARIDALES**

Family *CAPPARIDACEAE*

CAPER BUSH (*Capparis spinosa*)

General characters: Trailing shrub. Leaves alternate, up to $1\frac{1}{2}$″ long, egg-shaped or almost rounded, with small spiny point. Leaf-stalk short, with 2 spiny stipules at base. Flowers white, large, solitary in leaf-axils on thick stalks. Sepals 4, in 2 rows, outer sepals unequal with larger one hooded. Petals 4, reverse-egg-shaped, 2″ long. Stamens numerous (70–100), with long purple filaments. Ovary superior, supported on long stalk, 1-celled, with numerous ovules (placentation parietal).

Habitat: Dry sandy places.

Fruit: An ovoid berry, $1\frac{1}{2}$″ long, containing several seeds.

Seeds: Without endosperm. Kidney-shaped. With hard seed-coat.

Range: Mediterranean region. Tropical Australia.

Uses: Pickled flower buds are capers of commerce.

CAPER BUSH (*Capparis spinosa*)

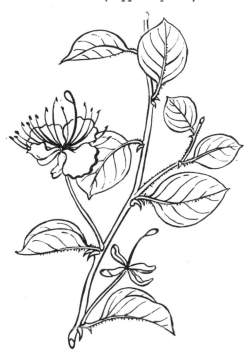

Order **TAMARICALES**

Family *FRANKENIACEAE*

SEA HEATH (*Frankenia laevis*)

General characters: Low woody perennial. Evergreen. Leaves narrow, opposite, short and crowded, heath-like, margins rolled downwards (often hiding lower leaf surface). Flowers small, solitary, pink, among upper leaves. Petals 5, free, long-clawed, limb spreading. Calyx tubular with 4–5 erect teeth. Stamens 6. Ovary superior, 1-celled, ovules numerous (placentation parietal).

Habitat: Sandy salt-marshes.

Fruit: A 3-angled capsule enclosed in persistent calyx, opening by valves with seeds attached to their centre.

Seeds: Very small. With endosperm.

Range: W. Europe (including Britain). Channel Islands. Mediterranean region. W. Asia.

Uses: No information.

Family *TAMARICACEAE*

Tamarisk (*Tamarix anglica*)

General characters: Shrub 3–9' high. Leaves small, scale-like, pointed, overlapping. Flowers small, pink or white, in cylindric many-flowered spike-like (almost catkin-like) racemes. Sepals 5, free. Petals 5, free. Stamens 5. Ovary superior, 1-celled, ovules 8–9.

Habitat: Sandy and marshy sea-coasts. In cultivation thrives inland in sunny places and soils which are not very shallow or chalky.

Pollination: By bees.

Fruit: An egg-shaped pointed capsule opening by 3 valves.

Seeds: Without endosperm. Crowned by tuft of hairs.

Vegetative reproduction: Readily propagated from cuttings.

Range: Coasts of S. and E. England, France, Spain, Portugal, N. America.

Uses: Attractive garden shrub. Useful sand-binder and wind-break on coast.

Order **VIOLALES**

Family *VIOLACEAE*

Sweet Violet (*Viola odorata*)

General characters: Perennial herb. Leaves 1–3″ long (longer ones in shady places), egg-shaped (sometimes almost circular), heart-shaped at base, apex rounded or bluntly triangular, long-stalked. Leaves and flowers from root. Flowers of 2 kinds, "open" and "closed" (cleistogamous). "Open" flowers sweetly scented, solitary on long stalks. Petals 5, violet or white (forms with petals purple, pink or apricot

occur rarely), lowermost petal with blunt round spur at base. Sepals 5, oblong. Stamens 5, anthers forming ring around ovary. Ovary 1-celled, ovules numerous (placentation parietal). "Closed" flowers remaining small, never opening, with reduced outer parts, looking like short-stalked flower-buds, produced after "open" flowers have ripened seed.

Habitat: Hedgebanks, woods, plantations, often on chalky soils.

Pollination: "Open" flowers cross-pollinated mainly by bees. Apparently self-pollination does not occur. "Closed" flowers self-pollinated.

Fruit: A globose capsule opening in 3 valves. Often lies on ground where seeds are shed.

Seeds: With fleshy endosperm. Dispersed by ants (which feed on seed's small fatty process) and probably by rain-wash.

Vegetative reproduction: By runners.

Range: Europe (including Britain). N. America. Asia Minor. N. Africa.

Uses: Grown for its flowers. Cultivated varieties source of essential oil used in perfumery and pomades. Candied flowers used in confectionery.

Special comments: Viola hirta × *odorata*, a hybrid, combines characters of parents.

SOME N. AMERICAN VIOLETS

Called Bird's-foot Violet, because narrow lobes of leaves are arranged so as to suggest bird's foot, *Viola pedata* is one of "stemless" group whose stems are short and thick and grow underground. Light blue flowers (in one form 2 upper petals are dark purple) are borne on stalks 3–10″ high. Whitish, yellowish or purple flowers of Johnny Jump-up (*Viola rafinesquii*) are small, but plant sometimes so abundant that fields and roadsides are coloured blue. Leaves are palmate in Wood Violet (*Viola palmata*) and Pine Violet (*Viola lobata*), and long narrow and woolly in Woolly Blue Violet (*Viola fimbriatula*).

Rinorea ilicifolia

General characters: Small evergreen tree or shrub up to 20′ high. Bark blackish. Twigs green, smooth. Leaves leathery, deep green and glossy above, up to 9″ long and 4″ across, lance-shaped to oblong-egg-shaped, pointed, margin with short sharp spines. Leaf-stalk about 1″ long. Flowers cream, nodding, in small clusters. Sepals 5, ribbed. Petals 5. Stamens 5. Ovary superior, 1-celled.

Habitat: Lowland rain forest in damp situations.

Fruit: A rounded capsule about ½″ long. Leathery. Becoming brown and very wrinkled.

Seeds: With fleshy endosperm.

Range: Tropical Africa.

Uses: Wood used for implement handles, walking sticks. Used as aphrodisiac, leafy twigs being crushed with salt and Capsicum pepper. Liquid extracted added to palm-wine and drunk.

Hybanthus enneaspermus

General characters: Erect perennial herb up to 1–1½′ high. Stems slightly ribbed. Leaves alternate, lance-shaped or narrowly so, pointed, margin toothed, about 2″ long. Stipules long, narrow. Flowers lilac or bluish, solitary in leaf-axils, stalked. Petals 5, lower petal much larger than others. Sepals 5, minute. Stamens 5. Ovary 1-celled. Style 1.

Fruit: A tiny capsule crowned with persistent style. Seeds about 6.

Seeds: With fleshy endosperm.

Range: Tropical Africa.

Uses: Used medicinally (given to pregnant women and infants).

Order **POLYGALALES**

Family *POLYGALACEAE*

SNAKEROOT (*Polygala senega*)

General characters: Herb 6-12″ high. Stems several from woody root-stocks, erect or ascending, simple or sparingly branched above. Leaves lance-shaped or oblong-lance-shaped, stalkless, 1-2″ long, toothed, the lowest small and scale-like. Flowers white or greenish, in racemes at top of stems.

Habitat: In rocky woods.

Range: Eastern N. America.

Uses: As Seneca Snakeroot used by Seneca Indians for snake-bites. Dried root used medicinally. Contains glucoside senegin.

MILKWORT (*Polygala vulgaris*)

General characters: Small perennial herb with woody tufted base and many erect or spreading branches. Leaves alternate, upper long and narrow, lower shorter and broader. Flowers bright blue, pink or white, in slender many-flowered racemes. Sepals 5, free, outer 3 small, inner 2 ("wings") much larger and petal-like. Petals 3, small, united with stamens. Stamens 8. Ovary superior, 2-celled, 1 ovule in each cell.

Habitat: Meadows, pastures, heaths, dunes.

Pollination: Cross-pollination by insects.

Fruit: Capsule with two 1-seeded cells. Narrowly winged. Flattened. Splitting at edges.

Seeds: Hairy. With 3-lobed strophiole (hard appendage outside seed-coat). Dispersed by ants, which are believed to eat strophiole.

Range: Europe (including Britain). N. Africa. W. Asia.

Uses: No recent information. Leaves boiled in ale once used as purge and dried root as sudorific.

Special comments: A variable species.

VIOLET TREE (*Securidaca longipedunculata*)

General characters: Shrub or tree up to 30' high. Bark smooth (often furrowed when old), light grey. Leaves alternate, oval, 1–2½" long, on short hairy stalks. Flowers reddish to magenta (occasionally white), very fragrant, scent like that of violets, in loose racemes at end of short side branchlets. Sepals 5, free, the 2 side ones larger and petal-like. Petals 5, two very small. Stamens 8.

Habitat: Open savanna woodland.

Fruit: Small dry oval nut ending in large stiff wing. 1-seeded.

Seeds: Apparently germinate well after ants have eaten away seed-coat.

Range: Tropical Africa.

Uses: Wood used as fuel or poles. Roots used for treatment of malaria. Fibre from bark.

Family *VOCHYSIACEAE*

Erismadelphus exsul var. *platyphyllus*

General characters: Large tree up to 110' high. Bole straight. Bark grey, peeling. Leaves opposite, 3–9" long, 2½–4½" broad, broadly ellip-tic, sometimes almost circular, leathery, glossy, on short stout stalk. Flowers irregular, greyish-green, in large panicles at ends of shoots, sur-rounded by broad persistent bracts. Sepals 5, unequal, outside one with 2 prominent pouches. Petals 5, pointed, ½" long. Stamens: only 1 fertile. Ovary inferior, 1-celled, 1 ovule. Style short, thick.

Habitat: Lowland rain forest.

Fruit: 1-seeded. With 2–3 wings (= enlarged sepals). Up to 3" long, 1" broad.

Range: W. Tropical Africa.
Uses: No information.

Order **LOASALES**

Family *TURNERACEAE*

Wormskioldia pilosa

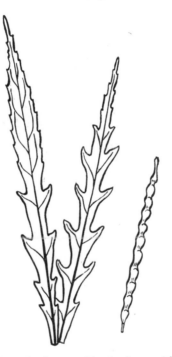

General characters: Branched annual herb about 1' high. Stems finely hairy and with many purple bristles. Leaves alternate, narrowly lance-shaped, toothed or lobed, up to 7" long and ½" broad. Flowers yellow, racemose. Calyx tubular, shortly 5-lobed. Petals 5, free, clawed, inserted on calyx-tube. Stamens 5, inserted at base calyx-tube. Ovary superior, 1-celled, numerous ovules (placentation parietal). Styles 3, slender. Stigmas fringed.

Pollination: Cross-pollination by insects. Failing this, self-pollination.

Fruit: A slender capsule opening by 3 valves. Seeds about 20.

Seeds: With endosperm. Straw-coloured. Small, pitted, with aril.

Range: W. Tropical Africa.

Uses: No information.

Family *LOASACEAE*
BLAZING STAR (*Mentzelia decapetala*)

General characters: Stout erect herb up to 2′ high. Leaves 2–6″ long, pinnately lobed, lobes pointed. Upper leaves stalkless, lower stalked. Flowers yellowish-white, 3–5″ across, mostly solitary at top of stems, opening in evening. Petals 10. Calyx-tube 5-lobed, usually bearing bracts. Stamens numerous. Ovary inferior, 1-celled. Style 1.

Habitat: Plains.

Fruit: An oblong capsule opening at top.

Seeds: Numerous. Flat. With scanty endosperm.

Range: U.S.A. (Great Plains and S.W.).

Uses: No information, but seeds of *Mentzelia albicaulis* were used as food by Indians in W. and S.E. United States.

Order **PASSIFLORALES**

Family *PASSIFLORACEAE*

PASSION FRUIT (*Passiflora incarnata*)

General characters: Woody vine climbing by coiling tendrils to height of 10–30′. Leaves alternate, stalked, 3–5″ broad, deeply 3–5-lobed, finely toothed. Flowers large and showy, $1\frac{1}{2}$–2″ broad, stalked, solitary in leaf-axils. Calyx-tube cup-shaped, narrowly 5-lobed, throat crowned with double-triple purple or pink fringe (corona). Petals 5, whitish, inserted on throat of calyx. Stamens 5. Ovary superior, 1-celled, ovules numerous.

Habitat: In thickets and in the open.

Pollination: By insects.

Fruit: An ovoid many-seeded berry about 2″ long. Yellow, fragrant, edible. Known as "Maypops" because of sound made when fruit is opened.

Seeds: With fleshy endosperm. Flat, egg-shaped, surrounded by pulpy aril. Seed-coat pitted.

Vegetative reproduction: Propagated by layering or cuttings.

Range: Eastern N. America.

Uses: Fruit made into jelly. Dried flowering and fruit tops used medicinally.

Special comments: In tropical America several other species of *Passiflora* valued for their edible fruits. *Passiflora edulis* widely cultivated in tropics and parts of subtropics, its juicy fruits containing vitamins A and C.

Order **CUCURBITALES**

Family *CUCURBITACEAE*

BRYONY (*Bryonia dioica*)

General characters: Herb rough with bulbous-based hairs. Rootstock perennial, thick, tuberous, branched. Stems annual, very long, climbing by spirally coiled tendrils. Leaves deeply divided into 5 lobes, heart-shaped at base. Flowers greenish, in cymes in leaf-axils, unisexual, sexes on different plants. Male flowers larger and more conspicuous than females. Calyx tubular, 5-lobed. Corolla 5-lobed. Stamens 5, two pairs joined by filaments, 1 stamen separate. Ovary inferior. Stigmas 3.

Habitat: Hedges, thickets, gardens.

Pollination: By insects.

Fruit: A small globular berry. 3–6-seeded. Red or orange. Eaten by blackbirds.

Seeds: Large, flattened. Without endosperm. Average weight: 0·00943 gm. Float for 3 days only. Dispersed by birds. Yield about 23% thick reddish-yellow oil.

Range: Europe (including Britain). N. Africa. W. Asia.

Uses: Root yields bryonin (used for certain bronchial troubles, rheumatism, gout).

Special comments: Highly poisonous in every part. Whole families poisoned by eating rootstock ("Devil's turnips") in mistake for turnips and parsnips. Produces root-shoots freely if injured. Plants with bisexual flowers grown at Kew from seed of bisexual parent.

CUCUMBER (*Cucumis sativus*)

General characters: Trailing annual with rough branching stems. Leaves alternate, large, roughly triangular or roundish in shape. Climbing by simple unbranched tendrils (believed to be modified leaves). Flowers unisexual, sexes on same plant, male greatly outnumbering female. Males on short stout stems in leaf-axils, usually in groups of 2 or 3. Females singly in leaf-axils, with elongated ovary.

Habitat: Cultivated for many centuries.

Pollination: Cross-pollination by bees. Pollination by hand when grown in glass-houses.

Fruit: A fleshy pepo (the cucumber of commerce). Types of cucumber in cultivation include those with small egg-shaped fruit and others with long fruits (some 2–3′ long). Rind thick and rough, thin and smooth, spiny. Fruit more than 95% water, but does contain vitamins A, B_1, B_2 and C, and minerals calcium, phosphorus, iron.

Seeds: Without endosperm.

Range: Widely cultivated throughout Old and New World.

Uses: Fruit pickled or eaten raw in salads. Where grown on field scale out of doors bees work flowers and honey crops obtained.

Special comments: Rapid grower, spreading up to 6′ in all directions in a season. In the open a warm-season crop injured by frost.

LOOFAH SPONGE PLANT (*Luffa aegyptiaca*)

General characters: Climber with tendrils. Leaves 4″ across, kidney-shaped or rounded, 5-angled or 5-lobed, toothed, usually rough, on stalk 2″ long. Flowers deep-yellow, unisexual, sexes on same plant. Male flowers at top long stalks, each on short stalk with small egg-shaped sticky bract. Calyx-tube top-shaped, 5-lobed. Petals 5, reverse-egg-shaped. Stamens 5. Female flowers solitary on stalk 1–3″ long. Calyx-tube shortly produced above ovary, 5-lobed. Petals 5. Ovary inferior, oblong, with numerous ovules. Style cylindric. Stigma 3-lobed.

Habitat: Moist river-banks. Also cultivated.

Fruit: Club-shaped, 5–12″ long, smooth, obscurely 10-ribbed, ultimately fibrous.

Seeds: Without endosperm. Usually black. Narrowly winged. About ⅜″ long.

Range: Cultivated in tropics.

Uses: Young fruit eaten as vegetable. Ripe fruit (dry, filled with network of fibres) used as bath sponge.

Family *CARICACEAE*

Papaw (*Carica papaya*)

General characters: Large herbaceous plant up to 25′ high, somewhat palm-like in appearance. Stem unbranched at first, but in old specimens sometimes branching from base and forming several erect stems. Each stem with crown of dark green foliage. Leaves very large, up to 2′ across, deeply divided into about 7 palmate lobes which are themselves pinnately lobed. Leaf-stalks long, cylindrical, hollow. Stems with smooth grey bark, bearing many large leaf scars, softly woody and fleshy, usually hollow. Plant with many latex vessels. Normally with male and female flowers on different plants, but individuals with bisexual flowers known. Male flowers in long pendulous racemes in

axils of upper leaves, calyx minute and 5-toothed, corolla pale yellow, tubular, 5-lobed. Stamens 10, inserted on corolla. Female flowers much larger, with calyx similar to that of male, 5 large petals united at base and twisted at tips. Ovary large, globular, green, usually 1-celled, with numerous ovules.

Habitat: Cultivated throughout tropics. Needs well-drained soil.

Pollination: Cross-pollination by insects.

Fruit: A pulpy berry up to 20″ long, weighing as much as 20 lb. Matures in about 18 months from time seed planted. "Tree melon" is green to orange when ripe, thin-skinned, with yellow to salmon-pink flesh 1–2″ thick and hollow central cavity containing numerous seeds enclosed in gelatinous membrane. Texture of ripe fruit soft and melting. Best types have delicious flavour. Edible. Source of vitamins A, B_1, B_2, C, and calcium.

Seeds: Rounded, dark green, brown or blackish. Retain viability for considerable time, but seeds may begin to germinate in ripe fruit. Germination takes 3–4 weeks. Contain about 25% pale yellow non-drying oil (not yet exploited commercially).

Vegetative reproduction: No satisfactory method of vegetative propagation known.

Range: Cultivated throughout tropics.

Uses: Fruit cooked as vegetable when green, but mainly eaten ripe in salads and desserts. Latex contains papain, proteolytic enzyme, used in U.S.A. to prevent cloudiness in beers during chilling, in preparation of canned meats, children's foods, chewing gums, patent medicines, and in leather tanning, shrink-resistance processes and meat tenderizing preparations (meat wrapped in papaw leaves said to lose some toughness).

Special comments: Grows rapidly. Complete sex reversal from male to female occurs, but female plants appear to be more stable.

Order CACTALES

Family *CACTACEAE*

BEAVER TAIL (*Opuntia basilaris*)

General characters: Succulent perennial with low spreading short-jointed stems. Joints flattened, reverse-egg-shaped, up to 6″ long, rough, plant branching at base of joints. Leaves small, fleshy, awl-shaped, soon falling. Areoles (structures situated in leaf-axils when leaves are present and from which branches, flowers, etc., develop) small, close together, spineless but with numerous short brown barbed bristles. Flowers reddish, rose, rarely white, stalkless, clustered at upper edge of joints. Perianth-tube cup-shaped, short, with scales. Perianth segments numerous, overlapping, in several rows, outer ones (sepals) thick, green or partly coloured, intergrading with inner coloured segments (petals). Stamens numerous, inserted on perianth-throat. Ovary inferior, 1-celled, numerous ovules (placentation parietal). Style 1.

Habitat: Dry places in scrub, deserts, rocky slopes.

Fruit: Dry when ripe, spineless, reverse-egg-shaped, brownish or greyish, about 1″ long.

Seeds: Bony, whitish, angled.

Range: Western United States.

Uses: No information. (Fruits, buds, flowers of certain other *Opuntia* species used as food. Stems sometimes fed to livestock after removal of spines.)

Special comments: Several varieties occur.

GIANT CACTUS (*Cereus giganteus*)

General characters: Erect succulent perennial 30′ or more high. Stems many times longer than thick, not jointed, leafless, simple or with few erect branches above, with 12–24 ribs bearing spines in clusters of 10–25. Flowers white, nocturnal, about 4″ long, in clusters on spine-bearing areoles near ends of branches. Ovary scaly.

Habitat: Gravelly slopes and flats.

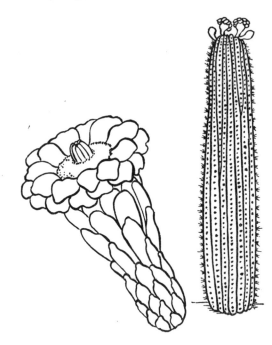

Fruit: A fleshy ovoid berry. Scaly. Up to 4″ long. Green outside, red inside.
Seeds: Numerous, small, black, shining.
Range: Western United States.
Uses: Fruit important food to Indians in Arizona.

FOXTAIL CACTUS (*Mammillaria alversonii*)

General characters: Small succulent plant 4–8″ high. Stems 1 or few, shortly cylindrical, with numerous spirally-arranged teat-like tubercles. Areoles spine-bearing, borne on tubercles. Flowers magenta with mid-vein deeper red, diurnal, about 1″ long, funnel-shaped, borne centrally in axils of young tubercles.
Habitat: Stony slopes in scrub.
Fruit: A smooth club-shaped berry.
Seeds: Black, minutely warty.
Range: Western United States.
Uses: No information.

Order **TILIALES**

Family *TILIACEAE*

LARGE-LEAVED LIME (*Tilia platyphyllos*)

General characters: Deciduous tree up to 100′ high. Crown spreading. Bark dark grey, fairly smooth. Leaves alternate, broadly egg-shaped, pointed, unequally heart-shaped at base, sharply toothed, short simple hairs on undersurface and in whitish tufts in axils of veins. Flowers yellowish-green, fragrant, 2–5 (usually 3) in pendulous cyme with large oblong bract. Sepals 5, free. Petals 5, free. Stamens numerous. Ovary superior, 5-celled, each cell with 2 ovules (placentation axile). Style slender, Stigma 5-lobed.
Habitat: Woods.
Pollination: Cross-pollination by bees and other insects.
Fruit: A small hairy nut. 1-celled, with 1–3 seeds. Ribbed. Shed with bract which acts as wing. Dispersed by wind. Eaten by jay and carrion crow. Average weight: 0·087 gm.
Seeds: With endosperm. Seeds rarely ripen in parts of range (e.g. Britain).
Vegetative reproduction: Propagated by layering.
Range: Europe (including Britain).
Uses: Lime one of best woods for carving, much of Grinling Gibbons's famous work executed in it. Bast ("raffia") from just below bark

was made into mats and cordage. An important honey plant, large amounts of nectar being secreted. Dried flowers used to make "tea" and large amounts collected in Britain during Second World War for medicinal purposes.

JUTE PLANT (*Corchorus capsularis*)

General characters: Little branched annual up to 15′ high. Stems thin, erect, round, sometimes branching near tip. Leaves alternate, 2–4″ long, tapering, pointed, toothed. Flowers 2–3 together opposite leaves. Sepals 5, narrow. Petals 5, small, yellow. Stamens numerous. Ovary 5-celled, ovules numerous.

Habitat: Cultivated on alluvial land.

Fruit: A small wrinkled almost globular capsule with flat ridged top. Splits into 5 segments to shed seeds.

Seeds: Small, oval, pointed, brown.

Range: Tropics. Main commercial cultivation in Bengal region of India and E. Pakistan, particularly in highland districts.

Uses: Jute, which is used in manufacture of 80 products, including sacking, carpets, rugs and matting, consists of extracted phloem fibres of plant. Best fibre obtained when plants harvested at flowering stage or before capsules ripen. Average crop yields 1,040 lb. fibre per acre. 2½–3 million acres cultivated in Pakistan and India, yielding 7–10 million 400-lb. bales fibre.

Special comments: Numerous varieties exist, differing in colour of stems, height, leaf-shape, degree of hairiness.

Family *STERCULIACEAE*

GENEESBESSIE (*Hermannia cuneifolia*)

General characters: Shrublet with hairy woody stems lying on ground and rising at end. Leaves alternate, small, wedge-shaped, shortly stalked, with small pointed persistent stipules. Flowers yellow or orange, pendulous. Calyx 5-lobed, lobes pointed, densely covered with short yellowish star-shaped hairs. Petals 5, free, erect. Stamens 5. Ovary superior, 5-celled, ovules numerous. Style 1.

Habitat: Sandy plains and dry rocky slopes.

Fruit: Dry, conical, 5-ridged, opening to allow seeds to escape.

Vegetative reproduction: Some *Hermannia* species propagated from root cuttings.

Range: S. Africa.

Uses: No information. (Dried leaves of *Hermannia hyssopifolia* were used as tea.)

Special comments: Several *Hermannia* species spread after fires.

AFRICAN TRAGACANTH (*Sterculia tragacantha*)

General characters: Deciduous tree up to 85′ high. Bark grey-brown, fissured. Branchlets densely covered with brown star-shaped hairs. Leaves egg-shaped to elliptic, up to 10″ long and 6″ broad, with dense small star-shaped hairs beneath, on stalks up to 3″ long. Flowers reddish-pink, in stalked inflorescence densely covered with brown star-shaped hairs, without petals. Calyx small, lobes adhering together at top.

Habitat: Open and drier parts of lowland rain forests.

Fruit: Of 4–5 boat-shaped carpels, each 2–3″ long, bright red and later brown, splitting along top side, bristly-hairy inside.

Seeds: Slate-coloured, shining, oblong-ellipsoid, about ¾″ long.

Vegetative reproduction: Propagated by cuttings (for live fences).

Range: Tropical Africa.

Uses: Bark yields pinkish gum used in confectionery, to adulterate gum arabic, etc. Wood used for huts, poles and domestic utensils. Young leaves eaten. Bark, shoots, leaves, fruiting carpels and seeds used medicinally.

African Tragacanth (*Sterculia tragacantha*)

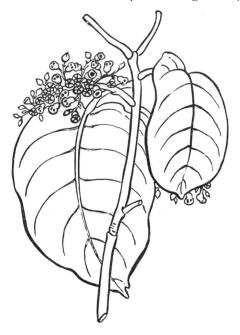

Family *BOMBACACEAE*

Silk Cotton Tree (*Bombax buonopozense*)

General characters: Deciduous tree up to 120′ high. Bark grey, rough, often armed with prickles. Leaves alternate, with 5–8 leaflets arranged digitately on common stalk up to 9½″ long. Stipules soon falling. Flowers deep pink or red, tulip-like, usually appearing before leaves, solitary, erect on branches. Calyx yellowish-green. Petals 5, free, 2½–3½″ long. Stamens numerous. Ovary superior, usually 5-celled. Style simple.

Habitat: Lowland rain forests.

Fruit: A cylindrical dark brown capsule 4–7½″ long. Splits open in 5 valves. Contains white or greyish "kapok."

Seeds: Numerous, embedded in "kapok." Contain an oil (? not used).

Vegetative reproduction: Propagated from cuttings.

Range: W. Tropical Africa.

Uses: "Kapok" used for stuffing cushions. Wood used for drums, doors, domestic utensils. Branches used for walking-sticks. Reddish-brown dye prepared from bark. Bark sometimes used for roofing huts, sheds. Flowers are mucilaginous and used in soups, sauces. Young

leaves fed to goats. Bark, leaves and flowers used medicinally (emollient properties).

Special comments: A sacred tree of the Tera tribe.

Order **MALVALES**

Family *MALVACEAE*

COMMON MALLOW (*Malva sylvestris*)

General characters: Perennial herb 1–3′ high. Leaves on long stalks, roundish, 3–7-lobed, lobes with blunt curved teeth, heart-shaped at base. Stems and stalks of leaves and flowers with long spreading hairs with swollen bases. Flowers rose-purple, stalked, in clusters in leaf-axils. Calyx 5-lobed, with 3 shorter segments (epicalyx) below, fringed with long hairs. Petals 5, joined at base to staminal tube. Stamens numerous, filaments united into staminal tube. Ovary superior, of about 10 united carpels, flat and disk-like. Style branches about 10 (same number as carpels).

Habitat: Waste places, roadsides, on walls and towers (sometimes at great heights).

Pollination: Cross-pollination by bees and other insects.

Fruit: A schizocarp, splitting up into 1-seeded nutlets.

Seeds: With little endosperm. Flattened, with v-shaped slit on one side.

Range: Europe (including Britain). Introduced into N. and S. America, Australia.

Uses: Source of nectar and pollen for honey bees. Leaves used as expectorant. Flowers used for gargling and mouth-washes.

MARSH MALLOW (*Althaea officinalis*)

General characters: Softly hairy perennial herb up to 4′ high. Leaves alternate, 3–4″ long and broad, stalked, shallowly 3–5-lobed, lobes pointed. Flowers pale pink, 1–1½″ broad, in upper leaf-axils, 1–3 together. Cup-like epicalyx of 7–9 narrow segments outside 5-lobed calyx. Petals 5, veiny. Stamens numerous, filaments united below. Ovary of 15–20 carpels.

Habitat: Salt marshes, along ditches near sea.

Pollination: Cross-pollination by insects. Failing this, automatic self-pollination.

Fruit: A disk-like group of hairy 1-seeded nutlets. Splitting up.

Seeds: With little endosperm. Kidney-shaped.

Range: Europe (including Britain). N. America. W. Asia, N. Africa.

Uses: Dried leaves and roots used medicinally to make soothing ointment and syrup. Mucilage from roots used in confectionery.

OKRA (*Hibiscus esculentus*)

General characters: Erect annual up to 6′ or more. Leaves large, on long stalks, divided into 3–5 pointed lobes with toothed margins (upper leaves usually more deeply divided than lower). Flowers bright yellow with red centre, solitary in leaf-axils on short stalks. Epicalyx of 8–10 narrow hairy bracteoles. Calyx 5-lobed, hairy. Petals 5, large. Stamens numerous. Ovary 5-celled.

Habitat: Moist but well-drained soil.

Pollination: By insects.

Fruit: A long ridged capsule. Mucilaginous and containing numerous seeds. Fresh fruit are rich in vitamin A and also contain vitamins B_1 and C, calcium, phosphorus, iron and little protein.

Seeds: Like small peas.

Range: Cultivated widely in tropics.

Uses: Popular vegetable in tropics. Young fruit eaten as vegetable or in soups and meat dishes. Young seeds cooked like peas. Seeds dried as coffee substitute. Fruit sometimes pickled or dried for winter use. Leaves cooked as pot herb. Stem fibres used locally but not commercially.

Special comments: Several varieties in cultivation, differing in form of fruit, degree of hardiness, flavour.

LACEBARK (*Hoheria lyallii*)

General characters: Graceful deciduous tree up to 30' high. Young branches and leaves with short star-shaped hairs. Leaves alternate, egg-shaped, pointed, thin and soft, up to 4" long, on slender stalks up to 2" long. Flowers white, about 1" across, numerous, on slender stalks in clusters of 3–5 in leaf-axils. Calyx 5-lobed, broadly bell-shaped. Petals 5. Stamens numerous, filaments united below. Ovary 10–15-celled, each cell with 1 ovule. Style branched above, with 10–15 slender branches.

Habitat: Subalpine forests.

Fruit: Globose. About ½" across. Consists of about 12 flattened 1-seeded carpels.

Seeds: Flattened.

Range: New Zealand.

Uses: Cultivated in several countries as attractive garden tree.

WILD HOLLYHOCK (*Sidalcea malvaeflora*)

General characters: Hairy perennial herb up to 2' high. Leaves rounded to kidney-shaped, 7–9-lobed, fleshy, long-stalked, up to 2" across, with small stipules. Flowers purple to rose-pink, usually white-veined, in racemes at top of stems. Calyx 5-lobed, hairy. Petals 5. Stamens numerous, filaments united. Ovary superior, of 5–9 carpels.

Habitat: Open grassy slopes, ditches, roadsides.

Pollination: By insects.

Fruit: 1-seeded carpels separating when ripe.
Range: California. Cultivated in other parts of world.
Uses: Important bee plant (nectar and pollen) in California.

Order **MALPIGHIALES**

Family *MALPIGHIACEAE*

BARBADOS CHERRY (*Malpighia glabra*)

General characters: Erect shrub or small tree up to 15′ high. Leaves opposite, oval, dark green, glossy, prickly, about 1″ long. Flowers pinkish white, ½″ across. Sepals 5, with 2 glands under each. Petals 5, clawed. Stamens 10, two larger than others. Ovary 3-celled, 1 ovule per cell.

Habitat: Cultivated in deep well-drained soil.

Pollination: Cross-pollination by bees.

Fruit: A round berry-like drupe. Bright red to crimson. Pulp juicy. Seeds in a 3-part stone, 3 angular pits lying together and looking like single stone. Fruit also known as acerolas, thin-skinned and delicate,

edible, very rich in vitamin C, larger amounts in green fruit less than half-ripe. Ripe fruit also contains carbohydrate, calcium, iron, and vitamins A, B_1 and B_2.

Seeds: Without endosperm.

Vegetative reproduction: Propagated by air layering, cuttings and grafting.

Range: Africa. Tropical America. West Indies. S. Texas.

Uses: Fruit eaten raw. Juice canned and made into jellies. Plant used for hedges.

Special comments: Several cultivated varieties developed in Puerto Rico and Florida.

Family *LINACEAE*

PALE FLAX (*Linum bienne*)

General characters: Slender branched annual, biennial or perennial herb up to 2' high. Leaves alternate, short, narrowly lance-shaped, stalkless. Flowers pale blue, in loose few-flowered cymes with small leaf-like bracts. Sepals 5, pointed. Petals 5, clawed, about $\frac{1}{2}''$ long. Stamens 5, filaments united at base. Ovary superior, 5-celled, each cell with 2 ovules.

Habitat: Waste places, dry grassland (mainly in limestone districts).

Fruit: A capsule, 10-toothed at top. Opening by 10 valves.

Seeds: Flat, egg-shaped, shining.

Range: Europe (including Britain).

Uses: No information.

Family *ERYTHROXYLACEAE*

COCA TREE (*Erythroxylum coca*)

General characters: Shrub with rusty brown slender branches. Leaves alternate, elliptical. Flowers yellow, small, in clusters of 3–5 in leaf-axils. Calyx bell-shaped, with 5 overlapping lobes. Petals 5, free, overlapping, with scale on inner side. Stamens 10, filaments united into a tube. Ovary superior, 3-celled (2 cells usually sterile, fertile cell with 1–2 ovules). Styles 3.

Habitat: Forests. Cultivated.

Fruit: A red 1-seeded drupe.

Seeds: With endosperm.

Range: S. America. Cultivated in Ceylon, Java and elsewhere in tropics.

Uses: Leaves infused as tea, chewed as stimulant in S. America, and used in manufacture of drug cocaine.

Family *ZYGOPHYLLACEAE*

PUNCTURE VINE (*Tribulus terrestris*)

General characters: Prostrate annual herb with hairy stems up to 2′ long. Leaves opposite, pinnate with 5–7 lance-shaped leaflets, stalked. Stipules small, thin, transparent, paired. Flowers yellow, stalked, solitary in leaf-axils. Sepals 5, free. Petals 5, free. Stamens 10. Ovary superior, 5-celled, 3–5 ovules in each cell (axile). Style 1.

Habitat: Waste ground, roadsides, shingle.

Fruit: Hard, flattened, 5-angled, with sharp woody spines. Not opening to allow seeds to escape. Sticks into feet of animals and tyres of motor vehicles and is thus dispersed.

Range: A widespread weed, particularly in the tropics.

Uses: Fruits used as diuretic.

Order EUPHORBIALES

Family *EUPHORBIACEAE*

PETTY SPURGE (*Euphorbia peplus*)

General characters: Annual herb with milky juice, 4–12″ high. Stems leafy, simple or branched from base. Leaves oval or reverse-egg-shaped, lower alternate with short slender stalks, upper becoming opposite and stalkless. Flowers very small, sometimes almost hidden by leaves, unisexual but sexes on same plant. Flower-heads small, green, each consisting of cup-shaped involucre with crescent-shaped long-pointed glands on margin and containing 1 female and several male flowers. Male consists of 1 stamen on jointed stalk. Female flower is simply a 3-celled ovary on a stalk (1 ovule in each cell).

Habitat: Cultivated and waste places.

Pollination: Mainly by flies, beetles and wasps (nectar secreted by glands of involucre).

Fruit: A small capsule splitting into 3 valves.

Seeds: Oblong, pale grey, deeply pitted. Average weight: 0·000497 gm. About 260 seeds produced on a plant.

Range: Europe (including Britain). Introduced into U.S.A., S. Africa.

Uses: Tincture and liquid extract of whole plant have been recommended for asthma and bronchial catarrh.

Special comments: Poisonous. Fatal poisoning occurred through a boy eating it. Tropical members of genus *Euphorbia* include trees and shrubs.

PARA RUBBER-TREE (*Hevea brasiliensis*)

General characters: Evergreen tree 60–100′ high. Trunk smooth, straight, bark light grey. Branches slender. Crown open. Leaves alternate, on long stalks, palmate with 3 long elliptical leaflets. Flowers small, greenish-white, strongly scented, mainly at ends of branches, unisexual. No petals. Calyx-tube 5-lobed. Males with 10 stamens. Females larger than males, with 3-celled ovary, each cell with 1 ovule.

Habitat: Tropical rain forests and elsewhere in tropics where rainfall at least 75″ annually and temperature 75–90° F. or more.

Pollination: By moths, bees and flies.

Fruit: A large 3-lobed 3-seeded capsule that opens explosively and scatters seeds.

Seeds: Large, brown, mottled. Seed-coat thick. Must be planted immediately as soon lose viability. Contain dark red drying oil sometimes used in soap-making.

Vegetative reproduction: Propagated by bud-grafting on to young seedlings.

Range: S. America (Amazon Valley). Cultivated in Malaya, Indonesia, W. Africa and the Congo.

Uses: Main source of world's natural rubber. Rubber a constituent of latex which is formed in latex vessels in cortex (derived from cambium). Latex collected from tree by tapping, a shallow incision being cut into bark so that latex flows down it to be collected in cup attached to trunk. Tapping starts when tree 4–7 years old.

Special comments: Improved varieties produced by breeding and selection. All trees now planted in Malaya yield at least twice as much as original introductions into S.E. Asia. (Seeds collected by Wickham in Brazil, 1876, planted at Kew Gardens, England, and young plants later sent to Ceylon.)

CASTOR-OIL PLANT (*Ricinus communis*)

General characters: Erect shrub (in tropics) or herb (in Europe) 6–35' high. Leaves alternate, on long stout stalks, palmately lobed with 5–11 large pointed lobes. Flowers in panicles at end of branches, unisexual, males at base of inflorescence, females in upper part. Petals none. Sepals 3 or 5, united at base. Stamens numerous, with much-branched filaments, anthers bursting explosively and scattering pollen. Ovary 3-celled, covered with green spiky outgrowths.

Habitat: Clearings, roadsides, rubbish-heaps throughout tropics and subtropics. Also cultivated.

Fruit: Globular, spiny, 3-celled, each cell with 1 seed. In wild types fruit explodes into 3 sections which open and drop seeds. Breeding has produced varieties whose ripe capsules do not shatter.

Seeds: Mottled. Colour varies from buff to black. Oval, flattened, with large caruncle. With copious endosperm. Oil content 35–55%. Some seeds are sea-borne (plants grown from seeds that floated 93 days in sea-water).

Range: Wild in many parts of tropics and subtropics. Cultivated in Brazil, Central Europe, India, U.S.A., U.S.S.R. Grown as decorative annual in Britain.

Uses: Castor oil from seeds used for medicinal purposes, soap-making, high-temperature lubricant, in manufacture of plastics, in fluids for hydraulic systems, as raw material for chemical manufacture. "Residue cake" (left after oil expressed) poisonous to livestock but used as fertilizer. Leaves yield insecticide. Pulp and cellulose from stems made into cardboard and newsprint.

CANDLE-NUT (*Aleurites triloba*)

General characters: Spreading tree up to 40' high. Young leaves and branches with short star-shaped hairs. Leaves alternate, stalked, up to 9" long, variable in shape (sometimes egg- to lance-shaped), entire or with 3–7 lobes. Flowers white, numerous, unisexual, sexes on same tree, in much-branched cymes at end of branches. Calyx very small, splitting into 2–3 segments. Petals 5, reverse-egg-shaped. Stamens 15–20. Ovary 2–5-celled, each cell with 1 ovule. Styles 2–5, two-cleft.

Habitat: Islands and places near coast. Also planted.

Fruit: A large fleshy drupe 2" across, with 1–3 seeds.

Seeds: With fleshy endosperm. Large. Seed-coat thick, wrinkled.

Range: Pacific Islands. Asia. Australia.

Uses: Seeds are source of drying oil used in varnishes, paints, soap, wood preservatives, burning oil. In Polynesia they are strung on sticks and burnt as candles.

Special comments: Rapid drying Tung oil of commerce obtained from seeds of *Aleurites fordii* and *A. montana*, natives of China now cultivated in several parts of world.

Order **THEALES**

Family *THEACEAE*

TEA PLANT (*Camellia sinensis*)

General characters: Evergreen shrub or small tree reaching 30–50' in wild but kept pruned to about 5' in cultivation. Leaves alternate, on

very short stalks, elliptical, 2–12″ long, margin toothed, leathery, stiff. Flowers white or pinkish, fragrant, up to $1\frac{1}{2}″$ across, solitary or in small groups in leaf-axils. Sepals 5. Petals 5. Stamens numerous. Ovary superior, 3–4-celled, each cell with 4–6 ovules (placentation axile).

Habitat: Hillsides in tropical forest areas.

Pollination: Cross-pollination by insects.

Fruit: A brownish-green capsule. Globular, woody, lobed. Diameter $\frac{1}{2}″$ or more. Opens when ripe.

Seeds: Brown, spherical or flattened. Period of viability very short. Contain about 20% of yellow non-drying oil (apparently not exploited commercially).

Vegetative reproduction: Mainly grown from seed, though cuttings sometimes used.

Range: Wild plants in Asiatic tropics. Cultivated in China, India, Ceylon, Java, Indonesia, E. Africa, Rhodesia, French Equatorial Africa, Brazil, Peru, Argentine, S. Russia.

Uses: Dried leaves used to make world's most popular non-alcoholic drink, tea, whose refreshing and stimulating properties are due to caffeine (tannin gives tea its "strength" and essential oils its flavour and aroma).

Special comments: Plucking of young shoots and leaves starts when plant 3–4 years old and continues at intervals until it is 40–50 years old.

Order **OCHNALES**

Family *OCHNACEAE*

Bo-kera (*Ochna wightiana* var. *moonii*)

General characters: Erect shrub or tree up to 15′ high. Much branched. Leaves alternate, lance-shaped, 3–6″ long, very shortly stalked, pointed, finely toothed. Stipules present. Flowers bright yellow, $\frac{3}{4}$″ across, 6–12 in umbellate panicles. Sepals 5, free, persistent, crimson and much enlarged in fruit. Petals 5, free. Stamens indefinite or 10, free. Ovary of 3–10 1-celled 1-ovuled carpels.

Habitat: Moist regions in low country.

Fruit: Ripe carpels distinct, fleshy, 1-seeded, smooth, purplish-black, not opening.

Seeds: With endosperm.

Range: Assam. Burma. Ceylon.

Uses: Timber used for walking-sticks.

Go-kera (*Ouratea zeylanica*)

General characters: Small much-branched tree up to 35′ high. Leaves alternate, lance-shaped, $2\frac{1}{2}$–5″ long, nearly stalkless, finely toothed,

shining, young leaves reddish, old olive-green. Stipules soon falling. Flowers yellow, numerous, about $\frac{1}{2}''$ across, on slender stalks in large pyramidal panicles in leaf-axils and at ends of shoots. Sepals 5, red, free, oval, persistent. Petals 5, free, clawed. Stamens 10, filaments very short. Ovary of 5 ovoid 1-celled carpels. Style stout, basal.

Habitat: Moist parts of low country.

Fruit: 5 or fewer ripe 1-seeded distinct carpels surrounded by persistent sepals. Purple-black, shining, small.

Seeds: Without endosperm.

Range: Ceylon. Malabar. Philippines. Singapore.

Uses: Wood used for posts (termite-proof).

Order **ERICALES**

Family *PYROLACEAE*

WINTERGREEN (*Pyrola minor*)

General characters: Perennial herb. Leaves towards base of stem, egg-shaped or oval, minutely and bluntly toothed, long-stalked. Flowers white or pinkish, small, drooping, in short-stalked racemes. Calyx 5-lobed. Petals 5, free. Stamens 10, free. Ovary superior, incompletely 5-celled, ovules numerous. Style simple, short. Stigma 5-lobed.

Habitat: Woods, moist shady places, moors.

Pollination: Cross-pollination by insects.

Fruit: A 5-lobed capsule splitting down middle of each cell. Edges of valves with web-like threads.

Seeds: Very small, numerous. Seed-coat loose, produced into short "tail" at each end. Endosperm copious. Dispersed by wind and rain-wash.

Range: Europe (including Britain). N. America. Asia.

Uses: No information. (Leaves of *Pyrola rotundifolia* used in medicine and as home-remedy for healing wounds).

Family *ERICACEAE*

COMMON RHODODENDRON (*Rhododendron ponticum*)

General characters: Evergreen shrub up to 15′ high. Leaves alternate, elliptic to narrowly oblong, dark glossy green above, paler beneath, pointed, smooth, up to 9″ long. Flowers purple, 2″ across, in large terminal clusters. Calyx small, 5-lobed. Corolla widely bell-shaped, 5-lobed. Stamens 10. Ovary superior, several-celled, ovules numerous. Style simple.

Habitat: Woods and open places on peaty and sandy soils.

Pollination: By insects.

Fruit: A dry woody capsule. Splits open.

Seeds: Numerous, minute, flat, winged. With endosperm. Dispersed by wind.

Vegetative reproduction: By taking root at branches.

Range: Europe. Asia Minor.

Uses: Makes a good hedge. Planted as cover for game and as shelter-belts. Young plants used as stocks on which garden varieties of rhodo-dendrons are grafted. Used by plant-breeders to produce hardy hybrid rhododendrons.

Special comments: Regarded as pest by foresters and horticulturists in some places, as spreads quickly by seedlings and vegetative means. Control is difficult and expensive. *R. ponticum* known to yield poison-ous honey in S.E. Europe.

STRAWBERRY TREE (*Arbutus unedo*)

General characters: Evergreen shrub or tree up to 40' high, but often much shorter. Bark brown, often with reddish tinge, rough, some-times peeling. Leaves alternate, shortly stalked, toothed, 2–3" long, rather leathery, typically oblong-lance-shaped. Flowers white tinged with green or pink, in many-flowered drooping panicles at end stems. Calyx deeply 5-lobed, lobes minute, triangular. Corolla pitcher-shaped, shortly 5-lobed. Stamens 10, anthers with 2 long appendages at back. Ovary superior, 5-celled, several ovules in each cell.

Habitat: Cliffs, rocky lake-shores, margins of oakwoods, steep rocky places.

Pollination: Cross-pollination by bees. Also self-pollination.

Fruit: A globular warty berry. Red. Flesh soft yellow. Eaten by thrushes, blackbirds, fieldfares and other birds, which probably help disperse seeds. Takes 13–14 months to mature.

Seeds: With endosperm. 20–40 seeds per fruit. Small. Ellipsoidal.

Vegetative reproduction: Apparently none.

Range: Ireland. Mediterranean region.

Uses: Berries made into preserves and liqueur. Leaves, fruit and bark (contains 45% tannin) used for tanning. Wood used mainly for charcoal.

Special comments: Planted in British gardens, withstanding gales in coastal districts.

SCOTCH HEATHER (Ling) (*Calluna vulgaris*)

General characters: Low much-branched evergreen shrub. Leaves opposite, very small, with 2 small projecting spurs at base, margins rolled downwards. Leaves on main stems widely spaced, but those on short shoots arranged in 4 rows. Flowers pale purple (very rarely white), small, in leafy racemes. Calyx deeply 4-lobed, coloured like

corolla. Corolla smaller, deeply 4-lobed, bell-shaped. Stamens 8, anthers tailed at base. Ovary superior, 4-celled, ovules numerous. Style simple, stout.

Habitat: Heaths, moors, bogs, open pinewoods, birchwoods and mixed oakwoods on acid soils. A greyish densely hairy form (variety *hirsuta*) grows on fixed sand-dunes.

Pollination: Pollinated by wind and such insects as bees and thrips. Both self- and cross-pollination probably occur.

Fruit: A small globose capsule opening by slits. 20–32 seeds per capsule.

Seeds: Minute. About 1 million seeds produced per square metre in a season near Bergen (Nordhagen's calculation). Dispersed by horse, cattle, elk (seeds in dung), wind and probably certain birds.

Vegetative reproduction: By prostrate branches rooting (usually in moist conditions).

Range: Europe (including Britain). Eastern N. America (according to tradition, introduced by emigrants from Scotland in heather-beds). Morocco.

Uses: A major honey plant, particularly in Scotland and N. England (heather honey with strong flavour, in great demand). Branches made into brooms, also used for thatching and packing. Shoots, flowers and seed-heads form staple food of red grouse. A valuable grazing plant for hill sheep and cattle, particularly in winter. Several cultivated varieties make attractive garden plants.

Special comments: Controlled burning of ling carried out to encourage new growth for grouse and sheep.

Family *MONOTROPACEAE*

YELLOW BIRD'S-NEST (*Monotropa hypopitys*)

General characters: Saprophytic herb without chlorophyll, living on dead organic matter, 6–12″ high, yellowish or whitish. Stems simple, with yellowish scales. Flowers pale yellow, in drooping raceme at top of stem. Sepals 4–5. Petals 4–5. Stamens 4–5. Ovary superior, deeply 4–5-lobed, incompletely 4–5-celled, ovules numerous. Root system much-branched, roots covered with hyphae of fungus (mycorrhiza) which aid absorption of ready-made food from decaying leaves.

Habitat: Beechwoods, pinewoods, woods and dunes with willows. Able to live in dense woods where light is insufficient for green plants.

Pollination: Cross-pollination by insects.

Fruit: A capsule opening by slits. About 1,970 seeds per capsule.

Seeds: Minute, tailed at ends. With endosperm. Average weight: 0·000003 gm. Average seed output per plant, 16,000. Viability low.

Range: Europe (including Britain). N. America, Asia.

Uses: No information.

Special comments: Monotropa hypophegea has filaments, style and inside of petals glabrous (with stiff hairs in *M. hypopitys*).

Order **GUTTIFERALES**

Family *HYPERICACEAE*

ST. JOHN'S WORT (*Hypericum perforatum*)

General characters: Erect perennial herb 1–3′ high. Stems 2-ridged. Leaves opposite, egg-shaped to oblong, stalkless, marked with transparent glandular dots (oil sacs). Flowers yellow, in many-flowered leafy cymes at top stems. Sepals 5, lance-shaped, with few gland-like dots or lines. Petals 5, glands on margin. Stamens numerous, joined at base into 3 bundles. Ovary superior, 3-celled, ovules numerous (placentation axile). Styles 3, free, slender.

Habitat: Margins of woods, roadsides, grassland.

Pollination: By insects. Apparently both cross- and self-pollination depend on insects which visit flowers for pollen (nectar absent).

Fruit: A capsule.

Seeds: Without endosperm. Small. Average weight: 0·00013 gm. Average annual seed output 26,000–34,000 seeds per plant. Dispersed by wind, plants growing high up on churches in France. Have retained viability for 10 years.

Vegetative reproduction: By adventitious shoots from lateral roots.

Range: Europe (including Britain). W. Asia. N. Africa. Introduced into Australia, New Zealand, U.S.A. (where it has become a dangerous pest).

Uses: Used medicinally against colds, coughs, etc. (tonic and astringent properties).

Special comments: In some countries spreads rapidly through dry pastures (excluded other vegetation on $\frac{1}{4}$ million acres in Victoria; infests $1\frac{3}{4}$ million acres ranges in U.S.A.). Contains poison affecting horses, cattle, sheep and goats. When bruised plant has aromatic odour.

Order **MYRTALES**

Family *MYRTACEAE*

MYRTLE (*Myrtus communis*)

General characters: Evergreen shrub or small tree up to 15′ high. Leaves opposite, egg- or lance-shaped, pointed, 1–2″ long, dotted with oil glands and fragrant when crushed. Flowers white, fragrant, solitary

on slender stalks in leaf-axils. Petals 5, rounded. Calyx 5-lobed. Stamens numerous, crowded. Ovary inferior, 3-celled, each cell with 3 ovules.

Habitat: Dry scrubby places.

Pollination: By insects.

Fruit: A purplish-black (white in one variety) berry $\frac{1}{2}''$ long. Eaten by birds.

Seeds: Without endosperm.

Vegetative reproduction: Propagated by cuttings.

Range: Europe. Asia.

Uses: Myrtle oil obtained by distillation from leaves and used as aromatic and tonic. Wood used for tool handles, walking-sticks. Sprigs of myrtle used in bridal bouquets (Myrtle was sacred to Aphrodite, goddess of love.)

SOUTHERN BLUE GUM (*Eucalyptus globulus*)

General characters: Large tree 150–180′ high. Trunk straight. Crown well-developed. Bark rough, grey, shed in long coarse strips, leaving smooth bluish-grey surface, bark persistent at base trunk. Leaves (adult) alternate, stalked, narrowly lance-shaped, often curved, glossy dark green, thick and leathery, aromatic, dotted with small immersed oil glands, up to 12″ long and 2″ broad. Flowers small, pale yellowish, solitary or rarely in 3s in leaf-axils. Sepals and petals 4–5, united to form double cap which covers stamens in bud and falls off in flower. Stamens numerous, conspicuous. Ovary inferior, 3–4-celled, each cell with numerous ovules.

Habitat: In Australia places near sea and moister valleys of hilly country.

Pollination: By insects, including bees. (In Australia species of *Eucalyptus* pollinated by nectar-eating honey mice.)

Fruit: A somewhat woody top-shaped or globose capsule opening at top.

Seeds: Without endosperm. Numerous, smooth, glossy, light. Dispersed by wind.

Range: Australia. Widely planted in other countries.

Uses: Timber used in both light and heavy construction. Also for poles, piles, sleepers. Fresh leaves are source Oil of Eucalyptus. Dried leaves used medicinally (antiseptic).

Special comments: Because of their quick growth and adaptability, many species of *Eucalyptus* are increasing in economic importance. Besides yielding timber and fuel, they are good pioneer plants and often thrive in high and arid places.

GUAVA (*Psidium guajava*)

General characters: Large evergreen shrub or small spreading tree up to 30′ or more high. Branching freely almost to ground. Trunk fairly thin. Bark scaly. Leaves opposite, almost stalkless, oval, up to 6″ long, dotted with oil glands. Flowers white, 1″ across, on short slender stalks, solitary or in groups of 2–3 in leaf-axils. Calyx-tube irregularly lobed. Petals 4, spreading. Stamens numerous. Ovary inferior, 4–5-celled, each cell with numerous ovules.

Habitat: Thickets. Cultivated.

Fruit: An edible berry 1–4″ long, 2″ or more across. Weight up to 16 oz. Apple- or pear-shaped. Skin smooth, greenish or yellow. Flesh white, yellow, pink or red, with many small seeds embedded in it. Flavour and smell often mild and pleasant, but sometimes acid and bitter. Rich in vitamin C. Also contains iron, calcium, phosphorus, and vitamins A, B_1, B_2.

Seeds: Numerous, flattened, kidney-shaped. Dispersed by birds.

Vegetative reproduction: Propagated by cuttings and grafting, but special treatment required. Also by air layering.

Range: Native of Central America, but now cultivated in many parts of tropics and subtropics, often escaping and becoming weed.

Uses: Fruit eaten raw, also made into jelly and guava cheese. Juice extracted and made into beverage.

Special comments: Named horticultural varieties being raised in Florida.

CLOVE TREE (*Eugenia caryophyllus*)

General characters: Evergreen tree up to 60–70′ in wild, 25–40′ when grown in plantations. Bark smooth, grey. Leaves opposite, lance-shaped, shortly stalked, up to 5″ long, 1″ or more broad, with numerous oil glands making crushed leaves aromatic. Flowers crimson, in 3s, on short stalks, in cymes at end branches. Calyx-tube fleshy, 4-lobed at top. Petals 4, soon falling. Stamens numerous.

Habitat: Wet lowland forests in tropics, often near sea.

Fruit: A 1-seeded drupe 1″ long. Topped by persistent calyx lobes.

Seeds: Soft. One side grooved. ¾″ long.

Range: Native of Moluccas, Zanzibar and Pemba (90% of world's clove supply). Dutch E. Indies. Madagascar. Java. West Indies.

Uses: Dried flower buds are cloves of commerce. Buds are hand-picked and dried in sun. Cloves used whole or in powder form to flavour food, pickles, sauces. Clove oil obtained by distilling flower buds, stems, fruit, and used in medicine, perfumes, and as antiseptic in dentistry. (Cloves employed in famous Vinegar of the Four Thieves, used by 4 men to ward off infection while they plundered homes of Plague victims in a French town about 1720.)

Special comments: Harvesting of flower buds starts when tree 8–9 years old and goes on for 60 years or more.

Order CELASTRALES

Family *AQUIFOLIACEAE*

HOLLY (*Ilex aquifolium*)

General characters: Evergreen shrub or tree up to 50′ or more. Stem smooth, later fissured, green or greyish. Leaves alternate, shortly stalked, thick and leathery, dark green, egg-shaped or oblong in outline, often with large spiny teeth and wavy margins, upper leaves sometimes entire. Flowers small, white, often unisexual with sexes on different plants, in small clusters in leaf-axils. Calyx small, of 4 lobes. Petals 4, united at base. Stamens 4, free. Ovary 4-celled, each cell with 1 ovule.

Habitat: Woods (often in shade), hedges.

Pollination: Cross-pollination by honey bees.

Fruit: A globose red drupe containing four 1-seeded stones. Eaten by thrushes, blackbirds and pheasants (one had 42 stones in gizzard).

Seeds: With endosperm. Dispersed by birds in excreta.

Range: Europe (including Britain).

Uses: Timber carves well, used for marquetry work, net-maker's needles. Birdlime made from bark. A valuable hedge plant. Cultivated varieties make attractive garden subjects. Berried foliage included in traditional Christmas decorations. Useful honey plant much-visited by bees.

Family *SALVADORACEAE*

Tooth-brush Tree (*Salvadora persica*)

General characters: Small erect much-branched tree. Branchlets long, slender, drooping. Bark rough, furrowed. Leaves opposite, numerous, oblong-oval or egg-shaped, shining on both sides, thick, shortly-stalked, $1\frac{1}{2}$–2″ long, with hot taste (tree also called Mustard-tree). Flowers small, greenish-white, very numerous on slender stalks in panicles at end shoots and in upper leaf-axils. Calyx small, bell-shaped, 4-toothed. Petals 4, united at base, persistent. Stamens 4, inserted in corolla-tube. Ovary superior, 1-celled, with 1 ovule. Style very short.

Habitat: Desert and dry regions, especially by coast.

Fruit: A small globose red drupe. 1-seeded.

Seeds: Without endosperm. Very small. Mustard-taste.

Range: Africa. Ceylon. India. Persia.

Uses: Fruit eaten and given as medicine to children. Leaves fed to camels. Twigs and roots used as tooth-brushes. Timber used for coffins.

Family *EMPETRACEAE*

CROWBERRY (*Empetrum nigrum*)

General characters: Evergreen heather-like shrub up to $1\frac{1}{2}'$ high. Much-branched. Leaves crowded, very short, edges rolled back. Flowers small, pinkish or purplish, solitary or in small groups in leaf-axils, unisexual, sexes on different plants. Perianth segments 6, free. Stamens 3. Ovary superior, globose, 6–9-celled, 1 ovule in each cell. Style short. Stigmas 6–9.

Habitat: Acid moorland.

Pollination: Wind-pollinated.

Fruit: Edible. A small black globular drupe containing several 1-seeded stones. Juicy, shining. Eaten by birds.

Seeds: With endosperm.

Range: Europe (including Britain). N. America.

Uses: Fruit eaten raw or made into beverage with sour milk.

Special comments: E. *nigrum*, moorland crowberry, a diploid plant (2n = 26), has been confused with E. *hermaphroditum*, mountain crowberry, a tetraploid plant (2n = 52), whose flowers are bisexual.

Family *CELASTRACEAE*

SPINDLE TREE (*Euonymus europaeus*)

General characters: Deciduous shrub or small tree 6–18' high. Much-branched. Bark smooth, grey. Twigs green, 4-angled. Leaves opposite, elliptic, pointed, toothed. Flowers greenish-white, in cymes in leaf-axils. Sepals 4, rounded. Petals 4, oblong. Stamens 4, inserted on disk. Ovary 4-celled, each cell with 1–2 ovules. Style simple, short.

Habitat: Woods, hedges, chalk scrub, limestone cliffs.

Pollination: Cross-pollination by small insects.

Fruit: A fleshy 4-lobed deep pink capsule which splits open.

Seeds: With copious endosperm. Enclosed in bright orange fleshy aril. Average weight: 0·0158 gm. Eaten by thrushes and blackbirds, which assist dispersal.

Range: Europe (including Britain). W. Asia.

Uses: Wood ("prickwood") made into skewers, toothpicks, knitting needles and artist's charcoal.

Special comments: Children, sheep and goats have suffered from eating leaves and fruit.

STAFF TREE (*Celastrus scandens*)

General characters: Deciduous climber with twining branches, ascending trees to height of 25' or more, or trailing on ground. Leaves

alternate, egg-shaped or oval, pointed, toothed, 2–4″ long. Flowers small, greenish or yellowish white, in racemes at ends branches, mostly unisexual, sexes on different plants. Calyx 5-lobed. Petals 5, with blunt curved teeth. Stamens 5. Ovary 2–4-celled, 2 ovules in each cell.

Habitat: Runs over trees, shrubs, hedges.

Fruit: A capsule with yellow or orange inner surface.

Seeds: With endosperm. Enclosed in bright scarlet aril.

Range: Eastern N. America. Cultivated in Europe.

Uses: A beautiful autumnal plant for covering unsightly objects.

Order **OLACALES**

Family *OLACACEAE*

MELLA (*Olax zeylanica*)

General characters: Shrub or small tree. Bark yellowish, ridged, with horizontal bands. Young branches sharply angled, yellow, finely ridged transversely. Leaves alternate, egg-shaped to oblong, 2–3″ long, shining, very shortly-stalked. Flowers small, few, stalked, in small racemes in leaf-axils. Calyx minute, cup-shaped, 4–5-lobed, much

enlarged in fruit. Petals 5, oblong, joined into tube. Stamens free, inserted at base petals, 3 fertile, 5 abortive (staminodes). Ovary 1-celled above, 3 celled below, ovules 3, ovary surrounded by small cup-shaped disk. Style long.

Habitat: Forests in moist low country.

Fruit: A small scarlet drupe with lower part in enlarged calyx. Ovoid, smooth, with stone 1-celled, 1-seeded.

Seeds: With endosperm.

Range: Ceylon.

Uses: Leaves eaten as salad.

Order SANTALALES

Family *LORANTHACEAE*

MISTLETOE (*Viscum album*)

General characters: Evergreen shrublet partially parasitic on various trees. Stems woody, green, with many forked branches. Leaves opposite, yellowish-green, leathery, narrow-oblong or narrowly reverse-egg-shaped, rounded at apex. Flowers unisexual, sexes usually on different plants, very small, yellow, almost stalkless in forks of branches. Petals 4, small. Calyx absent from male flowers, very small and 4-toothed in females. Stamens 4, stalkless on petals. Ovary inferior, 1-celled, ovules not distinct.

Habitat: Branches of many different kinds of broad-leaved trees and shrubs, including apple, poplar, oak, hawthorn and lime. Much rarer on coniferous trees, though recorded from pine, silver fir and spruce (also on trunk of this tree).

Pollination: Apparently by flies.

Fruit: A clear white globose berry. Viscous. 1-seeded.

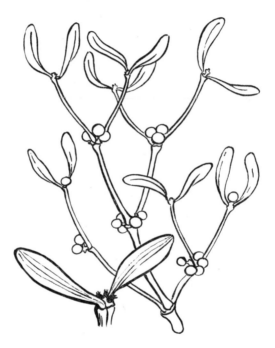

Seeds: With endosperm. Without seed-coat. 1–3 embryos in a seed. Need light for germination. Dispersed by birds which eat fruit and scrape sticky seeds on to branches.

Range: Europe (including Britain). Asia.

Uses: Source of drug used for nervous and hysterical complaints. Used as Christmas decoration in England, where "kissing under the mistletoe" still a feature of celebrations.

Special comments: Food-making carried on in leaves, water and other raw materials being derived from tree or shrub to which mistletoe attached by haustoria ("suckers").

Family *SANTALACEAE*

SANDALWOOD (*Santalum album*)

General characters: Semi-parasitic tree up to 30–40′ high. Leaves opposite, egg-shaped, pointed, shortly stalked. Flowers small, greenish, in clusters in leaf-axils. Calyx cup-shaped, united to ovary, with 4 pointed lobes at top. No petals. Stamens 4, arising from calyx-cup, each backed by several short hairs. Ovary 1-celled, ovules 1–3.

Habitat: In forests where its roots are attached by means of haustoria to roots of other species (over 100 host-plants known).

Fruit: A globose blackish-purple drupe. 1-seeded. $\frac{1}{4}''$ across.

Seeds: Without seed-coat. With copious fleshy endosperm.

Range: S. India. Malaya.

Uses: Wood sweetly scented and used for manufacture of boxes, chests and incense. Oil obtained from heartwood by steam distillation used medicinally and in perfumery.

Special comments: Cultivated in parts India. Slow-growing.

BASTARD TOADFLAX (*Thesium humifusum*)

General characters: Yellowish-green perennial herb, partially parasitic, attaching itself to roots of other plants by means of haustoria on own roots. Stems annual, slender, up to $1\frac{1}{2}′$ long. Leaves alternate, narrow,

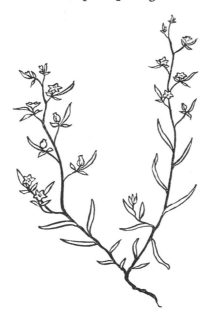

up to 1″ long. Flowers greenish-yellow, small, stalked, in racemes at top stems. Perianth funnel- to bell-shaped, of 5 triangular segments ("sepals"). Stamens 5. Ovary inferior, 1-celled, with 2 ovules.

Habitat: Meadows and pastures on chalk and limestone.

Fruit: A small green nut, ribbed, crowned by persistent calyx.

Seeds: With endosperm. Without seed-coat.

Range: Europe (England, Glamorgan, Belgium, France, Spain).

Uses: No information.

Order **RHAMNALES**

Family *ELAEAGNACEAE*

SEA BUCKTHORN (*Hippophaë rhamnoides*)

General characters: Thorny deciduous shrub or small tree, 3–20′ high. Much-branched. Covered with silvery scale-like hairs. Leaves alternate, narrow, often silvery on both sides. Flowers unisexual, sexes on different plants, very small, greenish, without petals. Male flowers appearing before leaves, in small catkin-like spikes, consisting of 4

stamens and 2 sepals. Female flowers appearing with first leaves, in short racemes in leaf-axils, with 2 minute sepals and a superior 1-celled ovary with 1 ovule.

Habitat: Sea cliffs and sand-dunes. Inland on gravel and sand banks.

Pollination: Wind-pollinated.

Fruit: Drupe-like, consisting of an achene enclosed in orange swollen fleshy receptacle. Fleshy pericarp very rich in vitamin C (120–860 mg/100 gm). Eaten by various birds.

Seeds: With endosperm. Germination epigeal. Average weight: 0·0015 gm. Dispersed by birds, remaining viable after ejection by hooded crow and starling.

Vegetative reproduction: "Suckering" by rhizome-like roots. Propagated by cuttings or layering.

Range: Europe (including Britain). Asia.

Uses: Wood sometimes used for turnery. Fruit made into jelly or sauce. Planted on coasts to form shelter-belts and to stabilize sand. Grown in gardens and on traffic islands for decorative value of foliage and fruit.

Special comments: Protected in Germany during Second World War because of high vitamin C content of fruit.

OLEASTER (*Elaeagnus commutata*)

General characters: Deciduous silver-scaly shrub up to 12' high. Much-branched. Young twigs covered with brown scurf, but becoming silvery. Leaves alternate, short-stalked, egg-shaped or oblong, 1–4" long, silvery on both sides. Flowers fragrant, in small clusters in leaf-axils. Perianth tubular below, 4-lobed above, silvery outside, yellow within. Stamens 4, borne on perianth-throat. Ovary 1-celled, 1 ovule.

Habitat: Rocky hillsides.

Pollination: Wind-pollinated.

Fruit: Drupe-like, thickened perianth-base enclosing achene. Oval. Silvery.

Vegetative reproduction: Stoloniferous.

Range: N. America. Cultivated in Europe.

Uses: Edible fruit.

Special comments: Received Award of Merit of Royal Horticultural Society, London.

Family *RHAMNACEAE*

BUCKTHORN (*Rhamnus catharticus*)

General characters: Thorny deciduous shrub or small tree up to 30' or more. Branching regular, branches in pairs almost at right angles to main stem. Leaves egg-shaped, toothed, stalked, 1–2½" long. Flowers unisexual, sexes on different plants, small, green, in dense clusters at base young shoots. Calyx tubular, 4-lobed. Petals 4, very small. Stamens 4. Ovary 3-4-celled, each cell with 1 ovule. Style 3-4-lobed.

Habitat: On alkaline fen peat, in scrub, hedgerows, ashwoods, oakwoods on limestone soils. Recorded from tops pollard willows.

Pollination: Cross-pollination by insects.

Fruit: A drupe containing 3-4 small 1-seeded pyrenes ("stones"), turning from green to black on ripening. Eaten by certain birds, but usually only in hard weather when other food scarce.

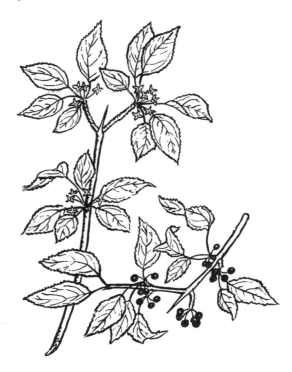

Seeds: With endosperm. Germination epigeal. Average weight: 0·01292 gm.

Vegetative reproduction: Not recorded.

Range: Europe (including Britain). W. Asia. N. Africa (at high altitudes in Morocco and Algeria).

Uses: Fruit were used in purgative medicine. Also to produce sap green for water colours. Wood used for charcoal for gunpowder.

Special comments: Charcoal in Neolithic deposits from Maiden Castle, Dorset.

Californian Lilac (*Ceanothus americanus*)

General characters: Deciduous shrub with several branched stems from deep reddish root (plant also called "Red-root"). Leaves alternate, stalked, egg-shaped, 1–3" long, pointed, toothed, finely hairy. Flowers small, white, in dense long-stemmed panicles at end shoots and in leaf-axils. Calyx-tube 5-lobed. Petals 5, hooded, narrowly clawed. Stamens 5. Ovary 3-celled, each cell with 1 ovule.

Habitat: Dry open woods.

Pollination: By insects.

Fruit: Dry, 3-lobed, nearly black, separating into 3 nutlets.

Seeds: With endosperm.

Range: E. North America.

Uses: American troops used leaves as tea ("New Jersey Tea"). Dried bark used medicinally (blood coagulant). Cultivated, the cross *americanus* × *coeruleus* having attractive sky-blue flowers.

Family *VITACEAE*

Grape Vine (*Vitis vinifera*)

General characters: Deciduous woody climber, climbing by tendrils. Stems with peeling bark. Leaves alternate, 3–6" wide and long, 3–5-lobed, coarsely toothed, long-stalked, often downy or felted below. Flowers small, greenish, in branched racemes opposite leaves, fragrant. Calyx small, 4–5-lobed. Petals 4–5, remaining united at top, becoming detached at base and falling as a cap. Stamens 4–5. Ovary usually 2-celled, each cell with 2 ovules.

Habitat: Warm sunny places.

Pollination: By wind. Also by insects in warmer climates.

Fruit: A berry with 1–4 seeds embedded in juicy pulp. Fresh grapes contain small amounts vitamins A, B, C, and some minerals but most of food value is in sugar.

Seeds: With endosperm. Source of drying oil. Grape seeds found on Swiss lake-dwelling sites and in ancient Egyptian tombs. Dispersed by people, birds, wild mammals (seeds in excreta of badgers and foxes).

Vegetative reproduction: Propagated from cuttings or by layering.

Range: Cultivated in all continents.

Uses: Grapes eaten raw as dessert fruit. Juice made into wine and champagne. Fruit dried to form raisins, sultanas, currants. Grape seed oil used in soap, paints, foods.

Special comments: Many varieties in cultivation grown for fruit, but others for ornamental autumn foliage.

Order **MYRSINALES**

Family *MYRSINACEAE*

CAPE BEECH (*Myrsine melanophloea*)

General characters: Small evergreen tree up to 15' high. Bark smooth, dark-coloured. Leaves alternate, oblong, stalked, dark green, leathery, about 4" long. Flowers creamy green, very small, stalkless, in leaf-axils. Calyx 5-toothed. Corolla 5-lobed, with very short tube. Stamens

5, without filaments, opposite petals. Ovary superior or half-inferior, 1-celled, with numerous ovules. Stigma without stalk.

Habitat: Forests, mountain ravines.

Pollination: By insects.

Fruit: Small, fleshy, spherical. Contains 1 or few seeds.

Seeds: With endosperm. Dispersed by elephants and birds which eat fruits.

Range: S. Africa.

Uses: Wood used for wagon building. Leaves used as astringent.

Family *AEGICERATACEAE*

GOAT'S HORNS (*Aegiceras corniculatum*)

General characters: Shrub or small tree. Leaves alternate, leathery, reverse-egg-shaped, up to 4″ long, shortly stalked, minutely dotted. Flowers white, fragrant, in dense clusters from ends of twigs or leaf-axils, on short stalks. Sepals 4–5. Corolla shortly tubular, 4–5-lobed. Stamens 4–5 (same number as corolla lobes). Ovary superior, 1-celled, with numerous ovules.

Habitat: Mangrove swamps.

Fruit: A cylindrical curved and pointed capsule (hence name), up to 2″ long, splitting open lengthwise.

Seeds: Without endosperm. Often germinate inside fruit. Long, curved.

Range: India. Malaya. Australia.

Uses: Bark used as fish poison. Wood made into knife-handles.

Order **EBENALES**

Family *EBENACEAE*

EBONY (*Diospyros ebenum*)

General characters: Large erect tree up to 60′ high. Crown dense, leafy. Bark dark grey. Leaves alternate, numerous, up to 6″ long, oblong-oval or oblong-lance-shaped, bright green and shining above, stiff, thickish, shortly stalked. Flowers small, pale greenish-yellow, unisexual, sexes on different trees, stalkless, in leaf-axils. Males in very shortly stalked clusters of 3–6, calyx 4-lobed, corolla tubular 4-lobed, stamens about 16 (filaments unequal, often joined in 2s or 3s). Female flowers solitary, larger than male, with 8 egg-shaped abortive stamens, superior 8-celled ovary, each cell with solitary ovule, stigmas 4.

Habitat: Forests mainly in dry regions.

Fruit: A small 3–8-seeded berry. Enlarged calyx forms shallow woody cup from back of which project large pointed thickened segments.

Seeds: With copious endosperm. Dull black, oblong, somewhat flattened, $\frac{3}{8}$″, with thin seed-coat.

Range: Ceylon. S. India. Malaya.

Uses: Hard jet-black wood used to make opium pipes and furniture.

PERSIMMON (*Diospyros virginiana*)

General characters: Deciduous tree up to 100′ high, but usually smaller. Bark hard, dark, furrowed. Leaves alternate, egg-shaped or

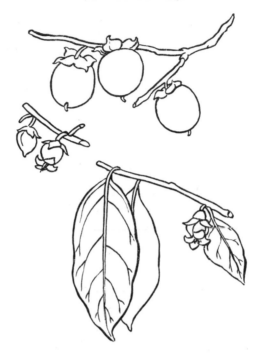

oval, becoming glossy, dark green above, pointed, 2–5″ long. Flowers inconspicuous, greenish-yellow, solitary or in small clusters, unisexual or bisexual, different flowers on same tree or on separate trees. Calyx 4-lobed. Corolla 4-lobed, pitcher-shaped.

Habitat: Fields and woods.

Pollination: Cross-pollination by bees.

Fruit: Large globose berry containing 4–12 seeds. Reddish-yellow and sweet when ripe, but green fruit have mouth-twisting effect described as "form of torture" (contain tannin).

Seeds: With endosperm. Flat, oblong, hard.

Vegetative reproduction: Produces suckers freely.

Range: Eastern N. America.

Uses: Young tender leaves sometimes picked, fermented and dried, and used like black tea. Hard strong wood used for carving, turnery, shoe-lasts, plane-stocks. Ripe fruit eaten raw, also used in puddings and cakes. (Fruit of related *D. kaki* contain vitamins A and C, calcium, sugar.)

Special comments: Little appears to have been done to improve this native persimmon in U.S.A., where Oriental persimmon (*D. kaki*), with much larger fruit, is grown in California and southern states.

Family *SAPOTACEAE*

STAR APPLE (*Chrysophyllum cainito*)

General characters: Evergreen tree 50–60' high. Crown narrow. Foliage dense. Leaves alternate, elliptic, pointed, shining red-silky below. Flowers small, white, on long stalks, in crowded clusters in leaf-axils. Calyx 4–8-lobed. Corolla 4–8-lobed, lobes overlapping. Stamens on petals. Ovary superior, many-celled, 1 ovule in each cell. Style simple.

Habitat: Forests. Also cultivated.

Fruit: A hard spherical berry 2–4" across. White to purple when ripe.

Seeds: With endosperm. Brown. Arranged in star-form, surrounded by white and pinkish-purple pulp.

Vegetative reproduction: Propagated by air layering or cleft grafting.

Range: Tropics.

Uses: Fruit pulp eaten. Wood used for cabinet-work.

Order **RUTALES**

Family *RUTACEAE*

SWEET ORANGE (*Citrus sinensis*)

General characters: Evergreen tree 25' or taller. Spreading. With slender blunt spines. Leaves egg-shaped-oblong, 3–4" long, pointed, dark green, shortly stalked. Flowers white, very fragrant, solitary or in small groups. Petals usually 5. Sepals 5, small, greenish. Stamens numerous. Ovary superior, of 8–15 united carpels.

Habitat: Well-drained sandy loams in sunny places.

Pollination: Self- and cross-pollination by insects.

Fruit: Familiar orange of commerce, a special form of berry, rounded. Skin ("peel") tight, contains chlorophyll and is green and photosynthetic at first, but as fruit ripens chlorophyll breaks down and skin turns deep yellow to orange as colour of carotenoid pigments xanthophyll and carotene becomes dominant. Skin with numerous oil glands containing essential oil. Flesh juicy, yellow to deep orange. Fruit contains vitamins A, B_1, B_2 and C, calcium, phosphorus, iron, sugar, citric acid.

Seeds: 0–28 (or more) per fruit, according to variety. Without endosperm.

Vegetative reproduction: Propagated by grafting or budding on to hardy and disease-resistant rootstock, rough lemon or bitter orange seedlings being commonly used for this purpose.

Range: Cultivated in tropics and warmer parts of subtropics.

Uses: Fruit eaten raw. Juice canned, bottled, frozen, used for flavouring. Oil extracted from flowers, leaves, young shoots, fresh peel and seeds and used in flavourings, perfume, soap. An important honey plant. "Agua de azahar," a kind of cordial, prepared from orange blossom in Spain (considered an excellent tonic for certain nervous disorders).

Special comments: Probably originated in S.E. Asia. Cultivated for a very long time (references to oranges in Chinese writing date back to about 2200 B.C.). Many varieties of Sweet Orange now cultivated. *Citrus aurantium,* Bitter or Seville Orange, produces sour fruit made into marmalade. Tangerine and Mandarin oranges, fruit of *Citrus reticulata,* are popular dessert fruits with very loose skin. Certain *Citrus* species hybridize readily, several natural and artificial hybrids being known. Tangors were produced by crossing Sweet Orange and Tangerines.

PRICKLY ASH (*Xanthoxylum americanum*)

General characters: Deciduous shrub or small tree up to 25′ high. Twigs and leaf-stalks prickly. Spines stiff, usually in pairs. Leaves alternate, 6–8″ long, odd-pinnate with 5–11 (sometimes 13) egg-shaped leaflets, heavy-scented when crushed. Flowers very small, yellowish-green, appearing before leaves, in clusters in leaf-axils. Calyx none. Petals 4–5. Stamens 4–5. Ovary of 2–5 distinct carpels, each with 2 ovules.

Habitat: Woods and thickets.

Fruit: A black fragrant 2-valved capsule. 1–2-seeded. Fleshy. Splits open.

Seeds: Black, shining, oblong.

Vegetative reproduction: Propagated by cuttings.

Range: Eastern N. America. Occasionally grown in Europe.

Uses: Dried bark used as cure for toothache (called Toothache Tree in U.S.A.).

RUE (*Ruta graveolens*)

General characters: Evergreen shrub about 3′ high. Branches erect, half-woody. Leaves alternate, 3–5″ long, blue-green, 2-pinnately dissected, aromatic. Flowers dull yellow, in cymes. Sepals 4–5. Petals 4–5, concave, edges jagged. Stamens 8–10. Ovary 4–5-celled, each cell with several ovules.

Habitat: Open places, cultivated and waste land.

Pollination: Cross-pollination by insects.

Fruit: A many-seeded capsule. Usually 4-celled.

Vegetative reproduction: Propagated by cuttings.

Range: Native of S. Europe. Now widely cultivated.

Uses: Rutin, essential principle of Rue, used in treatment of weakened blood vessels causing high blood pressure. Rue also used for nervous diseases and women's ailments. As bitter herb added sparingly to salads and stews. Oil of Rue, essential oil, distilled from green parts.

Special comments: Rue has long history of use in rituals and medicine, formerly being strewn about Law Courts and temples to discourage vermin and ward off plague.

Family *SIMAROUBACEAE*

TREE OF HEAVEN (*Ailanthus altissima*)

General characters: Deciduous tree up to 90–100′ high. Crown rounded. Older bark fissured. Leaves alternate, 1–3′ long, pinnate with 13–41 leaflets, with unpleasant smell. Leaflets 3–6″ long, egg-shaped, pointed, with few glandular teeth near base. Flowers small, greenish, in panicles at end branches, sexes often on separate trees. Calyx 5-lobed. Petals 5. Male flowers evil-smelling, with 10 stamens. Females with superior, deeply 2–5-lobed 2–5-celled ovary, each cell with 1 ovule.

Habitat: Woods, roadsides, fields, parks.

Pollination: By insects, including bees.

Fruit: A group of 1–5 reddish-brown samaras ("keys"), each about

1½" long, twisted, thin, 1-seeded in middle. "Key" revolves rapidly as it falls.

Seeds: Dispersed by wind.

Vegetative reproduction: Spreads extensively by suckers. Propagated by root cuttings.

Range: Asia. Widely naturalized in eastern N. America and parts Europe.

Uses: Wood used for building, furniture, fancy articles. Tree is source of surplus honey in parts Europe and N. America.

Special comments: A fine town tree. Smoke-resistant, hardy.

Order MELIALES

Family *MELIACEAE*

PERSIAN LILAC (*Melia azedarach*)

General characters: Tree up to 40' high. Leaves alternate, 9–18" long, 2-pinnate and occasionally 3-pinnate with pointed egg- or lance-

shaped leaflets $\frac{1}{2}''$ long. Flowers lilac, fragrant, $\frac{1}{4}''$ long, in panicles in leaf-axils. Calyx short, deeply 5–6-lobed. Petals 5–6, free, spreading, narrowly spoon-shaped. Anthers 10 or 12. Filaments united in a cylindrical staminal-tube which is purple, marked with 10–12 striations. Ovary superior, 5-celled. Ovules 2. Style slender.

Habitat: Forests, mountain slopes. Also widely cultivated.

Fruit: A drupe $\frac{1}{2}$–$\frac{3}{4}''$ across. 5-celled, 5-seeded or fewer by abortion.

Seeds: Bony. Dispersed by fruit-bats and birds which eat fruit.

Range: Baluchistan. Persia. India. Jamaica. C. America. Cultivated in Europe.

Uses: Various parts used medicinally. Stones of fruit made into necklaces and rosaries (hence name "Bead Tree"). Leaves used as fodder.

AFRICAN CEDAR (*Khaya senegalensis*)

General characters: Tree up to 100′ high. Bark grey, scaly, with reddish tinge. Leaves alternate, pinnate with 4–6 pairs oblong or oblong-elliptic leaflets. Flowers whitish with red disk around ovary, in loose panicles in leaf-axils. Sepals 4. Petals 4, free. Stamens 8, joined below into tube. Ovary superior.

Habitat: Savannah and fringing forest and in low-lying places beside streams.

Fruit: A woody capsule $2\frac{1}{2}''$ across. Generally 4-valved, globose, greyish brown.

Seeds: Flat, oblong-elliptic, about $2\frac{1}{2}''$ broad. Narrowly winged.

Vegetative reproduction: From suckers.

Range: Tropical Africa.

Uses: Timber resistant to insect and fungus attack and used for furniture, railway carriages, canoes. Bark yields brown dye. Bark sometimes used in tanning. Leaves fed to cattle and camels. Various parts used medicinally.

Order **SAPINDALES**

Family *SAPINDACEAE*

SOAPBERRY (*Sapindus marginatus*)

General characters: Tree 30–45′ high. Leaves alternate, pinnate with 7–13 lance-shaped leaflets. Flowers white or greenish (sometimes reddish), in panicles in leaf-axils or at end branches. Sepals 4–5, in 2 series. Petals 4–5, long-clawed. Stamens 8–10. Ovary superior, 2–4-celled, each cell with 1 ovule.

Habitat: Dry soil (often sandy) on hillsides and lower ground.

Fruit: Berry-like. Lobed. Contains saponin.

Seeds: Without endosperm.

Range: Southern United States and N. Mexico.
Uses: Timber used for light frames and baskets. Fruit pulp used as substitute for soap.

Family *ANACARDIACEAE*

SUMACH (*Rhus typhina*)

General characters: Small deciduous tree up to 40′ high, though often grown as shrub. Branchlets velvety-hairy, thick, yielding thick yellowish-white juice when broken. Leaves alternate, 1–2′ long, pinnate with 11–31 leaflets, each lance-shaped, long-pointed, toothed, 3–5″ long. Flowers small, greenish, in dense hairy and somewhat pyramidal panicles. Calyx 5-lobed, persistent. Petals 5. Stamens 5. Ovary superior, 1-celled, ovule 1.

Habitat: Dry or rocky soil.

Pollination: By insects.

Fruit: A small globose drupe densely covered with bright crimson hairs. Stone smooth, 1-seeded. Fruit in dense panicles.

Seeds: Smooth.

Vegetative reproduction: By shoots from root. Propagated by root cuttings.

Range: Eastern N. America. Cultivated in Europe.

Uses: In U.S.A. fruits made into "Indian lemonade" (plant called Lemonade Tree and sometimes Vinegar Tree!). Flowers are source of honey in America. Colourful autumn foliage.

MANGO (*Mangifera indica*)

General characters: Large spreading evergreen tree up to 90′ high. Leaves alternate, long-stalked, broadly lance-shaped, pointed, often stiff, dark shining green when mature, up to 12″ long. Flowers reddish, pink or whitish, both bisexual and male flowers in large panicles at end of branches. Calyx 4–5-lobed, falling. Petals 4–5. Stamens 5, usually only 1 fertile, others reduced as staminodes. Ovary small, 1-celled, with 1 ovule.

Habitat: Deep loamy soils and valleys near coast.

Pollination: Cross-pollination by short-tongued insects. Self-pollination probably occurs. About 33% bisexual flowers fertilized but only about 0·1–0·25% produce fruit.

Fruit: Edible. A large ovoid drupe 3–7″ long, 2–4″ wide. Skin smooth, thickish, yellow, green or red. Flesh light lemon to deep apricot, in best varieties smooth, juicy, peach-flavoured. Stone hard, fibrous, 1-seeded. Fruit known as "the tropical apple." Source of vitamins A, C, B_1, B_2, and niacin.

Seeds: Smooth. Light brown. Only 1 embryo in seeds of Indian varieties, but Hawaiian, Philippine and various other varieties are polyembryonic. Fruits eaten and seeds dispersed by monkeys, fox-bats and elephants (germinating seeds seen in elephant dung in Sumatra).

Vegetative reproduction: Propagated by grafting.

Range: Originated in S.E. Asia. Now cultivated or occurs in semi-wild state throughout tropics and parts subtropics.

Uses: Fruit important part of diet in S.E. Asia, where eaten fresh or cooked in chutney. Some fruit canned. Seeds cooked and eaten in India in time of famine. Indian Yellow, a light-resistant dye used in painting, obtained from urine of cows fed on Mango leaves.

Special comments: Many varieties in cultivation. Tree makes several growth flushes during year.

Family *ACERACEAE*

SYCAMORE (*Acer pseudoplatanus*)

General characters: Deciduous tree up to 105' but commonly 60-80' high. Bark grey, scaling in large strips from old trees. Leaves opposite, 3–6" broad, palmately 5-lobed to about half-way to base, lobes toothed and pointed. Flowers unisexual, sexes on same tree, small, yellowish-green, in pendulous racemes at end short branches. Sepals 5. Petals 5. Stamens 8. Ovary 2-celled, each cell with 2 ovules. Styles 2.

Habitat: Woods, hedges, gardens, plantations.

Pollination: By bees and probably certain large flies.

Fruit: A schizocarp separating into 2 samaras or winged "keys." Each samara normally 1-seeded but sometimes 2-seeded.

Seeds: Without endosperm. Dispersed by wind. Germination epigeal.

Vegetative reproduction: Sometimes by suckers.

Range: Europe (including Britain). Asia Minor.

Uses: Timber used for dairy utensils, rollers, turnery, carving, veneer. Flowers good source of nectar for honey bees.

Special comments: Stands exposure to wind and salt-spray very well. Fast-growing on suitable soils.

Family *HIPPOCASTANACEAE*

HORSE CHESTNUT (*Aesculus hippocastanum*)

General characters: Large deciduous tree up to 100' or more. Crown broad, rounded. Bark dark grey-brown. Buds large, egg-shaped, red-brown, very resinous ("sticky buds" of children). Leaves opposite, long-stalked, palmate with 5–7 large toothed leaflets. Flowers showy, in large panicles at end stems, male and bisexual flowers on same tree.

Calyx bell-shaped, 5-lobed. Petals 4–5, white with basal patch first yellow then red. Stamens 5–8, curved. Ovary superior, 3-celled, each cell with 2 ovules. Style simple, long. Stigma simple.

Habitat: Wild mountainous places. Planted in parks, gardens, roadsides.

Pollination: By bees.

Fruit: A large prickly 1–2-seeded capsule opening by 3 valves.

Seeds: Large, shining, brown. Without endosperm. Eaten by deer and rats.

Range: Europe. Planted in U.S.A.

Uses: A good bee plant (worked for both pollen and nectar). Wood used for brush backs, fruit storage racks. Seeds have been used as soap substitute. They contain aesculin, glucoside used in connection with treatment of bovine mastitis. During First World War they yielded acetone. In Second World War they were collected for their starch and for use in certain fire-fighting appliances.

Special comments: At one time people flocked to such places as Kew Gardens and Bushey Park, England, on Chestnut Sunday, Sunday before Ascension Day, to see Horse Chestnuts in flower.

Order **LOGANIALES**

Family *POTALIACEAE*

Desfontainea spinosa

General characters: Evergreen shrub up to 10′ or more high. Leaves opposite, holly-like, oval or egg-shaped, with sharp spiny edges, dark green, shiny and smooth, shortly stalked. Flowers scarlet and yellow, solitary on short stalks. Calyx 5-lobed. Corolla tubular, 5-lobed. Stamens 5, almost stalkless at base corolla lobes. Ovary superior, 5-celled, ovules numerous. Style 1.

Habitat: Moist somewhat shady places.

Fruit: A berry containing numerous seeds.

Seeds: With endosperm. Small, black.

Vegetative reproduction: Propagated by cuttings.

Range: Chile. Peru. Cultivated in Europe.

Uses: An attractive garden subject.

Family *LOGANIACEAE*

CAROLINA JESSAMINE (*Gelsemium sempervirens*)

General characters: Evergreen twining woody vine with slender stem up to 20′ long. Leaves opposite, lance-shaped on short stalks, 1½–3″ long. Flowers large, bright yellow, funnel-shaped, produced in 2 forms (one with short stigmas and protruding anthers; the other with longer stigmas and anthers not protruding), in 1-6-flowered cymes. Calyx 5-parted. Corolla funnel-shaped, 5-lobed. Stamens 5, inserted on inside of corolla-tube. Ovary 2-celled, ovules numerous in each cell. Style 2-lobed.

Habitat: Woods and thickets, mostly near coast.

Pollination: By insects.

Fruit: A flat capsule opening into 2 boat-shaped valves.

Seeds: With endosperm. Very flat. Broadly winged.

Range: S.E. United States.

Uses: Dried roots used medicinally (nervine, sedative, antispasmodic).

Special comments: Yields unwholesome honey.

Family *BUDDLEIACEAE*

BUTTERFLY BUSH (*Buddleia davidii*)

General characters: Deciduous shrub up to 10–15′ high. Branchlets angled, shortly and softly hairy. Leaves opposite, lance-shaped with long tapered points, finely toothed, dark green above, white-felted beneath, 4–10″ long. Flowers lilac or purple with orange-yellow ring at mouth, in dense long narrow panicles. Corolla tubular, 4-lobed. Calyx bell-shaped, 4-lobed. Stamens 4, inserted in corolla-tube. Ovary 2-celled, ovules numerous (placentation axile). Style 1.

Habitat: Mountains. In Britain: gardens, shallow chalk soils, waste places, roadsides, bombed sites, tops of old brick walls.

Pollination: By butterflies.

Fruit: A many-seeded smooth cylindrical capsule opening in 2 valves.

Seeds: With endosperm. Very small. Dispersed by wind, points of seed-coat being drawn out into elongated process gradually narrowed to tip.

Vegetative reproduction: Propagated by cuttings.

Range: Native of China. Naturalized in parts of Europe.

Uses: Attractive garden subject. (*Buddleia brasiliensis* and *B. curviflora* used to stupefy fish, while branches and leaves of *B. madagascariensis* are used to make native rum!)

Special comments: Several varieties in cultivation, including white-flowered ones.

Orange Ball Tree (*Buddleia globosa*)

Another widely cultivated shrub, reaching 15′ in the open and becoming even taller in sheltered places. Fragrant orange-yellow flowers produced in balls ¾″ diameter. Native of Chile and Peru. A good bee plant, flowers being useful source of nectar.

Family *STRYCHNACEAE*

Strychnine Tree (*Strychnos nux-vomica*)

General characters: Evergreen tree up to 50′ high. Trunk erect. Bark smooth, yellowish-grey. Twigs numerous, opposite. Leaves opposite, broadly oval, smooth, shining, thin, 2½–4″ long, shortly stalked. Flowers greenish-white, small, numerous on slender stalks in cymes at end shoots. Calyx small, hairy, 4–5-toothed. Corolla tubular, 5-lobed, lobes egg-shaped. Stamens 5, inserted in corolla-tube, filaments very short. Ovary superior, 2-celled, each cell with several ovules.

Habitat: Forests of dry regions.

Fruit: A globose berry 1–1¾″ across, shining, orange-red when ripe. Contains 1–6 seeds in pinkish-grey pulp.

Seeds: With copious endosperm. Large, flattened, silvery-grey, shining, button-shaped, ¾″ diameter, with dense covering very fine hairs.

Range: Burma. Ceylon. India.

Uses: Seeds are principal source poisonous alkaloids strychnine and brucine. Bark used as tonic and externally as remedy for skin-diseases. Timber used for carts and cabinet-work (termite-proof).

Family *OLEACEAE*
ASH (*Fraxinus excelsior*)

General characters: Deciduous tree often 45–75′ high but height of 148′ known. Bark grey, smooth at first, furrowed later. Buds large, black. Leaves opposite, pinnate with 3–6 pairs opposite lance-shaped leaflets and odd one at end. Flowers without perianth, purplish, in dense clusters, appearing before leaves. Male, female and bisexual flowers on same or different trees. Stamens 2. Ovary 2-celled. Style short, thick. Stigma 2-lobed.

Habitat: Woods, hedges, scrub, crevices in cliffs and limestone pavement, marshes. Characteristic of calcareous soils, being repelled by poor acid soils.

Pollination: Wind-pollinated.

Fruit: Borne in bunches. Familiar Ash "key" is a pale brown samara, a 1–2-seeded capsule whose top is produced into a wing. Dispersed by wind and rivers.

Seeds: With endosperm. Broad, flat, striated. Many seeds eaten by mice and voles.

Vegetative reproduction: Suckers observed occasionally.

Range: Europe (including Britain). N. Africa.

Uses: Timber used for furniture, hockey sticks, motor body frames, tool handles.

Special comments: Ash charcoal present in both Neolithic and Late Iron Age deposits from Maiden Castle, Dorset. Several varieties, including "Weeping Ash," grown in parks and gardens.

OLIVE (*Olea europaea*)

General characters: Small evergreen tree usually 20–40′ high. Becomes rugged with age. Leaves opposite, narrowly lance-shaped, leathery, dull green above, usually silvery below. Flowers small, white, in racemes in leaf-axils. Corolla 4-lobed. Stamens 2. Ovary 2-celled, each cell with 2 ovules.

Habitat: Hillsides in dry subtropical areas with Mediterranean climate, reaching 3,900′ on sunny slopes in Spanish province of Granada. Will grow well in tropics, but usually produces very little fruit there.

Pollination: By insects, including bees.

Fruit: A 1-seeded oily drupe. Oval, ¾″ long. Green at first, but black when ripe.

Seeds: Dispersed by birds which eat fruits.

Vegetative reproduction: By suckers. Propagated from cuttings, suckers or graftings.

Range: Apparently originated in Near East. Now grows wild in many places, but also cultivated in Mediterranean countries, N. Africa, S. Africa, Mexico, parts Australia, U.S.A. (Arizona and California). Grows in mildest parts Britain (fruit produced in garden near Plymouth).

Uses: Both green and black (but not fully ripe) fruit are pickled. Non-drying olive oil pressed from fully ripe fruit used for cooking, salad oils and creams, canning sardines, soap, cosmetics and toilet preparations, medicinal purposes. Pomace from pressed olives sometimes used as fuel. Olive wood hard and heavy and made into small articles. Tree is useful source of honey in Spain.

Special comments: A plant with a long history. Gathering of olives illustrated on Grecian vase of sixth century B.C. and the Bible includes many references to the Olive tree. Initial rate of growth slow, fruit-bearing often not starting until 15 years old, but trees yield fruit for centuries.

LILAC (*Syringa vulgaris*)

General characters: Deciduous shrub or small tree up to 20′ high. Leaves opposite, heart- or egg-shaped, smooth. Flowers fragrant, lilac or white, in pyramidal panicles. Corolla tubular, 4-lobed. Calyx bell-shaped, mostly 4-toothed. Stamens 2. Ovary 2-celled.

Habitat: Flourishes in warm open soils in sunny places.

Pollination: Mainly by bees, which work flowers when nectar produced abundantly and rises within their reach in corolla-tube.

Fruit: A smooth leathery capsule. 2-celled, 2 seeds per cell. Splits from top downwards when ripe.

Seeds: Flat. Slightly winged. Wind-dispersed.

Vegetative reproduction: By suckers. Propagated by layers and cuttings.

Range: Native of S.E. Europe. Cultivated and sometimes naturalized in Europe, U.S.A., and elsewhere.

Uses: Buds, leaves and bark yield lilacine, alkaloid valued in Europe for febrifugal qualities.

Special comments: Many varieties in cultivation, including single and double forms.

Order **APOCYNALES**

Family *APOCYNACEAE*

GREATER PERIWINKLE (*Vinca major*)

General characters: Evergreen creeping shrub with erect 1–2′ flowering stems and long trailing barren stems rooting at tips. Leaves

opposite, glossy, egg-shaped, pointed, edged with minute hairs. Flowers blue, solitary in leaf-axils. Corolla tubular at base, 5-lobed at mouth. Calyx narrowly 5-lobed, lobes fringed with hairs. Stamens 5. Ovary of 2 free carpels connected at top by styles. Ovules numerous.

Habitat: Gardens, hedgerows, woods, roadsides.

Pollination: By long-tongued bees.

Fruit: Consists of 2 follicles, 1-celled capsules diverging during ripening and opening by slit on inner side.

Seeds: Dark brown, long, narrow.

Vegetative reproduction: By runners rooting at tips and spreading as much as 7′ in a season.

Range: Europe.

Uses: Leaves used medicinally in tonic and in treatment of intestinal disorders.

Special comments: Grown in gardens to cover ground, banks, unsightly objects.

Family *PERIPLOCACEAE*

GRECIAN SILK VINE (*Periploca graeca*)

General characters: Deciduous climber up to 20–30′ high. Stems smooth, brown, twining, exuding poisonous milky juice when broken. Leaves opposite, egg-shaped or oval, pointed, shortly stalked, 2–4″ long. Flowers 1″ broad, in 8–12-flowered cymes at end short side-shoots, with somewhat unpleasant odour. Corolla shortly tubular, narrowly 5-lobed, downy, brownish-purple inside, greenish-yellow outside. Calyx 5-lobed. Stamens 5. Ovary of 2 separate carpels, ovules numerous. Styles 2. Stigma 1.

Habitat: Rocky and scrubby places.

Pollination: Cross-pollination by insects.

Fruit: Of 2 cylindrical follicles, each tapering to a point, 5″ long, opening lengthwise.

Seeds: With endosperm. Flattened, with tuft of long silky hairs at end.

Vegetative reproduction: Propagated by division of root, layers, cuttings.

Range: Europe.

Uses: Bark is source of periplocin (similar to digitalin, drug used for heart affections).

Family *ASCLEPIADACEAE*

SHOWY MILKWEED (*Asclepias speciosa*)

General characters: Perennial herb with stout simple stem up to 6′ high. Often with dense white or greyish hairs. Leaves opposite, thick, broadly egg-shaped or oval, stalked, 3–8″ long. Flowers purple-green, in many-flowered umbels. Corolla deeply 5-parted, segments bent backwards in open flower. Between corolla and stamens is corona of 5 concave hoods, each with a short incurved horn within. Calyx small, 5-parted. Stamens 5, filaments united into tube. Ovary of 2 separate carpels. Ovules numerous. Styles 2. Stigma 1.

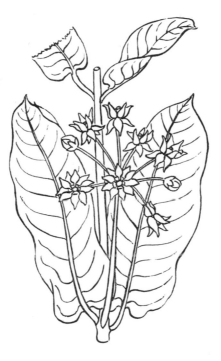

Habitat: Woodland openings. Prairies.
Pollination: Pollen in masses (pollinia). Cross-pollination by insects.
Fruit: Of 2 follicles, 3–4″ long, densely woolly and covered with soft spinose processes. Opening lengthwise.
Seeds: With endosperm. Flattened. Crowned with tuft of long silky hairs.
Range: N. America.
Uses: Buds, young shoots and leaves were eaten by Indians, who used latex as chewing gum.

Order **RUBIALES**

Family *RUBIACEAE*

COFFEE (*Coffea arabica*)

General characters: Small slender evergreen tree but usually cultivated as much-branched shrub up to 15' high. Leaves opposite, dark green, shining, oval, thickish, 3–6" long, 2" or more across, pointed, shortly stalked. Flowers white, fragrant, in dense clusters in leaf-axils, appearing in flushes several times a year, short-lived (lasting few hours). Epicalyx cup-shaped. Calyx of 5 small segments united into short tube. Corolla tubular, 5-lobed. Stamens 5. Ovary inferior, 2-celled, each cell with 1 ovule.

Habitat: Native to shady tropical rain forests. Widely cultivated (often under shade).

Pollination: Cross-pollination by insects. Self-pollination rarely occurs.

Fruit: A scarlet 2-seeded drupe with thin tough exocarp enclosing yellowish pulpy mesocarp and thin hard endocarp ("parchment") surrounding seeds. Fruit produced on bushes 3–40 years old.

Seeds: With endosperm. Grey-green, $\frac{1}{2}$" long, with thin seed-coat (the "silver skin"). Contain caffeol (volatile oil, gives beverage flavour), caffeine (alkaloid giving coffee stimulating properties), fatty oil, glucose, dextrin, protein. Seeds are "beans" of commerce.

Range: Native of Ethiopia, where used since very early times. Now grown in tropics of Old and New World. Brazil produces 75% of total world supply of coffee.

Uses: Seeds roasted, ground, and used to make popular beverage, coffee.

Special comments: Many varieties grown. Mocha coffee has smaller fruits, but seeds produce coffee of excellent flavour and aroma (grown in Arabia).

QUININE (*Cinchona officinalis*)

General characters: Small slender evergreen tree 25' or more high. Bark rough, brown. Leaves opposite, narrowly oblong, smooth, shining. Flowers dark pink, in panicles at end shoots. Sepals small, united into tube. Corolla tubular, 5-lobed. Stamens 5. Ovary 2-celled, ovules numerous.

Habitat: Wild in dense jungles and valleys (tropical Andes). Now cultivated in plantations.

Pollination: By insects.

Fruit: A 2-valved capsule.

Seeds: Very small, flat, winged.

Vegetative reproduction: Propagated by grafting and cuttings.

Range: S. America (Peru, Ecuador, Bolivia, Colombia).

Uses: Bark is the Crown or Loxa bark of commerce, source of quinine, alkaloid used medicinally as tonic, antipyretic, and cure for malaria. (Alkaloid content of bark varies from tree to tree and also with locality. Yield is highest when trees grown at altitude of at least 3,000'.)

Special comments: Several other species of *Cinchona* yield quinine, particularly *C. ledgeriana* (cultivated in Java, Ceylon, India).

NORTHERN BEDSTRAW (*Galium boreale*)

General characters: Perennial herb up to 3' high. Stems erect, firm, square, branched. Leaves lance-shaped, 4 in a whorl, 3-veined, up to $1\frac{1}{2}''$ long. Flowers white, in many-flowered panicles at top stems. Corolla 4-lobed, tube very short. Calyx reduced to minute ring-shaped border. Stamens 4. Ovary inferior, 2-celled, each cell with 1 ovule. Styles 2, joined below.

Habitat: Moist rocky places, streamsides, dunes.

Pollination: By insects.

Fruit: Dry, 2-lobed, each lobe 1-seeded, brown, with hooked white bristles.

Seeds: With endosperm. Dispersed in cattle dung (Sweden).
Range: Europe (including Britain). N. America. Asia Minor.
Uses: No information.

Order **BIGNONIALES**

Family *BIGNONIACEAE*

INDIAN BEAN TREE (*Catalpa bignonioides*)

General characters: Deciduous tree up to 60' high. Branches spreading. Bark thin, flaky. Leaves strong-scented, broadly egg-shaped, entire or 3-lobed, pointed, densely hairy below, 6–12″ long, on long stout stalks. Flowers large, white, mottled with yellow and purple within, in large panicles at end stems. Corolla bell-shaped below, expanded above, 2-lipped, 5-lobed. Calyx closed in bud, splitting into 2 lips in opening. Stamens 5 (usually only 2 fertile). Ovary superior, 2-celled, with numerous ovules.

Habitat: Woods, gardens.

Pollination: Cross-pollination by insects, including hive and humble bees.

Fruit: A narrow capsule 10–15″ long. Thin-walled. Drooping.

Seeds: Without endosperm. Flat. With long white hairs at ends.

Vegetative reproduction: Propagated by cuttings.

Range: Eastern U.S.A. Cultivated in Europe.

Uses: Wood used for fence posts and railroad-ties (durable in contact with soil).

Special comments: Extrafloral nectaries on undersurface of leaves secrete nectar. Bees collect this and nectar from flowers.

Order **VERBENALES**

Family *VERBENACEAE*

VERVAIN (*Verbena officinalis*)

General characters: Perennial herb with woody rootstock. Stems erect, 4-angled, with short bulbous-based hairs. Leaves opposite, deeply pinnately lobed with blunt or pointed lobes, upper leaves sometimes undivided. Flowers small, pale lilac, in slender spikes in leaf-axils and at top stems. Calyx small, hairy, 5-lobed. Corolla-tube with white hairs at mouth and 5 spreading lobes at top. Stamens 4. Ovary 4-celled, each cell with 1 ovule.

Habitat: Roadsides, waste places, cultivated land.

Pollination: Cross-pollination by insects or self-pollination.

Fruit: Of 4 reddish-brown 1-seeded nutlets, each weighing about 0·0004 gm. Dispersed in mud or in calyx which adheres to coats of animals or people's clothing.

Seeds: Without endosperm.

Range: Europe (including Britain). N. America. N. Africa. Asia.

Uses: Infusions of plant used for reducing temperature and in treatment of nervous disorders.

FRENCH MULBERRY (*Callicarpa americana*)

General characters: Deciduous shrub up to 10' high. Twigs, leaf-stalks and young leaves scurfy. Mature leaves smooth (or almost so), dotted with glands, opposite, egg-shaped, pointed, on slender stalks, 3–6" long. Flowers small, varying from white to pink or pale blue, in many-flowered cymes in leaf-axils. Calyx short, bell-shaped, 4-toothed. Corolla-tube short, 4-lobed. Stamens 4. Ovary 2-celled, each cell with 2 ovules.

Habitat: Moist woods and thickets.

Pollination: By insects, including bees.

Fruit: A small berry-like drupe. Globose, violet-blue, containing four 1-seeded stones.

Seeds: Without endosperm.

Range: S.E. and S. United States. Cultivated in Europe.

Uses: No information.

Division HERBACEAE

Herbs and woody plants derived from herbaceous ancestors.

Order RANALES

Family *PAEONIACEAE*

PEONY (*Paeonia mascula*)

General characters: Perennial herb up to $1\frac{1}{2}'$ high. Leaves large, twice divided into 3, with egg-shaped to elliptical leaflets. Flowers bright red (rarely whitish), large, up to 4" across, solitary at top of stout stalk. Sepals 5, free, green, persistent, outer ones often leaf-like. Petals 5–8, large, free, egg-shaped and sometimes almost rounded. Stamens very numerous. Carpels 3–5, free, densely hairy, the disk at their base fleshy.

Habitat: Hilly districts.
Pollination: Cross-pollination by insects.
Fruit: A group of 3–5 follicles.
Seeds: With copious endosperm. Round, black, shining, at first covered by a red aril.
Range: Europe. N.W. Africa.
Uses: Plant used as antispasmodic.

Family *HELLEBORACEAE*

BEAR'S-FOOT (*Helleborus foetidus*)

General characters: Perennial herb up to $2\frac{1}{2}'$ high. Lower leaves evergreen, long-stalked, divided into about 9 narrowly lance-shaped, pointed and toothed lobes. Flowers drooping, numerous, in panicle with large leafy bracts at top stem. Sepals 5, green bordered with red-purple, broadly egg-shaped, remaining erect until fruiting stage. Petals small, hidden by sepals, modified into 5–10 green tubular nectaries. Stamens numerous. Carpels usually 3, almost free, each with several ovules.

Habitat: Woods in chalky places.
Pollination: By insects.
Fruit: A group of beaked wrinkled follicles opening by inner margin.
Seeds: With endosperm. Black, with fleshy ridge. Dispersed by ants and snails. Average weight: 0·0088 gm.
Range: Europe (including Britain).
Uses: Formerly used medicinally. No current information.

143

Special comments: All parts poisonous, even when dried. Contains poisonous glucosides helleborin and helleborein, and alkaloid jervine.

Marsh Marigold (*Caltha palustris*)

General characters: Perennial herb with hollow stems. Leaves mainly from rootstock, heart-shaped, long-stalked, smooth, margin with blunt curved teeth. Stem leaves on very short stalks or clasping stem. Flowers large, about 2″ across, in few-flowered panicles at top stems. No petals. Sepals 5–8, bright golden-yellow, petal-like. Stamens numerous. Carpels 5–13, free, nectar-secreting, with numerous ovules.

Habitat: Water meadows, marshes, wet woods, lake margins.

Pollination: Cross-pollination by insects.

Fruit: Of 5–6 follicles, each containing about 9 seeds and splitting open along upper side.

Seeds: With endosperm. Constricted in middle. Average weight: 0·009 gm. About 2,700 seeds per plant. Float for 1–4 weeks, being provided with a floating organ.

Vegetative reproduction: By creeping rhizomes. Also by stems rooting at nodes.

Range: Europe (including Britain). N. America. Temperate Asia.

Uses: No current information. (Said to have been used as spring

vegetable, roots eaten, flower-buds pickled in vinegar and used as capers. However, people have been violently ill after eating it.)

Special comments: Cattle and horses have died from eating fresh plant, but when dried it is harmless.

Family *RANUNCULACEAE*

MEADOW BUTTERCUP (*Ranunculus acris*)

General characters: Perennial herb with much-branched hairy stem up to 3′ high. Basal leaves often long-stalked, 2–7-lobed, lobes them-selves divided into narrow pointed segments. Stem-leaves shortly stalked or stalkless, more deeply divided. Flowers bright yellow, 1″ across, on long hairy stalks. Sepals 5, yellowish-green, hairy, very rarely becoming reflexed. Petals 5, roundish, yellow, very glossy ex-cept for basal patch, with scale in front of nectary at base. Stamens numerous. Carpels numerous, each with 1 ovule.

Habitat: Damp grassland, damp rock ledges, roadsides.

Pollination: Cross-pollination by insects.

Fruit: A cluster of about 30 brown beaked achenes.

Seeds: With oily endosperm. Achene weighs about 0·0017 gm. Dispersed mainly around parent plant.

Vegetative reproduction: By branching of rhizome.

Range: Europe (including Britain). Introduced into N. America, S. Africa, New Zealand.

Uses: No information.

Special comments: A very variable species. Normally bisexual, but various sex forms have been found, including male, female and neuter flowers. Plant contains acrid poison, but is harmless when dried. Cattle have died after eating it fresh. In Europe pollen of certain buttercups is injurious to bees.

TRAVELLER'S JOY (*Clematis vitalba*)

General characters: Perennial woody climber. Deciduous. Leaves opposite, pinnate with 5 leaflets, each narrowly egg-shaped, pointed, often coarsely toothed. Leaf-stalks twining. Flowers fragrant (odour hawthorn-like), in loose panicles in leaf-axils. No petals. Sepals 4, white or greenish-white, densely hairy outside. Stamens numerous. Carpels numerous, free.

Habitat: Climbing over hedges, trees, shrubs, chiefly on calcareous soils.

Pollination: By insects.

Fruit: A small seed-like achene ending in long persistent style feathered with silky white hairs. Fruits grouped in large conspicuous heads (hence plant's other name "Old Man's Beard"). Average weight of fruit without style: 0·00139 gm.

Seeds: With copious endosperm.

Range: Europe (including Britain). N. Africa.

Uses: Stems used to make light baskets. Lengths of dry stems smoked like cigars in several parts Europe. In Paris the acrid juice was used by beggars to produce "ulcerous wounds" with which to excite pity (hence the name "herbe aux gueux").

Family *NYMPHAEACEAE*

YELLOW WATER-LILY (*Nuphar lutea*)

General characters: Aquatic perennial with stout branched rhizome. Floating leaves leathery, broadly elliptical, with long basal lobes, up to about 15″ long. Submerged leaves very thin, shorter-stalked, egg-shaped or roundish. Flowers yellow, held above water, long-stalked, cup-shaped when open, $1\frac{1}{2}$–$2\frac{1}{2}$″ across, smelling of brandy. Sepals 5 (very rarely 6), green and yellow outside, bright yellow inside. Petals 11–26, much shorter than sepals, yellow. Stamens numerous. Ovary bottle-shaped, circular stigmatic disk with entire margin at top, many-celled, each cell with numerous ovules.

Habitat: In lakes, ponds and streams.

Pollination: By insects.

Fruit: Berry-like, ovoid, ripening above water. Contains numerous seeds. Splits into parts. Eaten by fish and water-birds.

Seeds: With little endosperm. Olive-green, ovoid, smooth, shining. Sinking when free from fruit. Seeds germinated after removal from excreta of heron and from gut of fish.

Vegetative reproduction: By rhizome branching and breaking up.

Range: Europe (including Britain). Asia Minor. N. Africa.

Uses: Rhizome contains starch and has been recommended as emergency food.

Special comments: Also called "Brandy-bottle" (because of flower-scent or shape of fruit).

Order BERBERIDALES

Family *BERBERIDACEAE*

OREGON GRAPE (*Mahonia aquifolium*)

General characters: Evergreen shrub 3–6′ high. Leaves pinnate with 2–4 pairs leaflets and odd one at end. Leaflets leathery, egg-shaped, with sharply pointed teeth, dark green and glossy above. Flowers yellow, in many-flowered racemes at end stems. Sepals 6, yellow. Petals 6, yellow, with pair of nectaries towards base. Stamens 6, anthers opening by valves ("flaps"). Ovary of 1 carpel with about 6 ovules.

Habitat: Woods and thickets. Grown in parks and gardens.

Pollination: Cross-pollination by insects. (Stamens sensitive to contact and strike insect's head, covering it with pollen, which is taken to other flowers.)

Fruit: A 1-seeded globose berry. Dark blue with "bloom." Eaten by blackbirds, which disperse seeds.

Seeds: With endosperm.

Vegetative reproduction: By underground suckers.

Range: Native of western N. America. Naturalized in parts Europe.

Uses: Dried rhizome and roots used medicinally (bitter tonic, alterative).

Special comments: The State Flower of Oregon.

BARBERRY (*Berberis vulgaris*)

General characters: Deciduous shrub 6–10′ or even taller. Twigs greyish, slightly grooved, with yellowish wood. Long shoots with 3-forked spines (modified leaves). Leaves in clusters on short shoots inversely egg-shaped, stalked, sharply toothed on margin. Flowers yellow, in pendulous racemes 2–3″ long. Sepals 9, petal-like. Petals 6, each with 2 nectaries near base. Stamens 6, sensitive to touch, anthers opening by valves. Ovary of 1 carpel with few ovules.

Habitat: Hedges, thickets, sometimes grown in parks and gardens.
Pollination: Cross-pollination by insects.
Fruit: An oblong red berry. Edible, but acid. Eaten by cattle and certain birds, including blackbird, American crow, American waxwing.
Seeds: Average weight: 0·0117 gm. In U.S.A. dispersed by cattle (45 seedlings found in 1 piece cow dung).
Range: Europe (including Britain). N. America.
Uses: Hard yellow wood used for turnery and toothpicks. Wood and bark yield yellow dye. Fruit made into jam or jelly. Bark used medicinally (tonic, alterative).
Special comments: Shrub is host for aecidiospores of *Puccinia graminis*, a rust fungus affecting wheat.

Order **ARISTOLOCHIALES**

Family *ARISTOLOCHIACEAE*

ASARABACCA (*Asarum europaeum*)

General characters: Perennial evergreen herb with creeping rhizome. Stem very short, hairy. Leaves kidney-shaped, long-stalked, usually

2 paired on stem. Flower stalked, solitary between the 2 leaves at top stem. Calyx bell-shaped, deeply 3-lobed, brownish outside, persistent. No petals. Stamens 12. Ovary 6-celled, ovules numerous.

Habitat: Woods, hedgebanks.

Pollination: Cross-pollination by small flies. Also self-pollination.

Fruit: A leathery hairy capsule opening irregularly.

Seeds: With endosperm. Flat, with warted protuberance (caruncle) on one side. Collected and dispersed by ants.

Vegetative reproduction: By rhizome.

Range: Europe (including Britain).

Uses: Dried rhizome used medicinally ("purges violently, upwards and downwards!").

Special comments: Once widely cultivated as medicinal plant.

BIRTHWORT (*Aristolochia clematitis*)

General characters: Perennial herb $\frac{1}{2}$–$2\frac{1}{2}'$ high. Stems erect, somewhat zigzag. Leaves alternate, broadly egg-shaped, deeply heart-shaped at base, up to 5–6" long, stalked. Flowers greenish-yellow, stalked, in small groups in leaf-axils, upright at first, but later bending downwards. No petals. Calyx tubular with globular base, narrow tube, and egg-shaped or oblong limb. Stamens 6. Ovary 6-celled, inferior.

Habitat: Rocky places, ruins, neglected gardens.

Pollination: Cross-pollination by small flies which are trapped in the flower by downwardly-directed hairs that shrivel and release insects after anthers have opened.

Fruit: A globose 6-celled capsule 1″ across.

Seeds: With endosperm. Flat, triangular.

Vegetative reproduction: By rhizomes.

Range: Europe (including Britain). Asia Minor.

Uses. Was used medicinally (abortive effect), but no current information. (Roots of several other *Aristolochia* species used for snake bites, scorpion bites, tonics, and many other purposes.)

Family *CYTINACEAE (RAFFLESIACEAE)*

HASSELT'S RAFFLESIA (*Rafflesia hasseltii*)

General characters: Parasitic plant whose vegetative parts are hidden inside tissues of host-plant. Leaves none. Flower very large, about $1\frac{1}{2}'$ across, evil-smelling, fleshy, solitary on stem of host, the flower-bud breaking through bark. Petals none. Sepals 5, rounded, red with raised pinkish-white blotches, united below into broad tube covered inside with coarse branched hairs. Tube prolonged above sepals into a corona. Stamens numerous, stalkless, arranged round a short thick fleshy column in centre of flower. Flat top of column with numerous white conical styles. Ovary in basal part of column, with numerous ovules.

Habitat: On woody stems of lianes on or near ground in lowland forests.

Pollination: Cross-pollination by carrion flies.

Fruit: Fleshy.

Seeds: With cellular endosperm. Minute. Numerous.

Range: Malaya.

Uses: Used as medicine in child-birth.

Special comments: Rafflesia arnoldii has largest flower of any known plant, the diameter reaching 3' and weight 15 lb.

Family *NEPENTHACEAE*

PITCHER-PLANT (*Nepenthes rafflesiana*)

General characters: Climbing shrub. Stems tough. Leaves alternate. Fully-grown leaf consists of (1) an oblong or oval blade up to 1' long and 4" wide, with long channelled stalk; (2) a tendril, which is continuation of midrib of blade; (3) a hollow pitcher with lid. Pitchers large, lower ones somewhat mug-shaped, upper ones narrowly funnel-shaped, mottled with purple or reddish-purple. Flowers small, unisexual, sexes on different plants, crowded in many-flowered racemes. No petals. Sepals 4. Stamens 4–12, filaments united into a red column

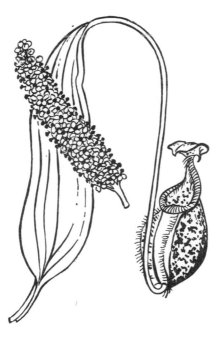

at top of which anthers are crowded in a ball. Ovary superior, with numerous ovules.

Habitat: Open places, roadsides, forest margins, swampy forest.

Fruit: A narrow capsule 1″ long. Splits lengthwise.

Seeds: With fleshy endosperm. Numerous. Long, narrow.

Range: Malaya.

Uses: No information. (Stems of some *Nepenthes* species made into baskets and coarse rope.)

Special comments: An ornamental species, long cultivated in Europe. One *Nepenthes* species from Borneo is said to have pitchers with capacity of 2 quarts. Pitchers serve to trap insects which fall into water at bottom. Insect is acted on by digestive juices secreted by glands in lower part of pitcher and thus plant secures part of its nitrogen requirements.

Order PIPERALES

Family *PIPERACEAE*

PEPPER (*Piper nigrum*)

General characters: Climbing vine. Stems reaching 30′ or more in wild, but growth controlled in cultivation. Short adventitious roots

arising from swollen nodes help anchor stems. Leaves alternate, smooth, egg-shaped, pointed, short-stalked, up to 10" long. Flowers minute, in long slender yellowish-green spikes opposite leaves. Perianth absent, young flower being protected by floral bract. Stamens 2–3. Ovary 1-celled with 1 ovule.

Habitat: In wild, climbing over trees. In cultivation, trained over low supports.

Pollination: Wind-pollinated.

Fruit: Known as peppercorn. Berry-like, comprising seed surrounded by thin pulpy mesocarp and thin red skin. Colour changing from green to red.

Seeds: With little endosperm and copious mealy perisperm. Small. Greyish-white.

Vegetative reproduction: Grown from stem cuttings.

Range: Native of S.W. India, but cultivated in tropics, particularly in S.E. Asia.

Uses: Black pepper (dried ground fruit), white pepper (dried ground seeds). Seeds are source of Oil of Pepper, used as flavouring, in perfumery and medicinally.

Special comments: Pepper has long been important spice, its pungency being due to presence of resins and the alkaloid, piperine.

Peperomia pellucida

General characters: Small fleshy herb up to 1' high. Stem rather thick and fleshy. Leaves alternate, triangular in outline, tip broadly pointed, to about 1" long and wide. Flowers minute, without perianth, in tiny round bracts, green, in slender spikes up to 2" long. Stamens 2. Ovary superior, 1-celled, with 1 ovule.

Habitat: Waste ground, gardens (as weed).

Fruit: A very small pale orange to blackish green berry.

Seeds: With copious mealy perisperm round the small endosperm. Small.

Range: Native of S. America. Naturalized in most tropical countries.

Uses: No information.

Family *SAURURACEAE*

LIZARD'S-TAIL (*Saururus cernuus*)

General characters: Perennial marsh herb. Stem erect, slender, sparingly branched, 2–5' high. Leaves alternate, thin, egg-shaped, pointed, deeply heart-shaped at base, on stout stalks, 3–6" long. Flowers small, white, fragrant, in long very dense spikes opposite leaves, end of spike drooping in flower. No perianth. Stamens 6–8. Ovary of 3–4 free carpels.

Habitat: Swamps. Shallow water.

Fruit: Slightly fleshy. Wrinkled when dry. Separating into 3–4 one-seeded carpels.

Seeds: Little endosperm. Copious mealy perisperm. Eaten by Wood Duck (up to 10,000 seeds found in stomach).

Range: Eastern N. America.

Uses: Used medicinally (sedative, astringent). Boiled roots were applied to wounds as poultice.

Yerba Mansa (*Anemopsis californica*)

General characters: Perennial herb up to 2′ high. Stems hairy, with broadly egg-shaped clasping leaf above middle and 1–3 small leaves in its axil. Basal leaves elliptic-oblong, heart-shaped at base, stalked. Stipules united to leaf-stalk. Flowers without perianth, each with small white bract, in dense conical spikes up to $1\frac{1}{2}''$ long, with persistent basal involucre of several white bracts. Stamens 6 or 8. Ovary of 3–4 united carpels. Stigmas 3–4.

Habitat: Wet, especially somewhat alkaline, places.

Fruit: A capsule.

Seeds: With copious perisperm.

Range: N. America.

Uses: Formerly used medicinally for diseases of skin and blood.

Order **RHOEADALES**

Family *PAPAVERACEAE*

FIELD POPPY (*Papaver rhoeas*)

General characters: Annual herb with erect branched stems up to 2' high. Leaves stiffly hairy. Lower leaves stalked, deeply pinnately divided, segments again cut or toothed. Upper leaves stalkless, 3-lobed. Flowers solitary on long hairy stalks, nodding in bud. Sepals 2, bristly hairy, falling off as flower opens. Petals 4, crumpled in bud, roundish, scarlet (occasionally pink or white), often with black blotch ("eye") at base. Stamens numerous. Ovary superior, 1-celled, with numerous ovules (parietal placentation). Milky juice (latex) exuded when plant broken or cut.

Habitat: Cornfields. Waste places.

Pollination: Cross-pollination by insects.

Fruit: A globose capsule crowned by persistent stigmatic disk. Opens by pores beneath overlapping lobes of disk.

Seeds: With copious endosperm. Average weight: 0·00013 gm. Small, dark brown, kidney-shaped, pitted and surface with network of ridges. Viability retained for at least 80 years when buried in soil. Single fruit contains more than 1,300 seeds. Some 17,000 seeds produced per plant. About 65% seeds may germinate within 8 months of being shed. Seeds found with barley grains in remains of Twelfth Dynasty at Kahun (more than 2,500 years B.C.) and also in Bronze Age deposits in Britain. Seeds eaten by birds, including blue and great tits, wood pigeons, but not all are destroyed as seedlings have been raised from excreta of birds.

Range: Europe (including Britain). Asia. N. Africa. Introduced into N. America, Australia, New Zealand.

Uses: Petals yield red pigment used for colouring wine and medicines. Flowers used medicinally (expectorant). A Norfolk chemist who died 1962 recalled boiling vast quantities poppies for making medicine. According to him, people kept babies quiet by giving them drop or two of laudanum (extracted from poppies) on lump of sugar, a practice now considered dangerous. Flowers are important source of pollen for honey bees.

Special comments: Poisonous alkaloids present in plant which can be very harmful to animals both in green state and when dried in hay. Poppies said to have stupefying effect on bees. During First World War poppies flourished in Flanders following disturbance of soil for trenches. Each year British Legion sells artificial "Flanders poppies" made in its poppy factory and people wear them on Remembrance Day.

GREATER CELANDINE (*Chelidonium majus*)

General characters: Perennial herb with erect branched stems 1–3′ high. Leaves irregularly pinnate with 5–7 egg-shaped coarsely toothed segments. Flowers bright yellow, in long-stalked umbel opposite to leaf. Sepals 2, free, soon falling. Petals 4, soon falling. Stamens yellow, numerous. Ovary superior, 1-celled, ovules numerous. Style very short. When broken plant exudes sticky orange latex with unpleasant smell.

Habitat: Hedgerows, waste places, old walls.

Pollination: Self-pollinated during dull weather (when flowers remain closed). Pollinated by bees on sunny days.

Fruit: A smooth cylindrical capsule up to 2″ long. Opens from below by 2 valves.

Seeds: With oily endosperm. Black with large white fleshy crest on one side. Dispersed by ants (attracted by oily nature of seed). Average weight: 0·0007 gm.

Range: Europe (including Britain). N. Asia. Introduced into N. America.

Uses: Used medicinally (purgative, for skin diseases and digestive ailments). Latex, which contains poisonous alkaloids, was used to cure warts.

CALIFORNIAN POPPY (*Eschscholzia californica*)

General characters: Annual herb 1' or more high. Stems erect or spreading. Leaves much-divided with narrow segments. Flowers yellow, orange or white, 2–3" across, solitary at end of stem. Sepals 2, forming a hood, falling as flower opens. Petals 4. Stamens numerous. Ovary superior, 1-celled, ovules numerous. Latex watery.

Habitat: Open spaces near sea and occasionally inland. Also much cultivated.

Pollination: By insects.

Fruit: A long narrow ribbed capsule. Opens from below by 2 valves.

Seeds: With endosperm.

Range: Western N. America. Cultivated in America and Europe.

Uses: Leaves were eaten by Indians of California, but no current information.

Special comments: The State Flower of California.

Family *FUMARIACEAE*

WHITE CLIMBING FUMITORY (*Corydalis claviculata*)

General characters: Annual climbing herb with many slender branches and branched tendrils. Leaves twice pinnate, with small narrowly elliptic leaflets. Flowers small, cream, about 6 on a long slender common stalk opposite leaves. Sepals 2, small, soon falling. Petals 4 in 2 whorls, upper petal with short round spur at base. Stamens 6 in 2 bundles. Ovary 1-celled, ovules numerous. Juice watery.

Habitat: Woods, rocks, stony places.

Pollination: Self-pollinated. Also pollinated by bees.

Fruit: A small black 2-valved capsule containing 2–3 seeds.

Seeds: With copious endosperm.

Range: Europe (including Britain).

Uses: No information.

RAMPING FUMITORY (*Fumaria capreolata*)

General characters: Climbing annual herb up to 3' long. Leaves pinnately cut, segments with oblong or wedge-shaped lobes. Flowers in dense racemes opposite leaves. Sepals 2, oval, pointed, toothed at base. Corolla of 4 petals in 2 whorls, creamy white, wings and tips dark reddish, upper petal laterally compressed, lower petal with narrow erect margins. Stamens 6 in 2 bundles. Ovary 1-celled, ovules 1–2.

Habitat: Hedgebanks. Cultivated and waste land.

Pollination: Self-pollinated. Flowers sometimes gradually turn pink or carmine after pollination.

Fruit: A small 1-seeded nutlet.
Seeds: With endosperm.
Range: Europe (including Britain). Introduced in S. America.
Uses: No information.

DUTCHMAN'S BREECHES (*Dicentra cucullaria*)

General characters: Delicate perennial herb 5–10″ high. Leaves all basal, on slender stems, finely divided, pale bluish-green. Flowers yellowish or whitish, nodding, in simple 4–10-flowered racemes at top slender stalks. Sepals 2. Petals 4, in 2 pairs, both outer petals spurred, inner petals minutely crested. Stamens 6, joined in 2 bunches. Ovary 1-celled.

Habitat: Woods, especially on rocky hillsides.
Pollination: By bees.
Fruit: A capsule opening to base by 2 valves.
Seeds: With fleshy endosperm. Crested.
Vegetative reproduction: By small tubers.
Range: Eastern N. America.
Uses: Dried tubers used medicinally (tonic, alterative).
Special comments: Said to be poisonous to livestock.

Order CRUCIALES

Family *CRUCIFERAE*

WILD RADISH (*Raphanus raphanistrum*)

General characters: Erect annual herb up to 3' high. Stiffly hairy. Lower leaves deeply pinnately lobed, end lobe large and rounded, others narrow and much smaller. Upper leaves small, narrow, sometimes almost undivided. Flowers in racemes at top stem, large, showy. Sepals 4, small, free. Petals 4, large, long-clawed, pale yellow, white or lilac, often dark-veined. Stamens 6, four long, two short. Ovary of 2 united carpels. Ovules numerous.

Habitat: Cultivated and waste places.

Pollination: By insects. Self-pollination said to be ineffective.

Fruit: A long beaked pod contracted between the 3–8 seeds. Not opening, but breaking into 1-seeded joints.

Seeds: Without endosperm. Rounded, reddish-brown, pitted. Average weight about 0·008 gm. Dispersed in excreta of birds and cattle. Very acrid and can cause intestinal troubles when eaten by animals.

Range: Europe (including Britain). N. & S. America. N. Africa. Australia. Japan.

Uses: A useful bee plant when present in quantity. May have given rise to cultivated radish (*Raphanus sativus*), a useful salad vegetable.

Special comments: Also called Runch and White Charlock, Wild Radish can be serious pest.

HONESTY (*Lunaria annua*)

General characters: Annual to biennial herb 1–3' high. Lower leaves long-stalked, pointed, broadly heart-shaped, coarsely toothed, rough and hairy. Upper leaves almost stalkless. Flowers reddish-purple (occasionally white), about 1" across, in loose racemes. Sepals 4, inner pair deeply pouched. Petals 4. Stamens 6. Ovary with 4–6 ovules.

Habitat: Dry soils, often in shady places.

Pollination: Cross-pollination by insects. Also self-pollination.

Fruit: A broadly elliptical or almost circular silicula with flat thin-walled translucent valves and thin shining white septum.

Seeds: Large, flat, winged.

Range: Europe.

Uses: Dried plants bearing silvery septa used for floral decorations. Roots said to be edible before development of flowers.

SHEPHERD'S PURSE (*Capsella bursa-pastoris*)

General characters: Annual to biennial herb up to 15″ high, but often much shorter. Leaves with both simple and star-shaped hairs. Basal leaves forming rosette, lobed or entire, tapered to base. Upper stem-leaves clasping stem with ear-like base. Flowers very small, white, in slender racemes at top of stems. Sepals 4. Petals 4, spoon-shaped. Stamens 6. Ovary ellipsoid, with 12–24 ovules.

Habitat: Cultivated and waste land.

Pollination: Either cross-pollination by insects or effective self-pollination may occur.

Fruit: A roughly triangular silicula opening by 2 valves.

Seeds: Pale brown, egg-shaped, flattened. Average weight: 0·0001 gm. Viability retained for at least 35 years. Seed-coat mucilaginous, swelling up when wetted. Seeds dispersed in excreta of birds (including sparrows), cattle, horses, and also on boots, tools, tyres and feet of birds.

Range: Cosmopolitan.

Uses: Used medicinally for kidney troubles and as stimulant.

Special comments: A most variable species, some botanists considering Shepherd's Purse to be an aggregate of species. Flowers during most months, sometimes producing 2–3 generations in a year.

Golden Alyssum (*Alyssum saxatile*)

General characters: Low branching perennial herb with short soft star-shaped hairs. Leaves greyish, inversely lance-shaped. Flowers small, yellow. Sepals 4. Petals 4. Stamens 6.

Habitat: Stony places, old walls, dry and poor soils.

Pollination: Visited by bees for pollen, but said to be mainly self-pollinated.

Fruit: A small oval or almost circular silicula.

Seeds: Without endosperm. Flattened. Winged.

Range: Europe.

Uses: A popular spring-flowering plant in European gardens.

Cuckoo Flower (*Cardamine pratensis*)

General characters: Erect perennial herb up to 1½' high. Basal leaves forming rosette, long-stalked, pinnate with 5–7 pairs egg-shaped or roundish leaflets and larger one at end. Stem-leaves with shorter stalks and narrow lance-shaped leaflets. Flowers mauve or white, in clusters of up to 20 at top stem. Sepals 4. Petals 4, clawed. Stamens 6. Ovary elongated.

Habitat: Moist meadows, sides of streams and brooks, damp woodlands.

Pollination: Cross-pollination by insects (said to be completely "self-sterile").

Fruit: A siliqua about 1″ long. 2 valves open suddenly, coil spirally from base and fling seeds 4–6′.

Seeds: Seed production often small.

Vegetative reproduction: By small plantlets from buds produced in leaf-axils (useful method of dispersal in damp and flooded areas).

Range: Europe (including Britain). N. America. Temperate Asia.

Uses: Sometimes eaten raw as salad vegetable. Recommended as emergency food-plant. Visited by honey bees for nectar and pollen.

Special comments: Several races of this species believed to exist (differing in chromosome numbers, height, size and colour of flowers).

WALLFLOWER (*Cheiranthus cheiri*)

General characters: Perennial herb with branched woody stems. Leaves narrow lance-shaped, with 2-armed hairs (short-stalked and roughly T-shaped). Flowers fragrant, yellow, orange-yellow, deep red, in racemes at top stems. Sepals 4, erect, narrowly lance-shaped. Petals 4, long-clawed. Stamens 6, four long, two short, nectary at base each short one. Ovary long and narrow.

Habitat: Old walls, ruins, rocky railway cuttings, cliffs, stony places.

Pollination: Cross-pollination by insects. Also self-pollination.

Fruit: A narrow flattened siliqua $1\frac{1}{2}$–$2\frac{1}{2}$″ long.

Seeds: Pale brown. Winged at apex. Average weight: 0·0013 gm.

Range: Europe (including Britain).

Uses: Flowers formerly used medicinally and as source of essential oil, but no current information. A useful bee plant in early spring.

Special comments: Numerous colour-varieties and double-flowered forms grown. A fashion flower of the Middle Ages when knights wore it as symbol of their devotion to the "mistress of their heart."

Order **RESEDALES**

Family *RESEDACEAE*

WILD MIGNONETTE (*Reseda lutea*)

General characters: Biennial to perennial herb 1–$2\frac{1}{2}$′ high. Stems erect or curving upwards, branched, ribbed. Stem leaves pinnately lobed, yellowish-green. Flowers greenish-yellow, in compact spike-like racemes. Sepals usually 6, sometimes 5, narrow. Petals usually 6, irregularly lobed. Stamens 12–20. Carpels united below into a 1-celled ovary which is open between the 3 apical lobes. Ovules numerous.

Habitat: Arable land, waste places, particularly on chalky soils.

Pollination: Cross-pollinated by insects. Also self-pollinated.

Fruit: An oblong 1-celled capsule open at top. As fruit ripens opening enlarges. Average of 14 seeds per fruit.

Seeds: Without endosperm. Oval, black, shining. Average weight: 0·00085 gm. Dispersed by birds and ants.

Vegetative reproduction: By adventitious shoots from roots (especially when shoots injured or plant eaten down by rabbits).

Range: Europe (including Britain). Asia Minor. N. Africa. Introduced into N. America.

Uses: A good source of nectar and pollen for honey bees.

Sweet Mignonette (*Reseda odorata*)

Closely related to previous species, this garden plant has wedge-shaped leaves, that are undivided or 3-lobed, and very fragrant flowers whose petals are deeply cleft. Very attractive to honey bees which collect both nectar and pollen from flowers. At one time an important source of an essential oil used in perfumery.

Order CARYOPHYLLALES

Family *ELATINACEAE*

Waterwort (*Elatine hexandra*)

General characters: Small aquatic or semi-aquatic annual herb with stems rooting at nodes. Leaves small, opposite, paddle-shaped. Flowers small, stalked, solitary in leaf-axils. Sepals 3, free, spreading. Petals 3, pinkish. Stamens 6, with short filaments. Ovary superior, 3-celled, with numerous ovules (axile placentation). Styles 3, free.

Habitat: In ponds and muddy places.

Pollination: Self-pollinated (anthers open inwardly to shed pollen on to stigmas).

Fruit: A 3-valved capsule.

Seeds: Without endosperm. Slightly curved, ribbed and transversely striated.

Range: Europe (including Britain).

Uses: No information.

Family *CARYOPHYLLACEAE*

RED CAMPION (*Silene dioica*)

General characters: Biennial to perennial herb with erect hairy flowering stems up to 3′ high. Leaves opposite, pointed, basal ones elliptical and tapering to long winged stalks, upper leaves egg-shaped or broadly elliptical, short-stalked or almost stalkless. Flowers unisexual, sexes on different plants. Calyx tubular, 5-toothed at apex, hairy, reddish. Petals 5, free, reddish-purple (rarely white), 2-lobed, with long claw and 2 coronal ligules. Stamens 10. Ovary superior, 1-celled, with numerous ovules. Styles 5.

Habitat: Woods, hedgebanks, bird-cliffs, sheltered mountain ledges.

Pollination: By insects (mainly bees and butterflies).

Fruit: An egg-shaped capsule opening widely at top by 10 short teeth which are rolled downwards.

Seeds: With endosperm. Black, kidney-shaped, densely warted (projections pointed). Dispersed by wind.

Vegetative reproduction: Leafy stolons sometimes important.

Range: Europe (including Britain). N. Africa. Introduced into eastern N. America.

Uses: No information.

Special comments: In certain recent Floras this and next species have been included in genera *Lychnis* and *Melandrium*.

WHITE CAMPION (*Silene alba*)

General characters: Annual, biennial or short-lived perennial herb. Similar to Red Campion, but teeth of capsule erect and flowers white, fragrant, opening in evening.

Habitat: A sun-lover of such open places as arable and waste land, pastures, verges, embankments, hedges. Frequent on chalky soils.

Pollination: By moths.

Fruit: A conical capsule. Opens narrowly.

Seeds: With endosperm. Kidney-shaped, greyish. Closely and bluntly warted. Up to 15,000 seeds per plant. Dispersed by wind, birds (seedlings raised from excreta), adhesion to boots and tools, in impure agricultural seed.

Vegetative reproduction: By stolons when rootstock is divided during ploughing of farmland.

Range: Europe (including Britain). N. Africa. Introduced into N. America.

Uses: Roots were used for washing clothes, but no current information.

Special comments: Fertile hybrids between Red and White Campions occur.

DEPTFORD PINK (*Dianthus armeria*)

General characters: Hairy annual or biennial herb 1–2' high. Stems erect, unbranched or sparingly branched. Leaves opposite, at swollen nodes, narrow, pointed, up to 3" long. Flowers in short-stalked clusters of 2–10, normally bisexual. Epicalyx of 2 pointed hairy scales. Calyx-tube cylindrical, woolly, with 5 sharply pointed teeth. Petals 5, bright red with pale spots, long-clawed. Stamens 10. Ovary 1-celled, with numerous ovules.

Habitat: Dry banks, waste places, dry pastures.

Pollination: Sometimes visited by lepidoptera, but automatically self-pollinated.

Fruit: A 1-celled cylindrical capsule opening at top by 4 teeth.

Seeds: With endosperm. Flattened, roughly egg-shaped. Average weight: 0·0026 gm.

Range: Europe (including Britain). Introduced into N. America.

Uses: No information.

MAIDEN'S BREATH (*Gypsophila paniculata*)

General characters: Much-branched slender perennial herb 2–3′ high. Leaves opposite, narrow, lance-shaped. Flowers white, small, very numerous, on thread-like stems in dense compound clusters. Calyx bell-shaped, deeply 5-lobed. Petals 5. Stamens 10.

Habitat: Deep well-drained soils, often in chalky districts.

Pollination: Cross-pollination by insects (mainly bees) or self-pollination.

Fruit: A capsule opening by 4 teeth.

Seeds: Kidney-shaped.

Vegetative reproduction: Propagated by division of roots, cuttings, grafting.

Range: Europe. Asia. Introduced into N. America.

Uses: Source of nectar for honey bees (single-flowered forms).

Special comments: Varieties with double white and double pink flowers in cultivation.

RAGGED ROBIN (*Lychnis flos-cuculi*)

General characters: Perennial herb with erect flowering stems up to 2½′ high. Leaves opposite, upper ones narrow, pointed, almost stalkless. Flowers red (rarely white), stalked, in loose clusters at top stems. Calyx-tube shortly 5-toothed, strongly 10-ribbed. Petals 5, deeply 4-lobed (lobes narrow), long-clawed with 2 scales near middle of claw. Stamens 10. Ovary 1-celled.

Habitat: Marshes. Damp meadows.

Pollination: By insects.

Fruit: An ovoid 1-celled capsule opening by 5 short teeth.

Seeds: Small, brown, kidney-shaped, closely warted.

Vegetative reproduction: By offsets (short runners).

Range: Europe (including Britain). Introduced into N. America.

Uses: No information.

SOAPWORT (*Saponaria officinalis*)

General characters: Perennial herb with stout branched or unbranched flowering stems up to 3′ high. Leaves opposite, egg- or lance-shaped, pointed, strongly 3-5-nerved. Flowers large, pink (sometimes nearly white), fragrant (especially in evening). Calyx-tube cylindrical, shortly 5-toothed. Petals 5, notched at top, long-clawed, claw with a 2-toothed scale on inside. Stamens 10. Ovary 1-celled with numerous ovules.

Habitat: Banks, roadsides, waste places, stream-sides.

Pollination: Mainly by hawk-moths.

Fruit: A capsule opening at top by 4 teeth.

Seeds: Kidney-shaped, blackish. Average weight: 0·0014 gm.

Vegetative reproduction: By stolons arising from creeping rhizome.

Range: Europe (including Britain). Asia. Introduced into N. America.

Uses: Used as soap, roots and leaves being boiled for this purpose. (Plant contains saponin, which causes intense frothing when stirred in water.) Recommended today for restoring ancient delicate fabrics, dried plants being placed in muslin bags and boiled in distilled water, the solution being used when cold.

Special comments: A double-flowered form occurs.

Family *FICOIDACEAE (AIZOACEAE)*

ICE PLANT (*Mesembryanthemum crystallinum*)

General characters: Prostrate much-branched succulent annual to biennial herb. Branches up to 2′ long with large glistening vesicles (little bladders or air cavities). Leaves largely alternate, egg-shaped to broadly spoon-shaped, flat, up to 4″ long. Flowers white to reddish, at end branches and in leaf-axils. Calyx-tube bell-shaped, joined to ovary, unequally 5-lobed. Petals numerous, narrow, inserted in calyx-tube. Stamens numerous.

Habitat: Saline places along coasts. Dry sunny places on poor soils.

Pollination: By insects, including bees.

Fruit: A 5-celled fleshy capsule opening when moist by valves at flattened top.

Seeds: Numerous, minute, somewhat flattened, brown.

Range: S. Africa. Western United States. Mediterranean region. Cultivated elsewhere.

Uses: Leaves eaten in salads and as cooked vegetable. A good bee plant in warm countries.

Family *PORTULACACEAE*

Spring Beauty (*Claytonia virginica*)

General characters: Perennial herb with deep tuberous root (corm). Stem unbranched, rarely with few branches, 6–12″ long. Basal leaves narrow, 3–7″ long. Flowering stems with 2 shorter opposite leaves. Flowers showy, white or pink, with darker pink veins, on slender stalks in loose racemes at top stem. Sepals 2, egg-shaped, persistent. Petals 5. Stamens 5. Ovary 1-celled, with few ovules.

Habitat: Moist woods.

Pollination: By insects.

Fruit: A 3–6-seeded capsule opening by 3 valves whose inner sur-faces contract during drying, shooting out seeds.

Seeds: With copious mealy endosperm.

Range: Eastern N. America. Cultivated in Europe.

Uses: Starchy corms were eaten by American Indians.

Order POLYGONALES

Family *POLYGONACEAE*

BLACK BINDWEED (*Polygonum convolvulus*)

General characters: Scrambling or climbing annual herb. Stems twin-ing, ribbed, up to 4′ long. Leaves alternate, stalked, long pointed, heart-shaped, almost triangular. Stipules sheathing stems. Flowers small, shortly-stalked, in clusters in leaf-axils. No petals. Sepals 5, green with white margins. Stamens 5. Ovary superior, 1-celled, ovule 1. Styles 3.

Habitat: Waste places, gardens, cornfields.

Pollination: Cross-pollination by insects. Also self-pollination.

Fruit: A small triangular black nut. Average weight: 0·005 gm.

Seeds: With mealy endosperm. Dispersed by cattle (in dung), ants, Californian ground squirrel.

Range: Europe (including Britain). N. Africa. Temperate Asia. Introduced into N. America, S. Africa.

Uses: A good bee plant.

Special comments: Seed and pottery impressions of seeds found in Bronze Age deposits in Britain.

CURLED DOCK (*Rumex crispus*)

General characters: Erect perennial herb up to 3′ high. Basal leaves narrow, up to 1′ long, margins crisped and waved, stalked. Upper leaves becoming smaller and stalkless. Flowers inconspicuous, small, green, in whorls on simple or little-branched flowering stem. Perianth segments 6, outer 3 small and thin, inner 3 heart-shaped with swollen tubercles on midribs. Stamens 6. Ovary 1-celled, ovule 1.

Habitat: Gardens, grassland, cultivated and waste places, seashore, occasionally in tops pollard willows.

Pollination: Wind-pollinated.

Fruit: A small 1-seeded nut. Triangular in section. Enclosed in persistent inner perianth segments. Weight about 0·002 gm. Large plants produce as many as 30,000 fruits a year. Dispersed by wind, fallow deer (in excreta), birds (seeds germinated after passing through a greenfinch), water (fruits float for up to 15 months).

Seeds: Seeds 60 years old have germinated.

Vegetative reproduction: By growth of shoots from pieces of tap-root broken off during cultivation and other disturbances.

Range: Europe (including Britain). Africa. Introduced and naturalized in many other parts of world.

Uses: Roots used medicinally (alterative, laxative, tonic).

Special comments: A serious weed which should not be allowed to become established in gardens or farmland or to bear fruit there.

Order CHENOPODIALES

Family *CHENOPODIACEAE*

GOOD KING HENRY (*Chenopodium bonus-henricus*)

General characters: Perennial herb up to 1½′ high. Leaves alternate, broadly triangular, margins wavy, surface mealy when young. Flowers small, greenish, numerous in small cymes forming a somewhat pyramidal inflorescence. Perianth 4–5-lobed. Stamens 4–5. Ovary 1-celled, ovule 1. Stigmas 2–3.

Habitat: Near houses and buildings, pasture verges, farmyards.

Fruit: A small nut.

Seeds: With endosperm. Reddish-brown, small, with rough seed-coat. Seeds occur in Bronze Age and Roman deposits in Britain.

Range: Europe (including Britain). N. America. Temperate Asia.

Uses: Young shoots still sometimes eaten as spinach.

SHRUBBY SEABLITE (*Suaeda fruticosa*)

General characters: Small evergreen shrub up to 4' high. Stem stout, erect, much-branched. Leaves alternate, small, crowded, narrowly oblong, rounded at ends, thick and fleshy. Flowers small, green, 1–3 in cymes in leaf-axils. Perianth 5-lobed, small. Stamens 5, opposite perianth segments. Ovary 1-celled, ovule 1.

Habitat: Well-drained shingle beaches exposed to sea spray. Salt-marshes near creeks and high-water mark.

Pollination: Self-pollination.

Fruit: A small nut.

Seeds: Small, egg-shaped, black, shining. Dispersed by sea-water.

Vegetative reproduction: By production of roots and shoots from branches buried in shingle.

Range: Europe (including Britain). Asia. America.

Uses: Fed to camels. Its ashes yield barilla, impure carbonate of soda used in glass- and soap-making.

SALTWORT (*Salsola kali*)

General characters: Prickly annual herb up to $1\frac{1}{2}'$ high. Stems much-branched, striped, spreading on ground. Leaves narrow, stalkless, thick and fleshy, ending in sharp spine. Flowers small, stalkless, solitary in leaf-axils, each with 2 sharp-pointed bracteoles. Perianth segments 5, thin but becoming tough and thickened in fruit. Stamens 5. Ovary 1-celled, ovule 1.

Habitat: Sandy shores and salt-marshes. Sometimes appears inland as a ballast plant.

Pollination: Wind-pollinated.

Fruit: A small nut enclosed by perianth segments.

Seeds: With very little endosperm. Dispersed by wind, in flood-water, in ballast.

Range: Europe (including Britain). America. Africa. Asia. Introduced into Australia, New Zealand.

Uses: Emergency food-plant (young shoots boiled). Ashes yield barilla formerly used in soap-making.

Special comments: Has become serious weed in some countries where entire plants are blown about by wind (hence name Roly-poly).

Family *AMARANTHACEAE*

PIGWEED (*Amaranthus retroflexus*)

General characters: Erect grey-green annual herb 1–10′ high. Stem stout, branched. Leaves egg-shaped, upper ones often lance-shaped,

3–6″ long, on long slender stalks. Flowers small, inconspicuous, green, unisexual, in dense stout spikes in leaf-axils and at top stem. Each flower with 3 awl-shaped bracts and 5 small perianth segments. Stamens 5, filaments united at base. Ovary superior, 1-celled, ovule 1. Stigmas 2–3, persistent.

Habitat: Cultivated and waste land.

Fruit: A 1-seeded capsule whose top comes off as lid.

Seeds: With copious endosperm. Weight about 0·003 gm.

Range: N. America. Introduced into Britain.

Uses: Young parts eaten as potherb. Seeds were eaten by Indians. (Seeds of cultivated *Amaranthus* species have been important crop since very ancient times.)

KIRI-HENDA (*Celosia argentea*)

General characters: Erect annual herb 1–3′ high. Leaves alternate, stalkless, 1–3″ long, narrowly lance-shaped, smooth. Flowers small, numerous, in dense spikes 1–5″ long at top stem, at first purplish-pink, later silvery-white. Perianth of 5 thin almost transparent erect segments. Stamens 5, filaments short and joined below. Ovary superior, globose, 1-celled, with several ovules. Style long, thread-like.

Habitat: Dry cultivated ground, sandy fields.

Fruit: A capsule whose top comes off as lid. Contains 4–8 seeds.

Seeds: With mealy endosperm. Kidney-shaped, flattened, black, polished.

Range: Tropics.

Uses: Young shoots and leaves eaten as vegetable.

Order **LYTHRALES**

Family *LYTHRACEAE*

PURPLE LOOSESTRIFE (*Lythrum salicaria*)

General characters: Erect perennial herb up to 3½′ high. Leaves opposite or in whorls of 3 (sometimes alternate towards top of stem), lance-shaped, pointed, stalkless. Flowers purple or pink, in dense spike-like raceme with small green bracts. Calyx tubular, hairy, toothed and ribbed. Petals 5–6. Stamens about 12. Ovary superior, 2-celled, ovules numerous (placentation axile).

Habitat: By sides of ponds, lakes, rivers. In wet ditches and marshes.

Pollination: Normally cross-pollination by insects (see *Special Comments*).

Fruit: A small capsule enclosed in calyx.

Seeds: Without endosperm. Seeds soon sink on falling into water, but come to surface after germination. Seedlings float and are dispersed by movement of water.

Range: Europe (including Britain). N. America. N. Africa. Asia. Australia.

Uses: Young shoots recommended as emergency food. A good bee plant (nectar and pollen).

Special comments: Exhibits phenomenon of tristyly, having on different plants 3 forms of flowers constructed thus:

1. Style short, half stamens medium length, remainder long (all stamens longer than style).

2. Style medium length, half stamens short (shorter than style), remainder long (longer than style).

3. Style long, half stamens short, remainder of medium length (all stamens shorter than style).

Long stamens produce largest pollen-grains, medium-length stamens medium-sized grains, and short stamens small grains.

Darwin showed that complete fertility results from only 6 of 18 ways in which pollination would seem possible. In each of these 6 cases anthers and stigma are at same level and cross-pollination is involved.

Family *ONAGRACEAE*

GREAT HAIRY WILLOW-HERB (*Epilobium hirsutum*)

General characters: Erect hairy perennial herb up to 5′ high. Stem branched. Leaves mostly opposite, upper ones becoming alternate, lance-shaped, toothed, stalkless. Flowers normally rose-purple (sometimes white or very pale pink), large, erect, in axils of upper leaves. Sepals 4, hooded, pointed, shortly united at base. Petals 4, free, notched. Stamens 8, 4 short and 4 longer. Ovary inferior, elongated, 4-celled,

ovules numerous (placentation axile). Stigmas 4. Three types flowers borne on separate plants (see *Pollination*).

Habitat: By streams and ditches and in marshes.

Pollination: Cross-pollination by insects in flowers whose long curved styles prevent self-pollination. Self-pollination in flowers with stigmas and stamens at same level and in flowers whose straight styles curve and touch anthers if cross-pollination fails.

Fruit: A long slender capsule opening into 4 recurved parts.

Seeds: Without endosperm. Numerous, tiny, each with plume of long fine hairs at top. Wind-dispersed.

Vegetative reproduction: By underground stolons.

Range: Europe (including Britain). Asia. Africa. Introduced into N. America.

Uses: No information.

Special comments: Vanishing in places because underground shoots are dug up and eaten by coypus, S. American mammals introduced into U.S.A. and Europe and bred for fur (nutria).

EVENING PRIMROSE (*Oenothera biennis*)

General characters: Erect annual or biennial herb up to 9′ high. Leaves alternate, lance-shaped, slightly toothed, up to 6″ long, basal ones stalked, others narrowed at base but not completely stalked. Flowers bright yellow, up to 2″ across, solitary in axils of upper leaves, opening in evening. Calyx tubular, tube long, slender, 4-lobed, lobes reflexed. Petals 4, free, broad, spreading. Stamens 8. Ovary inferior, 4-celled, ovules numerous (placentation axile). Style 4-lobed.

Habitat: Dry places, sand-dunes, waste places, near gardens, by river banks.

Pollination: By moths.

Fruit: An erect hairy capsule about $1\frac{1}{2}″$ long. Splits from top into 4 valves.

Seeds: Without endosperm. Small, numerous. About 160 seeds per capsule. Average weight: 0·0006 gm. Remaining viable in soil for 40 years or longer. Dispersed by wind and rain-wash.

Range: Native of N. America. Naturalized in Europe.

Uses: Young shoots eaten raw in salads. Boiled roots eaten.

Fuchsia excorticata

General characters: Deciduous shrub or tree up to 40′ high. Bark light brown, thin and papery, peeling. Leaves alternate, egg- to lance-shaped, pointed, thin, on slender stalks, green above but silvery below. Flowers reddish-purple, about 1″ long, solitary, pendulous on long slender stalks from leaf-axils. Calyx tubular, with 4 spreading lobes. Petals 4, small. Stamens 8. Ovary 4-celled, with numerous ovules. Style simple. (Long-styled, mid-styled and short-styled forms occur.)

Habitat: Forests, often on margins.

Pollination: Cross-pollination by small nectar-feeding birds.

Fruit: A juicy purplish-black berry about $\frac{1}{2}″$ long, whose 4 cells contain numerous seeds. Eaten by birds.

Seeds: Without endosperm. Dispersed by birds.

Range: New Zealand.

Uses: No information.

Family *HALORRHAGACEAE*

SPIKED WATER-MILFOIL (*Myriophyllum spicatum*)

General characters: Perennial water-plant with rhizome rooting on and in mud and only flowering spikes above water. Leaves pinnately divided into thread-like segments, usually in whorls of 4 along stem. Flowers inconspicuous, in whorls of 4 in axils of small bracts, forming erect spikes often including both unisexual and bisexual flowers (males usually at top spike, females at bottom, bisexuals between them). Sepals 4 in male flower. Calyx minute in female. Petals 4, very small, dull red. Stamens 8. Ovary inferior, 4-celled, each cell with 1 ovule. Stigmas 4.

Habitat: Lakes, ponds, ditches.

Pollination: Wind-pollinated.

Fruit: A group of four 1-seeded nutlets which become separate.

Seeds: With copious endosperm. Dispersed by birds (carried on feet and feathers).

Range: Europe (including Britain). N. America. Asia. N. Africa.

Uses: No information.

Order **GENTIANALES**

Family *GENTIANACEAE*

CENTAURY (*Centaurium erythraea*)

General characters: Erect annual herb up to $1\frac{1}{2}'$ high. Leaves opposite, basal ones often spoon-shaped, stem-leaves narrowly lance-shaped and pointed. Flowers pink, numerous in repeatedly forked cyme. Calyx deeply 5-lobed, lobes narrow. Corolla with narrow tube and 5 spreading lobes at top, lobes twisted in bud. Stamens 5, inserted in corolla-tube. Ovary superior, 1-celled, ovules numerous (placentation parietal).

Habitat: Dry pastures, sandy banks and dunes, roadsides, waste places.

Pollination: Cross-pollination by insects and self-pollination.

Fruit: A 2-valved capsule with numerous seeds.

Seeds: With copious endosperm. Average weight: 0·000026 gm. About 10,000–12,000 seeds per plant.

Range: Europe (including Britain). N. America. Asia.

Uses: Dried plant used medicinally as tonic (contains bitter principle).

EASTERN FRINGED GENTIAN (*Gentiana crinita*)

General characters: Erect annual to biennial herb 1–3' high. Leaves opposite, lower reverse-egg-shaped, upper lance-shaped, pointed, 1–2" long. Flowers bright blue (rarely white), solitary at top of each stem,

about 2″ long. Calyx tubular, usually 4-lobed, lobes lance-shaped. Corolla tubular, narrowly bell-shaped, mostly 4-lobed, lobes rounded, spreading, conspicuously fringed. Stamens 4. Ovary 1-celled, ovules very numerous.

Habitat: Moist woods and meadows.

Pollination: By insects.

Fruit: A spindle-shaped 2-valved capsule.

Seeds: With copious endosperm. Tiny, numerous.

Range: Eastern N. America.

Uses: No information.

Special comments: Western Fringed Gentian (*Gentiana thermalis*) is Official Flower of Yellowstone National Park, where it flowers in open in moist subalpine places.

Family *MENYANTHACEAE*

BUCKBEAN (*Menyanthes trifoliata*)

General characters: Perennial marsh herb. Leaves alternate, divided into 3 reverse-egg-shaped leaflets with rounded apex. Leaf-stalks up to 10″ long, sheathing at base. Flowers 10–20 in raceme on long leafless stem. Calyx deeply 5-lobed. Corolla 5-lobed, broadly tubular, pink outside, with many white hairs inside. Stamens 5. Ovary superior,

1-celled, with few ovules. Some flowers long-styled, others short-styled.

Habitat: Boggy places, in ponds, swampy lakesides (flowers and leaves above water).

Pollination: By insects.

Fruit: A capsule splitting irregularly from top.

Seeds: With copious endosperm. Few, slightly flattened, shining, light brown. Float for at least 2 months.

Vegetative reproduction: By rhizomes rooting at nodes.

Range: Europe (including Britain). N. America. Asia.

Uses: Dried plant used medicinally for tonic, rheumatism, skin diseases and reducing fever. Added to beer (contains bitter glucoside). Emergency food-plant in Russia.

Order **PRIMULALES**

Family *PRIMULACEAE*

PRIMROSE (*Primula vulgaris*)

General characters: Perennial herb. Leaves bright green, reverse-lance-shaped, or oblong, wrinkled, margins toothed and somewhat

wavy, softly hairy beneath. Flowers yellow, fragrant, on long hairy stalks arising from root. Calyx tubular, 5-toothed, 5-ribbed, hairy. Corolla tubular, 5-lobed, lobes notched, flat, twisted in bud. Stamens 5. Ovary superior, 1-celled, ovules numerous.

Habitat: Hedgebanks, open woods and grassy places.

Pollination: Cross-pollination by insects.

Fruit: An ovoid capsule opening at top by 5 teeth. Stalk bends towards ground.

Seeds: With endosperm. Average weight: 0·0007 gm. Dispersed by ants and in excreta of horses and cattle.

Vegetative reproduction: By offsets.

Range: Europe (including Britain). N. Africa. Asia Minor.

Uses: Roots are safe emetic. Leaves eaten in salads. Primrose ointment (petals simmered with fresh lard) still used for chapped hands.

Special comments: 1. Forms with pink, white and double flowers in cultivation. 2. Normally 2 kinds of flowers occur on separate plants: "pin-eyed" flower with long style, stigma at mouth corolla-tube, anthers near middle corolla-tube, smaller oblong pollen-grains, larger ovules, fewer seeds per capsule; "thrum-eyed" flower with short style, stigma at middle corolla-tube, anthers near mouth corolla-tube, larger spherical pollen-grains, smaller ovules, more seeds per capsule. Cross-pollination between the 2 kinds results in more seed being produced. Self-fertile "long-homostyle" flowers, with both stamens and stigma at top corolla-tube, also occur.

SCARLET PIMPERNEL (*Anagallis arvensis*)

General characters: Prostrate annual or perennial herb with square stems up to 1′ long. Leaves opposite, egg- to lance-shaped, stalkless, with dark spots (glands) beneath. Flowers normally red or pink in Ssp. *arvensis* and blue in Ssp. *foemina*, solitary on slender stalks in leaf-axils. Calyx deeply 5-lobed, lobes narrow and pointed. Corolla with very short tube and 5 rounded lobes. (Ssp. *arvensis* and its blue-flowered form have corolla-lobes fringed with 3-celled glandular hairs, but in Ssp. *foemina* these hairs are 4-celled.) Stamens 5, with hairy filaments. Ovary 1-celled, ovules numerous.

Habitat: Cornfields, gardens, roadsides, waste places, dunes.

Pollination: Cross-pollination by small insects. Self-pollination also occurs.

Fruit: A small globose capsule splitting transversely around the middle.

Seeds: With endosperm. Brown, angular, margins narrowly winged. Average weight about 0·0006 gm. Dispersed by birds in excreta.

Vegetative reproduction: By rooting of prostrate shoots.

Range: Temperate regions of world.

Uses: Dried plant used medicinally (kidney and liver medicine).

Special comments: 1. Flowers open on warm sunny days, but close in dull damp weather and when temperature falls (hence names Shepherd's Weather-glass and Poor-man's Weather-glass). 2. Also known as Poison Weed, Scarlet Pimpernel has been responsible for death of many sheep in Victoria.

SHOOTING STAR (*Dodecatheon meadia*)

General characters: Perennial herb up to 2′ high. Leaves basal, reverse-lance-shaped or oblong, narrowed into stalk, up to 1′ long and 4″ wide. Flowers lilac, pink or white, arranged in umbels at top stems. Individual flower-stalks recurved but becoming erect in fruit. Calyx deeply 5-lobed, lobes pointed. Corolla tubular, tube very short, 5-lobed, lobes sharply reflexed. Stamens 5, inserted on throat of corolla, joined at bases, anthers forming cone around stigma. Ovary 1-celled, ovules numerous.

Habitat: Prairies, open woods, meadows.

Pollination: Cross-pollination by insects. Failing this, self-pollination occurs.

Fruit: A small erect capsule.

Seeds: With copious endosperm. Numerous. Minute.

Range: Eastern N. America.

Uses: No information.

Family *PLUMBAGINACEAE*

SEA LAVENDER (*Limonium vulgare*)

General characters: Perennial herb with erect angular flowering stems and leaves forming basal rosette. Leaves often oblong-lance-shaped (but shape variable), narrowed at base into long slender stalk, bright green. Flowers small, numerous, in panicles at top stems about 1′ high. Calyx tubular, 5-lobed, blue, persistent. Petals 5, joined at base to form very short corolla-tube, blue-purple, withering. Stamens 5. Ovary superior, 1-celled, 1 ovule. Styles 5, free.

Habitat: Salt-marshes. Occasionally on maritime cliffs and rocks.

Pollination: Cross-pollination by insects. Apparently self-pollination also occurs.

Fruit: Dry. 1-seeded.

Seeds: With mealy endosperm.

Range: Europe (including Britain). N. America. N. Africa.

Uses: Roots used for tanning (Russia). Certain cultivated Sea Lavenders dried as winter decorations ("Statice").

LEADWORT (*Plumbago capensis*)

General characters: Erect perennial herb with somewhat woody stems. Often bushy. Leaves alternate, elliptic, 1–3½″ long. Flowers blue, in spike-like panicles at top stems. Calyx tubular, 5-lobed, with stalked glands. Corolla tubular, tube long, 5-lobed, lobes broad. Stamens 4–5. Ovary superior, 1-celled, 1 ovule. Styles 5.

Habitat: Open places, roadsides, waste places.

Fruit: A 1-seeded capsule.

Range: S. Africa. Cultivated and naturalized in other places.

Uses: No information.

Order **PLANTAGINALES**

Family *PLANTAGINACEAE*

RIBWORT (*Plantago lanceolata*)

General characters: Perennial herb. Leaves erect (or ascending) or forming flat rosette, lance-shaped, sometimes minutely and distantly toothed, 3–5-ribbed, gradually narrowed into leaf-stalk, up to 1′ long. Flowers small, in egg-shaped spikes at top deeply furrowed stalks up to 1½′ long. Sepals 4, greenish. Corolla tubular, 4-lobed, lobes thin, dry, with prominent brown midrib. Stamens 4, white, with long filaments and large anthers. Ovary superior, usually 2-celled, 1 or more ovules in each cell.

Habitat: Grassy places, pastures, by roadsides, waste places.

Pollination: Wind-pollinated.

Fruit: A small 1–2-seeded capsule opening transversely, top becoming detached.

Seeds: With fleshy endosperm. Brown. Average weight: 0·00155 gm. 8% buried seeds still viable after 10 years, 2% after 16 years. Dispersed in mud on boots and implements, in excreta of cattle, birds (including sparrows). 100% germination from seeds that had passed through birds.

Range: Most parts of world, especially temperate regions.

Uses: Young leaves recommended as emergency food. Leaves provide useful fodder for livestock, particularly in winter. Minerals in plant include cobalt (up to 24 parts per million), copper (15 or more p.p.m.) and magnesium (1% or more).

Order **SAXIFRAGALES**

Family *CRASSULACEAE*

WALL PEPPER (*Sedum acre*)

General characters: Succulent evergreen perennial herb growing in tufts. Short erect branches arising from creeping stems. Leaves mainly alternate, very fleshy, stalkless, ovoid, often densely arranged on shoots.

Flowers bright yellow (hence name Golden Stonecrop), in small cymes at end of shoots. Sepals 5, fleshy, united at base. Petals 5, free, lance-shaped. Stamens 10, in 2 rows. Carpels 5, free, each with nectariferous scale at base. Ovules numerous.

Habitat: Walls, rocks, shingle, dunes and other sandy places, dry grassland, roofs.

Pollination: Cross-pollination by insects.

Fruit: A group of follicles, each splitting along inner side.

Seeds: Minute. Dispersed by wind.

Range: Europe (including Britain). N. America. N. Africa. Temperate Asia.

Uses: Plant sometimes used as laxative.

Special comments: Called Wall Pepper because whole plant hot and bitter to taste.

RED CRASSULA (*Rochea coccinea*)

General characters: Perennial herb up to $1\frac{1}{2}'$ high. Stems thick, woody at base, erect or lying on ground and then ascending. Leaves opposite, oval, broad, crowded, stalkless, shiny and somewhat fleshy, edged with short projections (papillae). Flowers bright crimson, stalkless, crowded in flat-topped inflorescence at top stem. Sepals 5. Petals 5, with long claws whose bases are united and upper parts pressed together as a tube about 1″ long. Stamens 5. Carpels 5, free, superior, with numerous ovules.

Habitat: High mountain rocks.
Fruit: A group of follicles.
Seeds: Minute.
Range: S. Africa.
Uses: No information.

CAPE SNOWDROP (*Crassula capensis*)

General characters: Perennial herb about 6″ high. Leaves basal, rounded or broadly oval, usually 4, with shallow rounded lobes, stalkless or shortly stalked, green above, purple beneath. Flowers white (petals often pinkish outside), in a 1–10-flowered umbel at top stem, with small bracts. Sepals and petals 5–9, often 6. Stamens as many as petals. Carpels superior, free, as many as petals, red, with numerous ovules.

Habitat: Dry sheltered mountain slopes.
Fruit: A group of follicles.
Seeds: Minute.
Vegetative reproduction: By spherical tubers.
Range: S. Africa.
Uses: No information.

Family *SAXIFRAGACEAE*

MEADOW SAXIFRAGE (*Saxifraga granulata*)

General characters: Erect perennial herb up to 1½′ high. With long white hairs and shorter gland-tipped ones. Basal leaves forming rosette, kidney-shaped, coarsely toothed, long-stalked. Stem leaves few, some almost stalkless. Flowers white, in few-flowered cymes at top stems. Calyx deeply 5-lobed, covered with gland-tipped hairs. Petals 5, free. Stamens 10. Ovary partly inferior, 1-celled, ovules numerous. Styles 2.

Habitat: Moist but well-drained meadows (often on basic soils).
Pollination: Cross-pollination by insects.
Fruit: A capsule containing up to 600 minute seeds.
Seeds: With copious endosperm. Small, dark brown, covered with minute projections. Average weight: 0·000021 gm. Wind-dispersed.
Vegetative reproduction: By small bulbils at base of plant.
Range: Europe (including Britain).
Uses: Formerly used medicinally, but no current information.

ALUMROOT (*Heuchera americana*)

General characters: Perennial herb 2–3′ high. Stem stout, leafless or with few small leaves. Leaves mainly basal, long-stalked, 3–4″ broad, egg-shaped to rounded, with several rounded and toothed lobes. Flowers small, greenish, in panicles. Calyx-tube bell-shaped, 5-lobed.

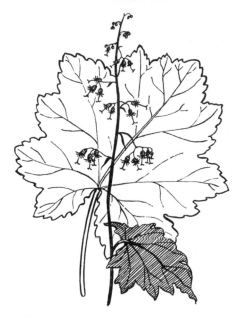

Petals 5, very small, spoon-shaped, inserted on throat of calyx. Stamens 5. Ovary 1-celled, ovules numerous.

Habitat: Dry or rocky woods.
Pollination: By insects, including bees.
Fruit: A 2-valved 2-beaked capsule.
Seeds: With endosperm. Numerous. Small.
Range: Eastern N. America.
Uses: No information.

Family *ADOXACEAE*

MOSCHATEL (*Adoxa moschatellina*)

General characters: Small perennial herb with pale green leaves. Basal leaves long-stalked, divided into 3 long-stalked parts, each again divided into 3. Flowering stems erect, unbranched, with pair of opposite leaves similar to basal ones. Flowers small, pale yellowish-green, usually in cluster of 5 at top stem, 1 facing upwards, others facing outwards in 4 directions (hence names Townhall Clock and Five-faced Bishop). Calyx 2-lobed in top flower, 3-lobed in side flowers. Corolla 4-lobed in top flower, 5-lobed in others. Stamens 4 or 5, but appearing as 8 or 10 owing to splitting of filaments. Ovary partly inferior, 3–5-celled, each cell with 1 ovule.

Habitat: Moist shady woods, rocky places.

Pollination: Visited by small insects, but self-pollination known to occur.

Fruit: A pale green 3–4-seeded drupe. Stalk with ripe fruit bends downwards.

Seeds: With copious endosperm. Average weight: 0·00071 gm.

Vegetative reproduction: By rhizome.

Range: Europe (including Britain). N. America. Asia.

Uses: No information.

Order **SARRACENIALES**

Family *DROSERACEAE*

SUNDEW (*Drosera rotundifolia*)

General characters: Perennial insectivorous (or "carnivorous") herb up to 10″ high. Leaves in a rosette, rounded, on long hairy stalks, upper surface covered and fringed with long crimson glandular hairs ("tentacles") which entrap insects (see *Special comments*). Flowering stems slender, erect, leafless, simple or branched. Flowers, each with small bract, arranged along top of stem and to one side of it, white, not opening or doing so for short period only. Calyx deeply 5-lobed. Petals 5, free. Stamens 5, free. Ovary superior, 1-celled, ovules numerous (placentation parietal). Styles 4.

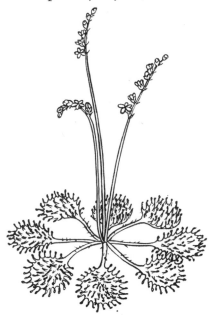

Habitat: In wet and boggy places, often among Sphagnum moss, on heaths and moors.

Pollination: Self-pollination.

Fruit: A capsule with numerous minute seeds.

Seeds: With fleshy endosperm. Winged, flattened, spindle-shaped. Weight about 0·000022 gm. Wind-dispersed.

Vegetative reproduction: Occasionally by stolons.

Range: Europe (including Britain). N. America. N. Asia.

Uses: Dried plant used medicinally (antispasmodic).

Special comments: Rounded glands at end glandular hairs or "tentacles" secrete sticky glistening fluid. This will hold insect or other small animal whose struggles stimulate other "tentacles" to bend towards it. Softer parts of captive's body digested by juices secreted by glands and absorbed and used by plant.

Order **PODOSTEMALES**

Tropical herbs growing submerged in fresh water. Flowers without petals. Without calyx or with 2–3 sepals. Stamens 1–4. Ovary 1–3-celled with numerous ovules. Styles 2–3. Fruit a capsule. Seeds without endosperm, minute. Apparently of no economic importance.

Order **UMBELLALES**

Family *UMBELLIFERAE*

Cow Parsley (*Anthriscus sylvestris*)

General characters: Erect biennial to perennial herb up to 4' high. Stems furrowed, hollow, branched. Leaves alternate, much-divided (2–3-pinnate), up to 1' long, lower leaves long-stalked, upper ones shortly-stalked, leaf-stalks with sheathing base. Flowers small, white, arranged in compound umbels consisting of 3–9 small umbels, each with 5–6 bracteoles. Calyx joined to ovary, minutely 5-toothed. Petals 5, outer ones of outer flowers of small umbels larger than inner petals. Stamens 5. Ovary inferior, 2-celled, each cell with 1 ovule. Styles 2.

Habitat: Borders of fields and woods, hedges, roadsides, waste places.

Pollination: By insects.

Fruit: Dry, narrow, with styles at top. Dividing into 2 mericarps.

Seeds: With copious endosperm.

Vegetative reproduction: By offsets.

Range: Europe (including Britain). N. America. N. Africa.

Uses: No information.

HEMLOCK (*Conium maculatum*)

General characters: Erect biennial herb up to 6' high. Stems branching, furrowed, hollow, with reddish-purple spots. Leaves much divided (2–3-pinnate), up to 1' long. Flowers small, white, arranged in compound umbels. Calyx joined to ovary, without teeth. Petals 5, with pointed inflexed tips. Stamens 5. Ovary 2-celled, each cell with 1 ovule. Styles 2, short. Plant with unpleasant smell when bruised.

Habitat: Damp places in hedges, open woods, waste places, roadsides.

Pollination: By insects.

Fruit: Greyish-brown, egg-shaped, with 5 wavy ribs on each half. Weight of half-fruit about 0·0005 gm.

Seeds: With copious endosperm.

Range: Europe (including Britain). N. America. Asia. N. Africa. Temperate S. America. New Zealand.

Uses: Dried leaves and seeds used medicinally as sedative and narcotic.

Special comments: Whole plant very poisonous mainly because of

alkaloid coniine in leaves (before flowering) and fruits. Children should be warned not to make "pea-shooters" from the hollow stems.

HARE'S EAR (*Bupleurum rotundifolium*)

General characters: Bluish-green annual herb 6–12″ high. Stem hollow, zigzag, branched, branches zigzag. Leaves simple, without stalks, lower ones elliptic and clasping stem at base, upper leaves elliptic to rounded and completely surrounding stem. Flowers yellow, very small, in compound umbels, the small (secondary) umbels surrounded by 4–6

large leafy yellowish bracteoles. Calyx joined to ovary, without teeth. Petals 5, with inflexed points. Stamens 5. Ovary 2-celled, each cell with 1 ovule. Styles 2, short.

Habitat: Cornfields, waste places.

Pollination: By insects.

Fruit: Small, dry, blackish when ripe. Of 2 carpels which separate.

Seeds: Average weight: 0·0023 gm (carpel).

Range: Europe (including Britain). N. America. N. Africa. Australia. New Zealand.

Uses: No information.

WILD CELERY (*Apium graveolens*)

General characters: Erect biennial herb with strong smell, up to 2′ high. Lower leaves pinnate with lobed and toothed segments, stalked, but becoming stalkless towards top of plant, where leaves are smaller and divided into 3 parts. Flowers greenish-white, very small, in compound umbels which are shortly-stalked or stalkless. Rays of main umbel unequal in length. Calyx joined to ovary, teeth often minute. Petals 5, point inflexed. Stamens 5. Ovary 2-celled, 1 ovule in each cell. Styles 2, very short.

Habitat: Marshy places, often near sea.

Pollination: By insects.

Fruit: Small, dry, egg-shaped. Each half with 5 slender ribs.

Seeds: Contain an essential oil.

Range: Europe (including Britain). N. & S. America. N. & S. Africa. Asia. New Zealand.

Uses: Celery is widely cultivated as vegetable. Fleshy root of variety *rapaceum*, celeriac or turnip-rooted celery, which is eaten raw or cooked, has delicate flavour, is rich in calcium and phosphorus, also contains vitamin C, iron, protein. Stalks and leaves of cultivated celery, variety *dulce*, are eaten raw or cooked. Green stalks of certain types are used, but stems of other varieties are first blanched. Stalks contain vitamins A, B_1, B_2 and C, also calcium, iron, phosphorus, protein. Seeds used medicinally and for flavouring. Celery proved to be a useful bee plant in California, where grown on large scale for seed.

WILD PARSNIP (*Pastinaca sativa*)

General characters: Hairy strong-smelling biennial herb up to 5′ high. Stems erect, furrowed, hollow. Leaves pinnate, with lobed and toothed egg-shaped segments, sheathing at base. Flowers small, yellow, in compound umbels. Calyx joined to ovary, teeth very small or absent. Petals 5, inflexed. Stamens 5. Ovary 2-celled, 1 ovule in each cell. Styles 2, very short.

Habitat: Pastures, roadsides, rough grassy places, especially in chalky districts.

Pollination: By insects.

Fruit: Dry, of 2 flattened carpels ("half-fruits"). Carpels oval, margin narrowly winged, outside with 5 slender ribs and 4 resinous canals (vittae). Weight of carpel about 0·003 gm.

Seeds: Germinate slowly. Soon lose viability.

Range: Europe (including Britain). N. & S. America. Australia. New Zealand.

Uses: Swollen tap-root of cultivated variety cooked and eaten as vegetable. Roots contain carbohydrate (about 18%), vitamins A, B and C, calcium, phosphorus, iron and protein.

WILD CARROT (*Daucus carota*)

General characters: Annual or biennial herb with tough tap-root. Stem erect, branched, solid, ribbed, with bristle-like hairs, up to 3' high. Leaves much divided (3-pinnate), bristly. Flowers in compound umbels, mostly white but sometimes pinkish and central flower of umbel often crimson-purple. Calyx minute. Petals 5, notched, point inflexed, unequally 2-lobed. Stamens 5. Ovary covered with short bristly hairs, 2-celled, each cell with 1 ovule. Styles 2. Subspecies *carota*: Fruiting umbel cup-shaped (hence name Bird's Nest). Subspecies *gummifer*: Fruiting umbel flat, leaves more fleshy and with shorter segments.

Habitat: Calcareous grassland, arable land (Ssp. *carota*). Maritime cliffs and dunes (Ssp. *gummifer*).

Pollination: By insects.

Fruit: Dry, of two 1-seeded carpels whose 4 secondary ridges bear spines with minute reflexed tips.

Seeds: Contain a volatile oil. Dispersed by animals (in excreta of cattle and roe deer), wind and by adhesion by spines.

Range: Most temperate and many tropical regions.

Uses: Dried plant used medicinally for liver complaints. Seeds sometimes used for digestive disorders. Ssp. *sativus*, cultivated carrot, whose thick fleshy tap-root is eaten raw or cooked, source of vitamins A, B_1, B_2 and C, calcium, phosphorus, iron, protein. Carrots also fed to farm livestock. Oil from seeds used in perfumery, liqueurs, flavourings. Coffee substitute made from roasted roots. In N. America both wild and cultivated carrots are useful honey plants.

Order VALERIANALES

Family *VALERIANACEAE*

CORN SALAD (*Valerianella locusta*)

General characters: Much-branched annual herb up to 1' high. Leaves opposite, sometimes toothed, lower ones spoon-shaped, upper leaves narrowly oblong. Flowers small, bluish-mauve, in head-like cymes at end branches. Calyx indistinct, joined to ovary. Corolla very small, funnel-shaped, with 5 spreading lobes at top. Stamens 3. Ovary inferior, 3-celled, 1 cell with 1 ovule, 2 cells sterile and empty. Style simple.

Habitat: Dry chalky arable land, dunes, waste places.

Pollination: Cross-pollination by insects. Failing this, automatic self-pollination.

Fruit: Small, dry, nut-like. 1-seeded. Fertile cell corky on back, with 2 empty cells. Weight about 0·001 gm.

Seeds: Without endosperm.

Range: Europe (including Britain). N. America. N. Africa. W. Asia.
Uses: Grown as vegetable, leaves being used mainly in salads.

Family *DIPSACACEAE*

TEASEL (*Dipsacus fullonum*)

General characters: Biennial herb up to 6′ high. Stems erect, branching, hollow, ribbed, prickly on ribs. Basal leaves forming rosette, somewhat prickly, oblong, shortly-stalked. Stem-leaves opposite, narrowly lance-shaped, joined at base and forming a water-collecting trough. Flowers small, rose-purple (occasionally white), arranged in an erect conical head bristly with spine-tipped bracts and surrounded by common involucre of spiny green bracts. Base of flower surrounded by cup-shaped epicalyx, above which is small cup-shaped calyx. Corolla tubular, 4-lobed. Stamens 4. Ovary inferior, 1-celled, 1 ovule. Style shortly and unequally 2-lobed.

Habitat: Banks of streams, roadsides, waste places, woodland margins and clearings.

Pollination: By insects.

Fruit: An achene enclosed in epicalyx and crowned by persistent calyx. Average weight: 0·005 gm. About 700 achenes per fruiting head. A favourite food of goldfinches.

Seeds: With endosperm.

Range: Europe (including Britain). N. America. N. Africa. Asia Minor.

Uses: Fruiting heads of Ssp. *sativus*, cultivated Fuller's Teasel, bear bracts ending in stiff hooks. These heads still used to comb woollen cloth to raise nap.

Special comments: A useful bee plant in America, where Teasel honey said to have good flavour.

FIELD SCABIOUS (*Knautia arvensis*)

General characters: Erect perennial herb up to 5' high. Stems rough with stiff downwardly directed hairs. Leaves opposite and joined at base around stem, bristly-hairy, lower ones reverse-lance-shaped and often undivided, upper ones deeply pinnately lobed. Flowers pale lilac or bluish, about 50 in each flat long-stalked head, outer flowers larger than central ones. Head with calyx-like involucre of hairy green bracts. Each flower surrounded at base by 4-angled epicalyx ("involucel"). Calyx cup-like, shallow, with 8 or 16 bristles. Corolla tubular, unequally 4-lobed. Stamens 4. Ovary inferior, 1-celled, ovule 1.

Habitat: Chalky fields, corn fields, hedgebanks.

Pollination: Cross-pollination by insects (mainly bees and butterflies).

Fruit: A small hairy achene enclosed in epicalyx. Weight about 0·004 gm. Dispersed by ants.

Seeds: With endosperm.
Range: Europe (including Britain). N. America.
Uses: No information.

Order CAMPANALES

Family *CAMPANULACEAE*

HAREBELL (*Campanula rotundifolia*)

General characters: Slender perennial herb up to $1\frac{1}{2}$–$2'$ high. Basal leaves rounded, long-stalked, often disappearing early. Stem-leaves alternate, narrow, pointed, stalkless. Flowers blue, rarely white, nodding on slender stalks, solitary or in loose panicle at top stem. Calyx-tube very short, with 5 narrow lobes. Corolla bell-shaped, with 5 broad lobes. Stamens 5. Ovary inferior, 3–5-celled, ovules numerous.

Habitat: Grassy places, heaths, fixed dunes, damp mountain rock-ledges.

Pollination: Cross-pollination by insects. Failing this, self-pollination.

Fruit: A 3–5-celled nodding capsule opening by pores near base.

Seeds: With endosperm. Average weight: 0·00006 gm. Dispersed by wind (plants growing on walls 20′ above ground) and rain-wash.

Range: Widely distributed in north temperate regions.

SHEEP'S-BIT (*Jasione montana*)

General characters: Annual or biennial herb (probably occasionally perennial) up to $1\frac{1}{2}'$ high. Stems simple or branched from base, with white bristly hairs. Leaves alternate, with long bristly hairs, narrowly oblong or lance-shaped, those on stem stalkless. Flowers small, pale blue (rarely white), up to about 200 arranged in rounded head surrounded by numerous triangular bracts. Calyx-tube narrowly 5-lobed. Corolla deeply 5-lobed, lobes narrow and spreading. Stamens 5, anthers joined at base. Ovary inferior, 2-celled. Stigmas 2.

Habitat: Grassy places, heaths, rough pastures.

Pollination: Cross-pollination by insects. Failing this, self-pollination.

Fruit: A capsule opening at top by 2 short valves.

Seeds: With endosperm. Very small.

Range: Europe (including Britain).

Family *LOBELIACEAE*

CARDINAL FLOWER (*Lobelia cardinalis*)

General characters: Perennial herb 2–6' high. Stem leafy, rarely branched. Leaves alternate, lance-shaped or oblong, pointed, up to 6" long, lower ones stalked, upper stalkless. Flowers bright scarlet (rarely white), numerous, 1–1½" long, arranged at intervals along upper part of stem. Calyx joined to ovary, with 5 narrow pointed lobes. Corolla-tube about 1" long, 2-lipped, upper lip 2-lobed, lower 3-lobed. Stamens 5, anthers united into tube around style. Ovary inferior, 2-celled, ovules numerous (axile).

Habitat: Along shaded streams and in moist thickets. Occasionally actually in shallow streams.

Fruit: A 2-valved capsule containing numerous seeds.

Seeds: With copious endosperm. Small.

Vegetative reproduction: By offsets.

Range: Eastern N. America.

Uses: Dried leaves and stem tops used medicinally (emetic, expectorant).

Order **GOODENIALES**

Family *GOODENIACEAE*

FAN FLOWER (*Scaevola spinescens*)

General characters: Rigid shrub up to 3' or more, with dense covering minute star-shaped hairs. Branchlets spiny. Leaves often reverse-lance-shaped, ¾" long, thickish, often clustered, each cluster with rigid spine. Flowers white, on short solitary stalks in leaf-axils, irregular. Sepals 5, minute. Corolla-tube slit to base on upper side, with 1-sided 5-lobed limb (fan-shaped). Stamens 5, free. Ovary inferior, 2-celled, each cell with 1 ovule. Style hairy, with stigma like small cup at apex.

Habitat: Dry places in hills.

Pollination: Cross-pollination by insects.

Fruit: A small egg-shaped-oblong drupe.

Seeds: With fleshy endosperm. Small, flat, oblong.

Range: Temperate Australia.

Uses: Fruits eaten by aborigines.

Family *BRUNONIACEAE*

BLUE PINCUSHION (*Brunonia australis*)

General characters: Perennial herb with numerous silky hairs. Leaves reverse-lance-shaped, up to 4" long and ½" wide, all from base of plant. Flowers blue, stalkless, in dense hemispherical heads at top leafless

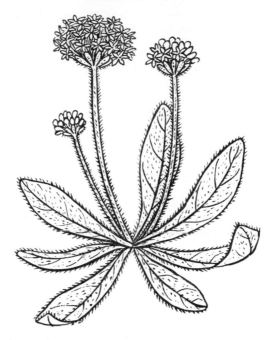

stalks 4–12″ long. Flower-head surrounded by calyx-like arrangement
of bracts and each flower by 4 bracteoles. Calyx tubular, with 5 awl-
shaped lobes, persistent in fruit. Corolla slightly 2-lipped, tubular, with
5 lance-shaped lobes. Stamens 5, inserted at base corolla, with anthers
forming tube round style. Ovary superior, 1-celled, 1 ovule, enclosed
by calyx-tube. Style simple. Stigma small, enclosed by cup-shaped
structure (indusium).

Habitat: Dry pastures.
Pollination: Cross-pollination by insects.
Fruit: Small, dry, 1-seeded, enclosed by persistent calyx-tube.
Seeds: Without endosperm. Small, egg-shaped.
Range: Temperate Australia. Tasmania.
Uses: No information.

Family *STYLIDIACEAE*

Phyllachne clavigera

General characters: Herb with stems close together, forming dense
cushions up to 2″ high. Leaves small, thick, leathery, densely overlapping, stalkless, narrowly oblong. Flowers white, small, stalkless, solitary. Calyx-tube joined to ovary, 5–6-lobed, lobes narrowly oblong.

Corolla-tube short, 5–7-lobed, lobes reverse-egg-shaped. Stamens 2, filaments joined into stout column surrounding style. Ovary inferior, 2-celled.

Habitat: Rocky places, peat bogs in hills and lower places.

Fruit: A top-shaped 6–8-seeded capsule.

Seeds: With copious endosperm. Minute.

Range: New Zealand.

Uses: No information.

Order **ASTERALES**

Family *COMPOSITAE*

SUNFLOWER (*Helianthus annuus*)

General characters: Annual herb 3–15' high. Stem stout, erect, woody, often roughly hairy, sometimes unbranched. Leaves large, mostly alternate, broadly egg-shaped, pointed, long-stalked, often rough. Flowers small (florets), arranged in large broad drooping heads with 2 types of florets, 1 marginal, the other central. Marginal or ray-florets golden-yellow, with large showy strap-shaped corolla, deciduous, sterile. Central or disk-florets numerous, purplish or brownish, with small tubular 5-lobed corolla, 5 stamens (anthers united into tube), and inferior 1-celled ovary with 1 ovule. (There are several races of "wild" sunflower and many cultivated varieties, differing in height, size of flower-head, colour of seeds, etc.)

Habitat: Prairies, railway yards, roadsides.

Pollination: Normally cross-pollination by insects.

Fruit: An achene about $\frac{1}{2}''$ long. Often flattened.

Seeds: Without endosperm. Containing 16–20% protein and 20–30% pale yellow semi-drying oil. Rich in B vitamins, calcium, iron, and phosphorus. Also contain vitamins A, C, D, E and K.

Range: Native of Central America, but widely cultivated, sometimes on large scale, in both temperate and tropical regions.

Uses: Sunflower seed oil used in cooking or table oils, margarine and compound fats. Inferior quality oil used as drying oil for paints or in soap. Oil cake, residue from oil extraction plants, is valuable cattle feed, as are leaves and stems. Fruit are nutritious food for people and poultry. Roasted, they make coffee substitute. Besides yielding silky fibres, stalks are burnt to extract high-grade potash salts for use in glass-making and as fertilizers. Flowers are source of yellow dye and stems of pith employed in making microscopical sections. Dried leaves used in Germany as tobacco. A good bee plant, sunflower honey being delicious.

Special comments: As name suggests, plant is sun-lover. Flower-head turns with direction of sun's rays, becomes erect after dark, bends over towards east before sunrise, and then continues daily movement.

BLACK-EYED SUSAN (*Rudbeckia hirta*)

General characters: Hairy annual to perennial herb. Stems erect, simple or sparingly branched, 1–3' high. Leaves alternate, lance-shaped or oblong, sometimes with few short teeth, up to 7" long, basal and lower ones stalked, upper narrower and without stalks. Flower-heads 2–4" broad, long-stalked, few or solitary, with calyx-like involucre of numerous hairy bracts. Ray-florets strap-shaped, bright yellow, neuter. Disk-florets tubular, brownish-black, bisexual, forming dark central cone (hence name Cone-flower).

Habitat: Fields, waste places.

Pollination: By insects, including bees.

Fruit: A 4-angled achene.

Seeds: Without endosperm.

Range: N. America. Naturalized in parts Europe.

Uses: No information.

RAGWORT (*Senecio jacobaea*)

General characters: Erect biennial or perennial herb up to 4½' high. Stems furrowed, branched in upper part. Leaves dark green, sometimes cottony beneath, deeply divided, basal and lower stem-leaves stalked, upper ones stalkless. Flower-heads bright yellow, in flat-topped clusters, each head with about 70 tubular bisexual disk-florets surrounded by 12–15 strap-shaped female ray-florets. Stamens 5. Ovary 1-celled, ovule 1.

Habitat: Waste places, poor pastures, sand-dunes, occasionally in tops pollard willows.

Pollination: Cross-pollination by insects.

Fruit: A small yellowish-brown ribbed achene with "parachute" of feathery hairs. Achenes from ray-florets smooth, others hairy. Average weight: 0·00028 gm. About 77,000 fruits per plant. Dispersed by wind, water, man and birds.

Seeds: Without endosperm. Normal germination about 80%.

Vegetative reproduction: By buds from roots and root fragments.

Range: Europe (including Britain). N. & S. America. W. Asia. New Zealand. Australia. S. Africa.

Uses: Leaves used as tonic and home-remedy for cramp. Source of nectar and pollen for bees, but ragwort honey strong flavoured and may render other honey unsuitable for human consumption.

Special comments: Toxic to cattle and horses (contains toxic alkaloids jacobine, jacodine and jaconine, which are not lost on drying. Sheep eat ragwort, but do not thrive on it and are occasionally poisoned by it.

GOLDEN-ROD (*Solidago canadensis*)

General characters: Perennial herb 2–8' high. Leaves alternate, lance-shaped, pointed, sharp-toothed (margins of upper ones sometimes without teeth), gradually decreasing in size from base of plant upwards. Flower-heads small, golden-yellow, of both ray- and disk-florets, surrounded by involucre of narrow bracts, crowded along upper side of curving branches of pyramidal flower cluster. Florets small, ray-florets female, disk-florets bisexual.

Habitat: Open places. In Europe, escaping from gardens and growing at roadsides, in waste places.

Pollination: Cross-pollination by insects.
Fruit: A ribbed achene crowned by pappus of short hairs.
Seeds: Without endosperm.
Range: Eastern N. America. Cultivated in Europe.
Uses: Recommended as emergency food-plant. Seeds of this and several other Golden-rod species were eaten by American Indians. In parts eastern N. America golden-rods are important autumn honey plants, providing winter stores for bees and fine flavoured surplus honey for human consumption.
Special comments: A very variable species.

NEW ENGLAND ASTER (*Aster novae-angliae*)

General characters: Branched perennial herb 2–8′ high. Stem stout, hairy, somewhat sticky. Leaves alternate, lance-shaped, pointed, hairy, clasping stem by ear-like basal lobes, up to 5″ long. Flower-heads numerous, 1–2″ broad, clustered at ends of branches, each with involucre of several rows of narrow green overlapping bracts. Disk-florets tubular, yellow, bisexual, corollas 5-lobed. Ray-florets strap-shaped, female, deep violet or purple, occasionally white, pink or red. Stamens 5. Ovary 1-celled, 1 ovule.

Habitat: Meadows, woodland openings, along swamps, often in coastal regions.

Pollination: Cross-pollination by insects.

Fruit: A hairy achene crowned by reddish-white pappus of hairs.

Seeds: Without endosperm.

Range: N. America. Cultivated in Europe (as Michaelmas Daisy).

Uses: A useful autumn bee plant and beautiful garden subject.

CHICORY (*Cichorium intybus*)

General characters: Perennial herb up to 3′ high. Stems erect, stiffly branched, grooved. Basal leaves pinnately lobed, lobes often slightly curved and toothed, short-stalked. Stem-leaves stalkless, upper ones

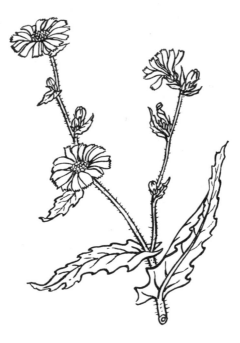

lance-shaped and sometimes toothed, clasping stem, becoming smaller upwards. Flower-heads of numerous florets, bright blue (rarely pink or white), 1-1½" across, single or in groups of 2-3 in axils of upper leaves. Florets all of 1 kind, bisexual, with strap-shaped corolla whose tip is 5-toothed. Stamens 5. Ovary 1-celled, ovule 1.

Habitat: Roadsides, fields, grassland, waste places (often on chalk and limestone).

Pollination: Cross-pollination by insects. Failing this, automatic self-pollination.

Fruit: A small ribbed achene crowned with ring of minute scales. Weight about 0·0013 gm.

Seeds: Without endosperm.

Range: Europe (including Britain). N. & S. America. Asia. Africa. Australia. New Zealand.

Uses: Roasted and ground, roots are added to coffee and even used as coffee substitute. Dried roots used medicinally as tonic and diuretic. Roots also sometimes cooked as vegetable. Blanched salad shoots obtained from roots by forcing. Grown as cattle fodder (contains magnesium and iron). A favourite of honey bees, flowers yielding nectar and pollen.

Special comments: Several varieties in cultivation.

BITTER LETTUCE (*Lactuca virosa*)

General characters: Erect biennial herb up to 6-7' high. With copious bitter milky juice. Leaves rigid, with wavy prickly-toothed margins, often prickly on midrib below. Basal leaves reverse-egg-shaped to oblong, stem-leaves oblong, stalkless, clasping, with deflexed ear-like lobes at base. Flower-heads numerous, small, yellow, consisting of 15-20 bisexual strap-shaped florets (no disk-florets), each head surrounded by a cylindrical involucre of overlapping bracts. Heads arranged in a much-branched inflorescence whose branches are slender and spreading.

Habitat: Hedgebanks, grassy places, cliffs near sea, gravel workings, roadside embankments.

Pollination: By insects.

Fruit: A blackish flattened and ribbed achene narrowed into slender beak bearing "parachute" of white spreading hairs. Average weight: 0·00095 gm. Wind-dispersed.

Range: Europe (including Britain). U.S.A. N. Africa. W. Asia. Australia.

Uses: Lactucarium from milky juice of leaves and stems used medicinally as sedative.

Special comments: Also known as Poisonous Lettuce and said to have had an injurious effect on cattle in Australia.

Mouse-ear Hawkweed (*Hieracium pilosella*)

General characters: Perennial herb with several long creeping stems (stolons) bearing small narrow hairy leaves. Leaves of basal rosette narrowly oblong to reverse-lance-shaped, tapered to base, with long stiff hairs, lower surface with white star-shaped hairs. Flower-head solitary at top hairy stalk 6–12″ high, surrounded by involucre of 2–3 rows hairy bracts, containing bisexual strap-shaped florets only, the strap-shaped ligules lemon-yellow above and often reddish below.

Habitat: Grassy places, banks, roadsides, heaths, walls.

Pollination: Honey bees work flowers for nectar and pollen. (Viable seed often produced without fertilization in *Hieracium*.)

Fruit: A purplish-black ribbed achene crowned by white pappus hairs. Dispersed by wind and birds (seedlings raised from excreta).

Vegetative reproduction: By stolons ending in overwintering rosettes.

Range: Europe (including Britain). N. America. W. Asia.

Uses: No information.

Special comments: This variable but distinctive member of large and puzzling genus *Hieracium* said to be occasionally harmful to livestock.

Common Dandelion (*Taraxacum officinale*)

General characters: Perennial herb with milky juice and fleshy tap-root. Leaves all from root, very variable in form, but often lobed and larger lobes curved towards base of leaf. Flower-head golden-yellow, up to 2″ across, solitary at top hollow leafless stem up to 1′ high, containing numerous bisexual strap-shaped florets, enclosed by cylindrical involucre of green bracts. Inner bracts erect, outer bracts narrow, shorter than inner ones, usually curved backwards.

Habitat: Fields, lawns, waste places, pastures, roadsides.

Pollination: All British dandelions are apomictic, viable seed being set without fertilization (pollination mechanism retained, but pollen development often very poor). However, dandelions reproducing sexually, with pollination and fertilization, do occur.

Fruit: A yellowish or olive achene, ribbed with ribs ending in spreading teeth. With long beak crowned by pappus of silky white hairs. Average weight: 0·0008 gm. Wind-dispersed (pappus hairs spreading open in dry weather and acting as "parachute").

Seeds: Germination often occurs soon after seeds are ripe and is frequently over 90%.

Vegetative reproduction: By adventitious buds from roots and root fragments.

Range: Northern hemisphere.

Uses: Dried root used medicinally as laxative and tonic. Roasted and ground root makes "coffee" valued by people with weak digestions.

Flower-heads made into popular country wine. Leaves eaten raw in salads or cooked like spinach. Cultivated varieties yield leaves rich in vitamins A, B_1, B_2 and C, and minerals (calcium, phosphorus, iron). Wild dandelions in pastures may contain more copper and iron than fodder grasses.

Special comments: A very variable plant, over 100 forms having been described in Britain alone.

Order **SOLANALES**

Family *SOLANACEAE*

DEADLY NIGHTSHADE (*Atropa bella-donna*)

General characters: Erect hairy perennial herb up to 6' high. Stem branched, solid. Leaves broadly egg-shaped, pointed, lower ones alternate, in unequal pairs further up stem. Flowers stalked, drooping, solitary in leaf-axils or forks of stem. Calyx bell-shaped, 5-lobed, lobes pointed. Corolla bell-shaped, purple (sometimes tinged with green), 5-lobed. Stamens 5, inserted in corolla-tube near base. Ovary superior, 2-celled, ovules numerous.

Habitat: Cliffs, slopes of calcareous woodlands, old quarry workings, gardens, meadows, felled woodland.

Pollination: Cross-pollination by insects, mainly humble-bees.

Fruit: A 2-celled purplish or blackish berry containing 120–150 seeds.

Seeds: With endosperm. Average weight: 0·00141 gm. Dispersed by birds (in excreta).

Vegetative reproduction: Sometimes by stolons. Also by shoots from root fragments.

Range: Europe (including Britain). N. America. W. Asia. N. Africa.

Uses: Dried leaves and roots used medicinally (contain toxic alkaloids atropine and hyoscyamine).

Special comments: All parts poisonous to man and certain animals.

BLACK NIGHTSHADE (*Solanum nigrum*)

General characters: Much-branched annual or biennial herb up to 2' high. Leaves alternate, egg- or diamond-shaped, pointed, narrowed at base, stalked. Flowers small, white, drooping, in stalked clusters. Calyx 5-lobed. Corolla shortly tubular, 5-lobed. Stamens 5, inserted in throat of corolla, anthers forming yellow cone. Ovary superior, 2-celled, ovules numerous.

Habitat: Arable land, gardens, waste places.

Pollination: Visited by insects, but self-pollination occurs.

Fruit: A small globose black berry containing 40–50 seeds (100 or more in large-fruited variety *macrocarpa*).

Seeds: With endosperm. Flattened, almost circular, minutely pitted. Weight about 0·0009 gm. 90% germination or more.

Range: Almost cosmopolitan.

Uses: Dried stalks used medicinally.

Special comments: 1. All parts said to contain poisonous alkaloids, amounts appearing to vary according to soil. Sometimes fruits have proved toxic to children, but on other occasions have caused little harm. In U.S.A. Luther Burbank developed the plant and for a time fruits (Wonderberries) of cultivated forms were used in pies. Recently an American economic botanist recommended Black Nightshade as emergency food-plant, but caution is obviously needed. 2. *Solanaceae* contains such valuable crop-plants as potato, *Solanum tuberosum* (edible tubers); egg-plant or aubergine, *Solanum melongena*; "pepper," *Capsicum frutescens*; tomato, *Lycopersicum esculentum* (last 3: edible fruits).

HENBANE (*Hyoscyamus niger*)

General characters: Hairy sticky annual or biennial herb up to 2½' high. With strong unpleasant odour. Basal leaves large, shortly stalked, coarsely and pinnately lobed. Stem-leaves smaller, stalkless, oblong, with few teeth or lobes. Flowers about 1″ across, yellowish veined with purple and with purple "eye." Calyx bell-shaped, 5-lobed, lobes pointed, becoming spine-like in fruit. Corolla 5-lobed. Stamens 5, inserted at base corolla-tube, anthers purple. Ovary superior, 2-celled, ovules numerous.

Habitat: Waste places, often near buildings, sandy places in the Prairies and near the sea.

Pollination: Cross-pollination by insects. Failing this, self-pollination.

Fruit: A 200–500-seeded capsule whose top splits off. Enclosed in calyx.

Seeds: With endosperm. Brownish, flattened, almost circular, ribbed. Weight about 0·0008 gm. Poisonous. Sometimes found as impurity with Red Clover seeds.

Range: Europe (including Britain). N. America. W. Asia. N. Africa.

Uses: Dried leaves used medicinally (narcotic, hypnotic).

Special comments: Poisonous. Contains alkaloids hyoscyamine and scopolamine.

Family *CONVOLVULACEAE*

BINDWEED (*Convolvulus arvensis*)

General characters: Prostrate or climbing perennial herb. Stems climbing by twisting spirally round other plants. Leaves alternate,

stalked, often halberd-shaped but variable. Flowers pink or white (sometimes striped), about 1″ across, scented, 1–3 on stalks arising from leaf-axils. Calyx deeply 5-lobed. Corolla funnel-shaped, with 5 very shallow lobes, soon withering. Stamens 5, inserted at base corolla-tube. Ovary superior, 2-celled, each cell with 2 ovules. Style slender. Stigmas 2. Stems exude milky juice (latex) when broken.

Habitat: Gardens, fields, waste places, roadsides.

Pollination: Cross-pollination by insects. Also self-pollination.

Fruit: A small 2-celled capsule containing 1–4 seeds.

Seeds: With endosperm. Minutely pitted. Weight up to about 0·02 gm. Often found as impurity in wheat.

Vegetative reproduction: By means of underground stems and shoots arising from stem and root fragments.

Range: Temperate regions of world.

Uses: No information.

Special comments: A troublesome weed and difficult to eradicate (hence name Devil's Guts). Root system spreads quickly (covering 30 square yards in a season) and penetrates to depths of up to 23′.

SEA BINDWEED (*Calystegia soldanella*)

General characters: Perennial herb with angular stems lying loosely on sand and sometimes buried in it. Leaves alternate, often kidney-shaped, long-stalked. Flowers pink or pale mauve, solitary on long sharply 4-angled stalks from leaf-axils. Calyx of 5 sepals, enclosed by 2 sharply keeled bracts. Corolla funnel-shaped, about 2″ broad, 5-lobed. Stamens 5, inserted near base corolla-tube. Ovary superior, with 4 ovules. Style slender. Stigmas 2, thick.

Habitat: Sandy and shingly seashores.

Pollination: Cross-pollination by insects (mainly humble-bees). Self-pollination also occurs.

Fruit: An egg-shaped capsule.

Seeds: With endosperm. Sea-dispersed, floating unharmed for 6–18 months.

Vegetative reproduction: By rhizomes.

Range: Europe (including Britain). N. & S. America. N. Africa. Asia. Australia. New Zealand.

Uses: Dried plant used as diuretic and purgative.

SWEET POTATO (*Ipomoea batatas*)

General characters: Perennial herb existing in many varieties. Stems long, trailing or twining, or shorter and more erect. Leaves alternate, stalked, showing much variation in shape and size, but often almost rounded, apex pointed. Flowers large, reddish-purple, on long stout stalks from leaf-axils. Calyx shortly tubular, 5-lobed. Corolla funnel-shaped, sometimes 5-lobed but often scarcely lobed. Stamens 5, inserted near base corolla-tube, filaments of varying length. Ovary 2-celled, sometimes 4-celled in cultivated varieties, each cell with 2 ovules.

Habitat: Prefers light sandy soils (sometimes grown under irrigation in dry districts).

Pollination: Cross-pollination by insects.

Fruit: A globular capsule.

Seeds: Small, black, somewhat flattened. Seed-coat thick. Plants often fail to set seed.

Vegetative reproduction: Propagated from stem cuttings.

Range: Cultivated throughout tropics and also in cooler climates.

Uses: Root tubers important food and major source of starch for tropical peoples. Tubers also contain sugar, fat, protein, calcium, phosphorus, iron, vitamins A (rich source), B_1, B_2, C. Tubers yield alcohol. They are used in U.S.A. for production of flour, starch and glucose syrup. Tubers sometimes canned. Young leaves used as green vegetable. Stems and foliage fed to livestock.

Order **PERSONALES**

Family *SCROPHULARIACEAE*

GREAT MULLEIN (*Verbascum thapsus*)

General characters: Erect biennial herb up to 7' high. With dense whitish covering of star-shaped hairs. Leaves oblong-lance-shaped, thick, pointed, narrowed at base, 4–12" long. Leaves of basal rosette with margined stalks. Stem-leaves alternate, base continued downwards, forming a wing on stem. Flowers yellow, up to 1" broad, numerous, in dense spike-like raceme at top stem. Calyx deeply 5-lobed. Corolla with short tube, broadly 5-lobed, lobes spreading. Stamens 5, three upper filaments covered with yellowish or whitish woolly hairs. Ovary superior, 2-celled, ovules numerous.

Habitat: Fields, waste places, banks, woodland clearings.

Pollination: Cross-pollination by insects or self-pollination.

Fruit: An egg-shaped capsule opening by 2 valves.

Seeds: With fleshy endosperm. Numerous, small, wrinkled. Possess narcotic properties and used to stupefy fish. Average weight: 0·00009 gm. Believed to retain viability after burial in soil for 58 years.

Range: Europe (including Britain). N. America. Asia.

Uses: Dried leaves and flowers used medicinally in soothing ointments and in liquid form for chest and bronchial ailments.

GREAT MULLEIN (*Verbascum thapsus*)

YELLOW TOADFLAX (*Linaria vulgaris*)

General characters: Perennial herb 1–3′ high. Stems erect, branched, leafy, rounded and shining. Leaves alternate, long, narrow, pointed. Flowers yellow, in dense racemes at top stem. Calyx deeply 5-lobed, sepals sharp-pointed. Corolla 2-lipped, lower lip 3-lobed with bulging orange "palate," upper lip 2-lobed, tube prolonged into straight pointed spur. Stamens 4, hidden below upper lip. Ovary superior, 2-celled, ovules numerous.

Habitat: Fields, gardens, waste places, roadsides, hedgebanks.

Pollination: Cross-pollination by bees.

Fruit: An egg-shaped capsule containing about 70 seeds and opening at top.

Seeds: With fleshy endosperm. Blackish, rounded, flattened, with small warts in centre and thin border ("wing"). Average weight: 0·00014 gm. Wind-dispersed.

Vegetative reproduction: By production of shoots from roots and root fragments.

Range: Europe (including Britain). N. America (where called Butter-and-eggs). W. Asia.

Uses: No information.

FIGWORT (*Scrophularia nodosa*)

General characters: Erect square-stemmed perennial herb up to 3–4′ high. Leaves opposite, stalked, egg-shaped, sharply pointed, toothed. Flowers dull purplish, in a loose panicle whose branches are covered with short gland-tipped hairs. Calyx 5-lobed. Corolla 2-lipped, with 5 small lobes, tube greenish and almost globular. Stamens 4. Staminode (infertile stamen) present at back corolla-tube. Ovary superior, 2-celled, ovules numerous.

Habitat: Moist shady places, woods, hedgebanks.

Pollination: Cross-pollination by insects (mainly wasps).

Fruit: An egg-shaped pointed capsule.

Seeds: With fleshy endosperm. Small, brown, egg-shaped, wrinkled. Wind-dispersed.

Vegetative reproduction: By short stolons.

Range: Europe (including Britain). Temperate Asia.

Uses: Dried plant used medicinally as anodyne and for internal inflammation. A good bee plant, providing abundant nectar.

FOXGLOVE (*Digitalis purpurea*)

General characters: Erect biennial (occasionally short-lived perennial) herb up to 5′ high. Leaves lance-shaped, up to 1′ long, hairy above, densely covered with soft white hairs below, tapering at base into winged stalk. Basal leaves forming rosette. Flowers numerous, drooping, in racemes at top stem. Calyx deeply 5-lobed. Corolla up to 2″ long, with bell-shaped tube, shortly 5-lobed, light purple (rarely white), spotted inside with purple or crimson. Stamens 4. Ovary superior, 2-celled, ovules numerous.

Habitat: Clearings and burnt areas in woods, woodland margin, heaths.

Pollination: Cross-pollination by humble-bees.

Fruit: An egg-shaped capsule.

Seeds: With fleshy endosperm. Numerous, very small. Average weight: 0·00009 gm. Large plants may produce over 500,000 seeds. Germination in light sometimes 100%. Wind-dispersed.

Range: Europe (including Britain). N. America.

Uses: Dried leaves and seeds used medicinally, being source of drug digitalin used for heart trouble.

Special comments: All parts poisonous (hence name Dead Men's Bells).

FOXGLOVE BEARD-TONGUE (*Pentstemon digitalis*)

General characters: Perennial herb 2–5′ high. Leaves opposite, basal and lower ones oblong or oval, 2–7″ long, narrowed into margined stalks. Upper leaves egg- or lance-shaped, pointed, stalkless, somewhat

clasping at base. Flowers white, in loose many-flowered cluster towards top of stem. Calyx deeply 5-lobed. Corolla tubular, about 1″ long, abruptly enlarged, 5-lobed, the 2 lips often indistinct. 4 fertile stamens and a bearded sterile one. Ovary superior, 2-celled, ovules numerous.

Habitat: Prairies, open woodlands.
Pollination: Cross-pollination by insects.
Fruit: A capsule.
Seeds: With fleshy endosperm. Numerous, small.
Range: N. America.
Uses: No information.

Family *OROBANCHACEAE*

GREATER BROOMRAPE (*Orobanche rapum-genistae*)

General characters: Parasitic herb (without chlorophyll), growing on roots of host-plant. Stem unbranched, up to $2\frac{1}{2}'$ high, with numerous scales and gland-tipped hairs, yellowish. Flowers yellowish-purple, in a long dense spike, each flower with a pointed bract. Calyx laterally 2-lipped, each lip deeply 2-lobed. Corolla tubular, tube curved; 2-lipped, upper lip shortly 2-lobed (sometimes entire), lower 3-lobed. Stamens 4, in 2 pairs, inserted at base corolla-tube. Ovary superior, 1-celled, ovules numerous.

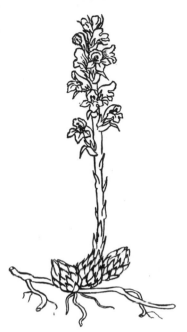

Habitat: Parasitic on roots of Gorse (*Ulex*), Broom (*Sarothamnus*) and certain other *Papilionaceae*.

Fruit: A capsule.

Seeds: With oily endosperm. Numerous, very small. Apparently wind-dispersed.

Range: Europe (including Britain). N. Africa.

Uses: No information, but roots of N. American *O. californica*, *O. ludoviciana*, and *O. tuberosa* are used as food by Indians.

Special comments: Unable to make own food. Lives entirely as parasite. Some Broomrapes greatly weaken their hosts.

Family *LENTIBULARIACEAE*

BUTTERWORT (*Pinguicula vulgaris*)

General characters: Insectivorous ("carnivorous") perennial herb about 6″ high. Leaves yellow-green, all in spreading basal rosette, stalkless, margins rolled upwards, egg-shaped to oblong, covered with small sticky glands which catch minute insects. Flowers violet, few, each on a leafless stalk from basal rosette. Calyx unequally 5-lobed. Corolla spurred, 2-lipped, upper lip 2-lobed, lower 3-lobed. Stamens 2. Ovary superior, 1-celled, ovules numerous.

Habitat: Wet rocks, bogs, wet heaths.

Pollination: Cross-pollination by insects (mainly bees).

Fruit: An egg-shaped capsule opening by 2 valves.

Seeds: Without endosperm. Numerous, small, oblong, wrinkled.

Range: Europe (including Britain). N. America. N. Asia. N. Morocco.

Uses: Leaves said to be used as coagulant of milk.

Special comments: When insect is caught leaf-margins roll over further and enclose it. Proteins of insect body digested by enzymes secreted by glands on leaf. Digested proteins (containing nitrogen) absorbed by leaf-surface and leaf unrolls again.

Bladderworts (*Utricularia* species), rootless herbs living in water, trap small animals in bladders borne on leaves.

Order **GERANIALES**

Family *GERANIACEAE*

Herb Robert (*Geranium robertianum*)

General characters: Annual or biennial herb up to $1\frac{1}{2}'$ high. Stems with slender hairs, often reddish. Leaves opposite, stalked, hairy, pinnately divided into 3 main parts which are themselves divided. Stipules

hairy. Flowers reddish-purple to pink (rarely white), in pairs on long common stalk from leaf-axil. Sepals 5, erect, 3-nerved, with long slender point. Petals 5, with long claw. Stamens 10. Ovary superior, 5-lobed, 5-celled, each cell with 1–2 ovules. Style stiff, erect. Stigmas 5, small.

Habitat: Woods, hedgebanks, walls, shingle beaches, rocks, waste places.

Pollination: Cross-pollination by insects. Self-pollination possible.

Fruit: Consists of 5 one-seeded carpels whose surface is covered with coarse network. Above seed-chambers is beak $\frac{1}{2}$–1" long which splits suddenly so that carpels with seeds are flung up to 20' from plant.

Seeds: Smooth.

Range: Europe (including Britain). N. & S. America. Asia. N. Africa.

Uses: No information.

Musk Storksbill (*Erodium moschatum*)

General characters: Musk-scented annual herb covered with white hairs and stalked glands, up to $1\frac{1}{2}$' high. Leaves pinnate, leaflets egg-shaped and toothed (sometimes deeply). Flowers rosy-purple, several in long-stalked umbels. Sepals 5, with short narrow point. Petals 5. Stamens 10, five fertile, but those opposite petals sterile (without anthers). Ovary superior, 5-lobed, 5-celled, each cell with 1–2 ovules. Stigmas 5, united.

Habitat: Sandy places, often in coastal districts.

Pollination: Cross-pollination by insects. (Both cross-pollination by insects and self-pollination occur in Common Storksbill, *Erodium cicutarium*.)

Fruit: Consists of 5 one-seeded carpels topped by long beak, which splits into 5 segments. Beak segment twists spirally and becomes detached with carpel and seed attached.

Seeds: Average weight: 0·00222 gm. Average 5,000–6,000 seeds per plant. Germination may average 95%. Twisted beak segments become entangled in fleece of sheep and seeds dispersed in wool and wool waste.

Range: Europe (including Britain). N. & S. America. S. Africa. Australia. New Zealand.

Uses: A good bee plant (nectar and pollen).

Pelargonium myrrhifolium

General characters: Hairy perennial herb $\frac{1}{2}$–1' high. Stems slender, spreading, with few branches. Leaves egg-shaped-oblong in outline, pinnately divided with narrow or wedge-shaped segments which are themselves often divided, long-stalked, up to 3" long. Stipules broad, pointed. Flowers pink or white, in 2–6-flowered umbels arising from leaf-axils. Calyx 5-parted with narrow pointed segments with prominent purple ribs, with a spur (nectar tube) united with flower stalk. Petals 4 or 5, free, 2 upper longer and broader than lower and with purple veins. Stamens 10, joined at base, 5–7 fertile, others sterile. Ovary superior, 5-lobed, 5-celled, each cell with 1–2 ovules.

Habitat: Dry sandy plains and mountains.

Fruit: Consists of 5 one-seeded beaked carpels which separate at maturity when beaks twist spirally.

Range: S. Africa.

Uses: No information. (Geranium oil distilled from leaves of *Pelargonium graveolens, P. odoratissimum, P. capitatum, P. roseum* and other species, for soaps and perfumes.)

Family *OXALIDACEAE*

Wood Sorrel (*Oxalis acetosella*)

General characters: Perennial herb. Leaves all from root, long-stalked, consisting of 3 yellow-green reverse-egg-shaped leaflets with notched apex. Flowers white, single on long stalks with 2 bracts half-way up. Sepals 5. Petals 5, free, reverse-egg-shaped, apex notched, white with violet lines. Stamens 10. Ovary superior, 5-celled, each cell with several ovules. Styles 5, free.

Habitat: Shady woods, hedgebanks.

Pollination: Most seed produced by cleistogamous flowers which do not open and are self-pollinated.

Fruit: An egg-shaped 5-angled capsule containing about 10 seeds.

Seeds: With copious fleshy endosperm. Average weight: 0·0024 gm. Seed enclosed by fleshy aril which suddenly turns inside out and thus ejects seed.

Vegetative reproduction: By slender rhizome.

Range: Europe (including Britain). N. America. Asia.

Uses: No information.

Special comments: Leaflets bend downwards at night and in cold weather. Flowers close in dull or cold weather.

Family *TROPAEOLACEAE*

Nasturtium (*Tropaeolum majus*)

General characters: Smooth succulent dwarf or climbing herb. Leaves alternate, roundish, stalk attached in middle. Flowers showy, yellow or red, up to 2½″ wide, solitary in leaf-axils. Sepals 5, one produced into spur 1–1½″ long. Petals 5, clawed, 2 upper unlike others. Stamens 8, free, unequal. Ovary superior, 3-lobed, 3-celled, each cell with 1 ovule. Style 1. Stigmas 3.

Habitat: Much-cultivated. Escaping to waste places, dumps, coastal areas, etc.

Pollination: By insects.

Fruit: Of 3 one-seeded carpels which separate from central axis when mature.

Seeds: Without endosperm.

Range: Native of S. America. Cultivated in many parts of world.

Uses: Flower buds and young fruits pickled and used as capers.

Family *BALSAMINACEAE*

JEWELWEED (*Impatiens capensis*)

General characters: Erect annual herb 2–5′ high. Leaves alternate, thin, egg-shaped or elliptic, 1½–3½″ long, toothed, on long slender stalks. Flowers orange mottled with reddish-brown within, on 2–4-flowered stalks from leaf-axils, individual flowers on slender stalks. Sepals 3, 2 lateral ones small, lower 1 petal-like, spurred. Petals 5, upper 1 large, lower united to form 2 pairs. Stamens 5, filaments joined above, anthers joined round ovary. Ovary superior, 5-celled, ovules numerous.

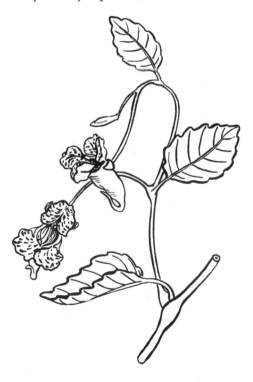

Habitat: Moist ground in ravines and along rivers and streams.

Pollination: Normal blossoms pollinated by insects, but flowers sometimes all cleistogamous and self-pollinated.

Fruit: An explosive fleshy capsule splitting open violently at slightest touch into 5 valves which curl up and scatter seeds several feet from plant. (Hence name Touch-me-not.)

Seeds: Without endosperm. Brown, ellipsoidal. Seeds sometimes dispersed by water.

Range: N. America. Europe (including Britain).

Uses: No information.

Order **POLEMONIALES**

Family *POLEMONIACEAE*

WILD BLUE PHLOX (*Phlox divaricata*)

General characters: Perennial herb with stems ascending or loosely spreading and prostrate sterile shoots. Leaves opposite, those of sterile shoots egg-shaped or oblong, leaves of flowering stems lance-shaped and usually pointed. Flowers bluish (sometimes white or pink), faintly scented, in clusters at top stems. Calyx tubular, with 5 awl-shaped teeth bearing fine glandular hairs. Corolla tubular, tube narrow, with 5

spreading inversely heart-shaped lobes. Stamens 5. Ovary superior, 3-celled, 1–4 ovules in each cell. Style 1. Stigmas 3.

Habitat: Moist open woods and meadows.

Fruit: A small 3-valved capsule.

Seeds: With endosperm.

Range: N. America (where known as Wild Sweet William, name associated with *Dianthus barbatus*).

Uses: No information.

Special comments: Cultivated as handsome garden plant.

SCARLET GILIA (*Gilia aggregata*)

General characters: Biennial herb 2–4′ high. Stem simple or sparingly branched. Leaves alternate, 1–3″ long, pinnately divided into narrow segments. Flowers scarlet or red (rarely almost white), in small stalked clusters forming inflorescence up to 1′ long. Calyx tubular, 5-lobed. Corolla 1–2″ long, tubular-funnelform, 5-lobed. Stamens 5. Ovary superior, 3-celled, ovules numerous.

Habitat: Dry soil.

Pollination: Cross-pollination by insects. Failing this, self-pollination sometimes occurs.

Fruit: A 3-celled capsule.

Seeds: With endosperm. Seed-coat mucilaginous when wetted and emitting spiral threads.

Range: Western N. America.

Uses: No information.

Family *CUSCUTACEAE*

DODDER (*Cuscuta europaea*)

General characters: Rootless annual parasitic herb attached to host-plant by suckers. Stems thread-like, much-branched, twining, brownish-red or pale yellowish (lacks green colouring). Leaves reduced to small scales. Flowers small, pinkish-white, in dense heads about ½″ broad. Calyx 5-lobed, fleshy. Corolla bell-shaped, 5-lobed, lobes spreading. Stamens 4–5, hidden in corolla-tube, with a ring of small scales below them. Ovary superior, completely or incompletely 2-celled, containing 4 ovules. Styles 2, free.

Habitat: On Stinging nettle, *Urtica dioica*, Hop, *Humulus lupulus*, and certain other plants, in hedges and shady places near rivers and streams.

Pollination: Self-pollination.

Fruit: A 2-celled capsule containing up to 4 seeds.

Seeds: With endosperm.

Range: Europe (including Britain). N. America. Asia.

Uses: No information.

Special comments: At one time Dodder was serious pest in European hop plantations.

Order **BORAGINALES**

Family *BORAGINACEAE*

HOUND'S-TONGUE (*Cynoglossum officinale*)

General characters: Erect biennial herb 1½–3′ high. Stems simple or branched, stout, leafy. Leaves spirally arranged, lance-shaped, usually pointed, with short soft hairs (old leaves sometimes rough), lower leaves stalked, upper stalkless. Flowers dull purple-red (rarely white) in branched cymes in axils of leaves. Calyx deeply 5-lobed. Corolla funnel-shaped, 5-lobed, mouth almost closed by 5 scales opposite rounded lobes. Stamens 5, inserted on corolla and alternate with its lobes. Ovary superior, deeply 4-lobed. Style from middle of lobes, simple.

Habitat: Open waste places, roadsides, edges of woods, sand-dunes near sea.

Pollination: Cross-pollination by insects (mainly bees). Failing this, self-pollination.

Fruit: Consists of 4 separate nutlets covered with hooked bristles. With thickened border.

Seeds: Average weight: 0·032 gm.

Range: Europe (including Britain). N. America. Asia.

Uses: Leaves and roots used medicinally (sedative, demulcent). Young leaves sometimes used as vegetable.

BORAGE (*Borago officinalis*)

General characters: Erect stiffly hairy annual or biennial herb up to 2′ high. Leaves alternate, egg-shaped to oblong, narrowed into margined stalk, upper ones often stalkless, up to 8″ long. Flowers bright blue, pendulous, in loose forked cymes in leaf-axils and at top of stem. Calyx deeply 5-toothed, densely and stiffly hairy. Corolla 5-lobed, lobes pointed and spreading at right angles to very short corolla-tube, mouth closed by short scales. Stamens 5, inserted in corolla-throat, forming an erect cone, with purple-black anthers. Ovary superior, deeply 4-lobed, style from middle of lobes.

Habitat: Dry places, banks. Long cultivated and escaping from gardens to waste places.

Pollination: Cross-pollination by insects (mainly bees).

Fruit: Consists of 4 wrinkled 1-seeded nutlets, each weighing about 0·014 gm.

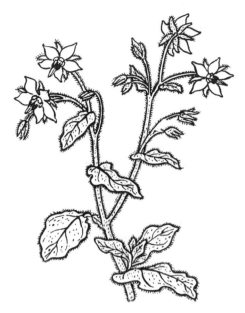

Seeds: Said to be dispersed by ants attracted by oil-body attached to nutlets.

Vegetative reproduction: Propagated by root division.

Range: Europe (including Britain). N. America. Australia.

Uses: Used medicinally for chest and throat complaints, leaves and stalks containing much mucilage. Young leaves included in salads (slight cucumber flavour). Flowers added to salads and certain beverages and formerly candied. A good bee plant.

WATER FORGET-ME-NOT (*Myosotis scorpioides*)

General characters: Hairy perennial herb. Stems ascending or lying on ground and end ascending. Leaves alternate, reverse-lance-shaped or oblong, narrowed at base, up to 3″ long. Flowers blue (rarely white), in a 1-sided inflorescence coiled in bud stage. Calyx bell-shaped, 5-toothed. Corolla 5-lobed, lobes flat and spreading at right angles to short straight tube, closed or partly closed at mouth by 5 notched scales. Stamens 5, inserted on corolla-tube between and below scales. Ovary superior, 4-lobed, style between lobes.

Habitat: Wet ditches, by sides of ponds and streams.

Pollination: Cross-pollination by insects. Also self-pollination.

Fruit: Consists of 4 small shiny black nutlets.

Vegetative reproduction: By stolons. Detached branches float and grow when stranded on mud.

Range: Europe (including Britain). N. America. N. Africa. Asia.
Uses: No information.

VIRGINIA COWSLIP (*Mertensia virginica*)

General characters: Perennial herb 1–2' high. Stem erect or ascending, sometimes branched. Leaves alternate, oval or reverse-egg-shaped, up to 5" long, upper ones stalkless, lower with margined stalks. Flowers blue-purple (pink in bud), about 1" long, in short racemes. Calyx small, 5-lobed. Corolla trumpet-shaped, with narrow tube and slightly 5-lobed limb whose sides are indented. Stamens 5, inserted on corolla-tube. Ovary superior, 4-lobed, ovules 4. Style simple, thread-like.
Habitat: Open woods, meadows and along streams.
Pollination: By insects.
Fruit: Consists of 4 one-seeded rounded nutlets.
Range: Eastern N. America.
Uses: No information.
Special comments: Often cultivated.

Order LAMIALES

Family *LABIATAE*

WATER MINT (*Mentha aquatica*)

General characters: Strongly scented perennial herb up to 3' high. Stems erect, hairy, often branched. Leaves opposite, egg-shaped, hairy, with minute glands below, shortly stalked, margin toothed. Flowers pink, small, in whorls at top stem and in axils of upper leaves. Calyx tubular, 5-lobed, 10-ribbed. Corolla tubular, 4-lobed. Stamens 4. Ovary superior, of 2 deeply lobed carpels, ovules 4. Style slender, arising from base of ovary-lobes. Stigma 2-lobed.
Habitat: Wet places in woods and marshes, at sides of rivers, lakes and ponds.
Pollination: Cross-pollination by insects.
Fruit: Consists of 4 smooth egg-shaped nutlets.
Seeds: Dispersed by wind and water (nutlets float 6–12 months).
Vegetative reproduction: By creeping rhizome. Also by detached stems rooting in mud where they are carried by rivers and streams.
Range: Europe (including Britain). Asia. N. & S. Africa.
Uses: Flowers yield late nectar for honey bees. (Some other Mints are cultivated as flavouring herbs and as sources of essential oils.)
Special comments: A very variable species which hybridizes with certain other Mints.

WILD THYME (*Thymus drucei*)

General characters: Extremely variable prostrate faintly aromatic perennial herb. Flowering stems almost square in cross-section, with numerous hairs on 2 sides and few (or none) on other 2. Leaves opposite, variable in shape (almost round, reverse-lance-shaped, paddle-shaped), shortly stalked, leathery, with or without hairs, generally arranged horizontally. Flowers purplish, in whorls forming a head at top stem. Calyx 2-lipped, upper lip 3-toothed, lower narrowly 2-lobed. Corolla 2-lipped. Stamens 4. Ovary superior, of 2 deeply lobed carpels, each with 2 ovules. Style arising from base of ovary-lobes.

Habitat: In the open on limestone soils, heaths, grassland, chalk downs and cliffs, screes, shingle, rock crevices, sand-dunes.

Pollination: By insects (particularly bees).

Fruit: Consists of 4 smooth nutlets enclosed in persistent calyx whose mouth is closed by a ring of hairs. Nutlets can be ejected to distance of 1-2'. They are sometimes wind-dispersed.

Seeds: 80-100% of fresh seeds germinate in light, but only 5% in darkness.

Vegetative reproduction: By runners.

Range: Europe (including Britain).

Uses: Dried leaves and flowers used medicinally for digestive and bronchial troubles. A good bee plant (nectar).

LYRE-LEAVED SAGE (*Salvia lyrata*)

General characters: Erect biennial or perennial herb 1-3' high. Stem slender, unbranched or with few branches. Leaves mostly basal and few on stem. Basal leaves divided with large end-lobe, long-stalked, up to 8" long. Stem-leaves often like basal ones, but stalkless or with short stalks. Flowers violet, large, in several well-spaced whorls at top of stem. Calyx bell-shaped, 2-lipped, upper lip 3-toothed, lower 2-toothed. Corolla tubular, strongly 2-lipped, upper lip short, lower bigger and 3-lobed. Stamens reduced to 2. Ovary superior, of 2 deeply lobed carpels, each with 2 ovules. Style arising from base ovary-lobes. Stigma 2-lobed.

Habitat: Dry woods and thickets.

Pollination: By nectar-feeding birds. (Some other *Salvia* species are useful bee plants.)

Fruit: Consists of 4 smooth 1-seeded nutlets.

Range: Eastern N. America.

Uses: Roots made into salve for treatment of sores.

Special comments: Sometimes cultivated.

WHITE DEAD-NETTLE (*Lamium album*)

General characters: Erect perennial herb up to 2′ high. Stems square in section. Leaves opposite, egg-shaped, pointed, coarsely toothed, up to 2½″ long, stalked, each pair of stalks joined across stem. Flowers white, stalkless, in whorls in leaf-axils. Calyx bell-shaped, narrowly 5-lobed. Corolla about 1″ long, 2-lipped, upper lip hood-like, lower lip 3-lobed (the 2 side-lobes very small). Corolla-tube cylindrical at base only, enlarged above. Oblique ring of hairs in tube. Stamens 4. Ovary superior, of 2 deeply lobed carpels, each with 2 ovules. Style 2-lobed, inserted between ovary-lobes.

Habitat: Roadsides, fields, hedgebanks, waste places, walls.

Pollination: By humble-bees and other long-tongued bees.

Fruit: Consists of 4 small brownish nutlets.

Seeds: Believed to be largely dispersed by ants which are attracted by oil-body attached to nutlet.

Vegetative reproduction: By prostrate rooting stems.

Range: Europe (including Britain). N. America. N. Asia. N. Africa.

Uses: Sometimes eaten as vegetable. Flowers and roots have been used medicinally (catarrh, dropsy, etc.).

BEEBALM (*Monarda didyma*)

General characters: Erect aromatic perennial herb 2–5′ high. Stem stout, often branched. Leaves egg-shaped or broadly lance-shaped,

pointed, sharply toothed, stalked, up to 6″ long and 3″ wide. Flowers scarlet, large, in a dense solitary cluster at top stem with leafy bracts often tinged with red. Calyx tubular, narrow, 5-toothed, teeth awl-shaped. Corolla 1½–2″ long, tubular, 2-lipped, upper lip long and curved, lower lip 3-lobed with long middle lobe. Stamens 2. Ovary superior, of 2 carpels, ovules 4.

Habitat: Moist soil in woods and along streams.

Pollination: By butterflies and humming-birds.

Fruit: Consists of 4 smooth egg-shaped 1-seeded nutlets.

Range: Eastern N. America.

Uses: Leaves sometimes used for flavouring and to make a tea (hence name Oswego Tea). Source of volatile oils used in perfumes and pomades.

Special comments: Widely cultivated.

Subphylum **MONOCOTYLEDONES**

Embryo with 1 seed-leaf (cotyledon). Leaves usually parallel-veined. Vascular bundles of stem usually in several series and some-what scattered. Flowers with parts usually in 3s.

Division **CALYCIFERAE**

Flowers with a distinct calyx and corolla.

Order **BUTOMALES**

Family *BUTOMACEAE*

FLOWERING RUSH (*Butomus umbellatus*)

General characters: Perennial herb up to 4½′ high. Leaves long, narrow, pointed, triangular in section, all from base. Flowers pink, on long stalks in many-flowered umbel at top tall leafless stem, umbel with several pointed bracts at base. Perianth of 6 petal-like segments in 2 whorls. Stamens 9, red. Ovary superior, of 6 red carpels cohering at base, the numerous ovules scattered on inside walls of carpels.

Habitat: Muddy margins of rivers, ponds and canals.

Pollination: Cross- or self-pollination.

Fruit: Ripe carpels (follicles) each contain 80–90 seeds in England (a much smaller number in northern part of range).

Seeds: Without endosperm. Numerous, very small.

Vegetative reproduction: By rhizomes.

Range: Europe (including Britain). N. America. Temperate Asia.

Uses: Rhizomes eaten in Russia.

Family *HYDROCHARITACEAE*

FROG-BIT (*Hydrocharis morsus-ranae*)

General characters: Free-floating herb whose leaves, flowers and roots are produced at intervals along long slender stems. Leaves in clusters, floating, kidney-shaped or almost circular, long-stalked, with large stipules. Flowers white, stalked, unisexual, sexes on different plants, males 2–3 from a stalked spathe, females solitary from a stalkless spathe. Sepals 3, green. Petals 3, free, broadly reverse-egg-shaped. Stamens 12 (sometimes fewer). Ovary inferior, 1-celled (partially 6-celled), with numerous ovules. Styles 6, free, 2-branched.

Habitat: Ditches and ponds.

Fruit: A somewhat fleshy capsule containing 2–6 seeds.

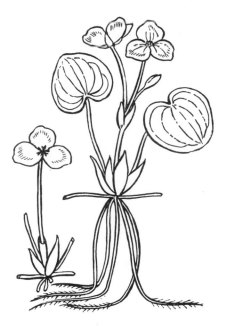

Seeds: Without endosperm. Numerous (but very rarely produced in some parts of plant's range, e.g. Britain).

Vegetative reproduction: By turions ("winter buds") which become detached from ends of stolons in late autumn, sink to bottom of ditch or pond, and rise to surface in spring.

Range: Europe (including Britain). Asia.

Uses: No information.

WATER SOLDIER (*Stratiotes aloides*)

General characters: Aquatic herb which floats during growing season and sinks to bottom of water in autumn. Leaves stalkless, forming large rosette, up to 1½' long and about 1" wide, pointed and with sharp teeth. Flowers white, 1–1½" wide, usually unisexual (sexes on different plants), though bisexual flowers have been found. Flowers opening above water within a pair of bracts at top of erect stem, males stalked and in small groups, females stalkless and solitary. Sepals 3, green. Petals 3, white, thickish, almost circular. Stamens 12 (in male flowers only). Infertile stamens numerous (in both male and female flowers). Ovary inferior, 1-celled (partially 6-celled), with numerous ovules. Styles 6, two-branched.

Habitat: Ponds, ditches, lakes. Prefers chalky districts.

Fruit: Smooth, egg-shaped, somewhat succulent.

Seeds: Without endosperm. Ripe seed never produced in parts of plant's range (e.g. Britain).

Vegetative reproduction: Spreads rapidly by means of "daughter plants" which become detached.

Range: Europe (including Britain). N.W. Asia.

Uses: In some places plants dredged from water and used as manure.

CANADIAN PONDWEED (*Elodea canadensis*)

General characters: Submerged herb. Stems brittle, branched, often several feet long. Leaves dark green, narrowly lance-shaped or oblong stalkless, up to ½" long, translucent, lower leaves opposite, others in whorls of 3–4. Flowers purplish, small, floating, solitary in small spathes in leaf-axils, unisexual, sexes on different plants. Sepals 3. Petals 3, narrow. Male flower with 3–9 stamens. Female flower with long thread-like axis; ovary inferior, 1-celled, with numerous ovules. Styles 3, free.

Habitat: Lakes, ponds, canals, reservoirs, slow rivers and streams.

Pollination: Water-pollinated.

Fruit: Rarely produced in parts of plant's range (e.g. Britain, where male plant very rare).

Seeds: Without endosperm.

Vegetative reproduction: By means of "winter buds," which fall to bottom in late autumn and float to surface the following spring. Also by fragments of shoots which become detached and grow on mud or when floating.

Range: Europe (including Britain). N. America.

Uses: No information.

Order **ALISMATALES**

Family *ALISMATACEAE*

Water Plantain (*Alisma plantago-aquatica*)

General characters: Erect perennial herb up to 3′ high. Leaves egg-shaped, pointed (often bluntly so), long-stalked, leaf-blades usually well above water-level. Flowers small, pale lilac, on slender stalks, in many-flowered much-branched panicles. Sepals 3, free, green, oblong. Petals 3, free, rounded. Stamens 6. Ovary superior, of numerous free carpels arranged in a single whorl. Style lateral, persistent.

Habitat: Mud at bottom of ponds and ditches and at margins of slow-flowing rivers and streams.

Fruit: A head of about 20 flat achenes, which float for 6–15 months and are also dispersed by water-fowl.

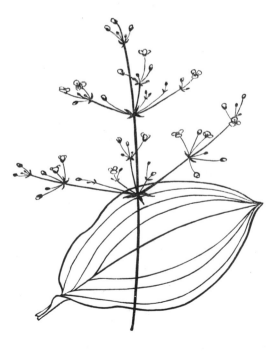

Seeds: Without endosperm. Small, curved. Drying of seeds (as during summer droughts) appears to induce germination.

Range: Europe (including Britain). N. America. Temperate Asia. Australia. New Zealand.

Uses: Rhizomes have been used as food.

ARROW-HEAD (*Sagittaria sagittifolia*)

General characters: Erect perennial herb up to 3′ high, with submerged ribbon leaves, floating leaves of varying shape (lance- to egg-shaped) and arrow-shaped aerial leaves with long stalks. Flowers white, 1″ across, stalked, in whorls of 3, unisexual, sexes on same plant, male whorls at top of stem, females below them. Sepals 3, pouched. Petals 3, rounded. Stamens numerous (usually about 25), with arrow-shaped anthers. Ovary superior, of numerous free carpels, each with 1 ovule.

Habitat: In rivers, streams, ponds, ditches and canals.

Fruit: A hemispherical head containing numerous flattened achenes which float 6–12 months.

Seeds: Without endosperm.

Vegetative reproduction: By bulb-like turions ("winter buds") produced in autumn at ends of runners.

Range: Europe (including Britain). N. America. Asia.

Uses: Cultivated in Asia, where turions eaten as vegetable.

Order **TRIURIDALES**

Tropical saprophytic herbs with leaves reduced to colourless scales. Flowers minute, unisexual, with perianth of 3–8 segments. Stamens 2–6. Carpels free, several, 1-celled, 1-ovuled. Fruiting carpels opening lengthwise. No information as to useful products.

Order **JUNCAGINALES**

Family *JUNCAGINACEAE*

MARSH ARROW-GRASS (*Triglochin palustris*)

General characters: Erect slender herb up to 1½′ high. Leaves from base, narrow, somewhat fleshy, semi-cylindrical, upper surface furrowed at base. Flowers small, yellowish-green, stalked, in racemes. Perianth segments 6, free, egg-shaped, 3 inner erect, 3 outer often spreading. Stamens 6, anthers shortly stalked. Ovary superior, of 6 united carpels (3, the alternate ones, sterile). Each fertile carpel with 1 ovule. Style absent. Stigmas 3, feathery.

Habitat: Marshes. Wet meadows.

Pollination: Wind-pollinated.

Fruit: A club-shaped capsule opening from base upwards, the carpels separating from central axis but remaining attached to it at top.

Seeds: Without endosperm.

Range: Europe (including Britain). Northern parts of America, Asia and Africa.

Uses: No information. (*T. maritima*, Sea Arrow-grass, whose young leaves are eaten as vegetable, has been recommended as emergency food-plant.)

Order **APONOGETONALES**

Family *APONOGETONACEAE*

CAPE PONDWEED (*Aponogeton distachyos*)

General characters: Perennial herb with long-stalked oblong-elliptic floating leaves up to 8″ long. Flowers white and fragrant (hence name Water Hawthorn), arranged in double rows along whitish branches of 2-forked inflorescence which projects above water. Each flower with 1 egg-shaped perianth segment about ½″ long, 6–18 stamens and an ovary of 3–6 free carpels (with 2 or more ovules in each).

Habitat: Ponds, lakes.

Pollination: Self-pollination occurs.

Fruit: Consists of the ripe carpels which open along inner margin.

Seeds: Without endosperm. With buoyant fleshy green outer coat. Sometimes germinating on surface of water.

Vegetative reproduction: By tuberous rhizome.

Range: S. Africa. Planted in other parts of world (e.g. Britain) where sometimes naturalized.

Uses: Rhizome and flowering spikes (pickled or cooked) eaten.

Family *ZOSTERACEAE*

EEL-GRASS (*Zostera marina*)

General characters: Submerged perennial herb with slender stems. Leaves flexible, long, narrow, up to 3′ long on sterile shoots but shorter and narrower on flowering stems, sheathing at base. Flowers without perianth, unisexual, sexes alternating in 2 rows on 1 side of flattened axis, which is at first enclosed in a leaf-sheath. Male flower reduced to 1 anther. Female flower consisting of an ovary with 1 ovule and 2 stigmas.

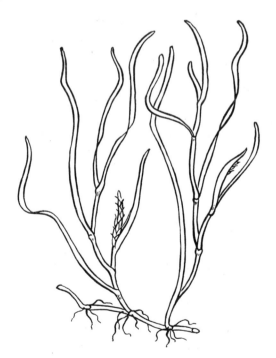

Habitat: On mud, gravel or muddy sand in sea lochs, bays and sheltered places along coasts.

Pollination: Water-pollinated (pollen is thread-like).

Fruit: Egg-shaped. 1-seeded. Splitting open to release seed.

Seeds: Without endosperm. Small, ellipsoid, ribbed. Dispersed by water movements and fish.

Vegetative reproduction: By dispersal of fragments of rhizome.

Range: Europe (including Britain). N. America (Atlantic and Pacific coasts).

Uses: Dried plants used as packing material, for heat and sound insulation, and for stuffing pillows and cushions.

Special comments: Between 1931 and 1934 large expanses of Eel-grass were destroyed by disease in Western European and Eastern U.S. waters. In many places the species does not seem to have recovered.

Order **POTAMOGETONALES**

Family *POTAMOGETONACEAE*

BOG PONDWEED (*Potamogeton polygonifolius*)

General characters: Aquatic perennial herb with unbranched slender stems up to 1½′ long. Leaves mainly alternate, stalked, with stipules.

Size and shape of leaves varying according to depth of water. Submerged leaves often narrowly lance-shaped, thin, flexible, translucent. Floating leaves often broadly elliptical, opaque, somewhat leathery. Flowers small, inconspicuous, arranged in dense cylindrical spikes on stalks arising from leaf-axils and projecting above water. Perianth of 4 rounded segments. Stamens 4, inserted on short claws of perianth-segments, without stalks. Ovary of 4 free 1-celled carpels each with 1 ovule.

Habitat: Ponds, ditches, shallow streams.
Pollination: Wind-pollinated.
Fruit: Drupaceous. Small, somewhat flattened, reddish, 1-seeded.
Seeds: Without endosperm.
Vegetative reproduction: By fragments of rhizome. Also by turions ("winter buds").
Range: Europe (including Britain). Eastern N. America. N. Africa.
Uses: No information.

Family *RUPPIACEAE*

DITCH-GRASS (*Ruppia maritima*)

General characters: Submerged perennial herb with branched thread-like stems. Leaves thread-like, with sheathing base. Flowers small, in short racemes, without perianth, each consisting of 2 almost stalkless stamens and a superior ovary of four 1-ovuled free carpels.

Habitat: Pools on salt-marshes, creeks, brackish ditches.
Pollination: Water-pollinated.
Fruit: Fruiting carpels 1-seeded, stalked, not opening.
Seeds: Without endosperm.
Range: Europe (including Britain). N. America. W. Asia. N. Africa.
Uses: No information.

Order **NAJADALES**

Family *ZANNICHELLIACEAE*

HORNED PONDWEED (*Zannichellia palustris*)

General characters: Variable submerged perennial herb with branched thread-like stems. Leaves mostly opposite, very narrow, translucent. Flowers very small, without perianth, unisexual, each small group (often 1 male and few females) in cup-shaped spathe in leaf-axil. Male flower of 1 stamen. Female flower of 1 curved carpel containing 1 ovule.

Habitat: Fresh or brackish water.
Pollination: Water-pollinated.
Fruit: A small achene crowned by persistent style. Often shortly stalked. Dispersed by water-birds (entangled in plumage).

Seeds: Without endosperm.
Vegetative reproduction: By fragments of creeping rhizome.
Range: Cosmopolitan.
Uses: No information.

Family *NAJADACEAE*

NAIAD (*Najas flexilis*)

General characters: Submerged annual herb with slender branched stems. Leaves in whorls of 2–3, narrow, translucent, base sheathing, margins often with few very minute teeth. Flowers very small, solitary or in small groups in leaf-axils, unisexual, sexes on same plant. Male flower with 1 stamen enclosed in a spathe. Female flower without perianth (sometimes with a very thin one), ovary of a 1-ovuled carpel with 2–4 stigmas.

Habitat: Lakes.

Pollination: Water-pollinated.

Fruit: Fruiting carpel 1-seeded, small, narrow, not opening.

Seeds: Without endosperm.

Range: Europe (including Britain). N. America.

Uses: Dried plants used as packing material. Fresh plants sometimes spread on land as manure.

Order COMMELINALES

Family *COMMELINACEAE*

WANDERING JEW (*Tradescantia fluminensis*)

General characters: Perennial herb with jointed stems lying on ground. Leaves alternate, stalkless, oval, pointed, up to 2″ long, with short basal sheath. Flowers white, in 4–5-flowered groups at end stems with 2 leaf-like bracts. Sepals 3. Petals 3, large, free. Stamens 6, all fertile, filaments with long hairs. Ovary superior, 3-celled, each cell with 2 ovules. Style simple.

Habitat: Sheltered stream banks, swampy forest.
Pollination: Cross-pollination by insects.
Fruit: A capsule.
Seeds: With abundant mealy endosperm.
Range: S. America. New Zealand. S. Africa.
Uses: No information.

SLENDER DAY FLOWER (*Commelina erecta*)

General characters: Perennial herb 1–3′ high. Stems jointed, slender, erect or ascending, often tufted. Leaves narrowly lance-shaped, pointed,

up to 6″ long and 1″ wide, with closed basal sheath. Flowers blue, in cymes at top stem with sheathing bracts. Sepals 3, unequal. Petals 3, unequal, 2 larger than third. Stamens 6, usually only 3 fertile. Ovary superior, 3-celled, each cell with 1 ovule. Style simple.

Habitat: Moist soil.

Fruit: A papery capsule of 3 one-seeded cells.

Seeds: With abundant endosperm.

Range: Eastern and Central U.S.A. Tropical America.

Uses: No information.

Order **ERIOCAULALES**

Family *ERIOCAULACEAE*

PIPEWORT (*Eriocaulon septangulare*)

General characters: Perennial herb with rootstock creeping in mud. Leaves tufted, narrow, up to 4″ long, sharply pointed. Flowers minute, unisexual, males surrounded by females in small heads with bracts at top of stalks 2′ or more high. Perianth of 4 segments in 2 series, 2 inner free and each with minute black spot (gland) near top. Male flower with 4 stamens. Female flower with superior 2-3-celled ovary (each cell with 1 ovule) and short style with 2-3 stigmas.

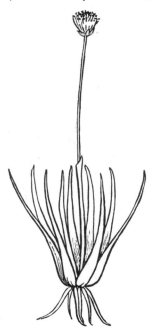

Habitat: Shallow lakes, wet peaty soil.

Fruit: A thin capsule with 2–3 one-seeded cells.

Seeds: With copious endosperm.

Range: Isles of Skye and Coll, Scotland. W. Eire. N. America.

Uses: No information.

Order **XYRIDALES**

Annual or perennial herbs of marshes in tropics and subtropics. Flowers small, in heads at top of leafless stems. Perianth segments in 2 series, inner joined and forming a tube. Stamens 3 or 6. Ovary superior, 1- or 3-celled (sometimes imperfectly 3-celled). Ovules few or numerous. Fruit a capsule opening by 3 valves. Seeds with copious endosperm.

Uses: Root of *Xyris communis* used medicinally in Brazil. Stems of *Xyris melanocephala* made into mats in Indonesia.

Order **BROMELIALES**

Family *BROMELIACEAE*

SPANISH MOSS (*Tillandsia usneoides*)

General characters: Silvery-scurfy epiphytic herb with slender thread-like stems up to 20′ long. Leaves thread-like, 1–3″ long. Flowers yellow,

stalkless, solitary (rarely 2 together) in leaf-axils. Sepals 3, small. Petals 3, clawed, free. Stamens 6. Ovary superior, 3-celled, ovules numerous. Style slender. Stigmas 3.

Habitat: Hangs from branches of trees.

Fruit: A narrow 3-valved capsule.

Seeds: With copious mealy endosperm. Plumed, wind-dispersed.

Vegetative reproduction: Portions of branches carried by wind and birds (nesting material) to other trees where they grow.

Range: Southern United States. West Indies. S. America.

Uses: Plants used as packing material and in upholstery.

Special comments: Tillandsia only uses branch as support and is not parasitic. Water absorbed by scaly hairs covering plant.

PINEAPPLE (*Ananas comosus*)

General characters: Biennial or perennial herb up to 4' high. Leaves forming a rosette, 3' long and 3" broad, sword-shaped, stiff, sharp-pointed, fleshy, fibrous, margins sometimes spiny, upper surface grooved, base clasping stem. Flowers numerous, reddish-purple, stalk-less, arranged spirally around the stem, each with a pointed bract. Perianth segments free, in 2 series, outer 3 short and calyx-like, inner 3 larger and petal-like. Stamens 6. Ovary inferior, 3-celled, 10–15 ovules in each cell. Style slender. Stigmas 3.

Habitat: Well-drained sandy soils.

Pollination: The different varieties of Pineapples are self-incompatible (seedless fruits). Most of them are cross-compatible and set seed when cross-pollinated. In Hawaii, important centre of pineapple production, introduction of humming-birds is prohibited because they are believed to cause cross-pollination among pineapple varieties (with formation of unwanted seedy fruits).

Fruit: Barrel-shaped Pineapple of commerce represents entire inflorescence, consisting of thickened central stem and numerous small berries which form from flowers and come together to form multiple fruit.

Seeds: Fruits of cultivated pineapples generally seedless.

Vegetative reproduction: Propagated by means of tuft of leaves growing at top of fruit, suckers from lower leaf-axils, or small shoots ("slips") arising from stem under fruit.

Range: Tropics and subtropics. (Native of tropical S. America.)

Uses: Fruit eaten raw, canned, candied, as juice. Fresh fruit is good source of vitamin C, also containing vitamins A, B_1, B_2, calcium, phosphorus, iron, sugar, citric and malic acids. Leaves yield strong durable white fibres used to make pina cloth. Juice is source of alcohol and *vin d'ananas,* an alcoholic drink.

Special comments: Numerous varieties are in cultivation.

Order ZINGIBERALES

Family *MUSACEAE*

BANANA (*Musa paradisiaca*)

General characters: Large perennial herb. Pseudostem ("aerial shoot") 15–30′ high, stout, cylindrical, consisting of leaf bases rolled round one another. Leaves forming a crown at top pseudostem, large, oval, with stout midrib and stalk, edges often torn. Flowers numerous, clustered in axils of large bracts which are arranged spirally round a long un-branched stem that emerges through centre of pseudostem and then bends over and downwards. Female flowers at base inflorescence, each with elongated inferior 3-celled ovary and a short orange-yellow perianth of 6 segments (5 joined, 1 free). Male flowers at tip inflorescence, with 5 stamens, soon falling.

Habitat: Moist well-drained soil. Sometimes grown under irrigation in arid places.

Pollination: Seedless fruits of edible bananas form without pollination, but many edible bananas will produce a few seeds if pollinated (anthers rarely contain pollen). Pollination by bees or birds is essential in wild bananas whose fruits contain numerous seeds.

Fruit: An elongated berry whose pulpy contents include carbohydrates, vitamins A, B_1, B_2, C and niacin. The bunch of bananas produced from the inflorescence weighs 25–70 lb. and contains 100–200 separate fruits.

Seeds: Rarely produced by cultivated bananas. Those of other *Musaceae* have thick hard seed-coat and copious endosperm.

Vegetative reproduction: Propagated by cuttings from rhizome or suckers from parent plants.

Range: Tropics and subtropics.

Uses: Fruit important food in tropics. Elsewhere eaten mainly as dessert. Alcoholic drinks made from fruit (Banana beer of nutritional value). Leaves used for shade and as wrapping material. Chopped pseudostems fed to cattle.

Family *STRELITZIACEAE*

BIRD OF PARADISE FLOWER (*Strelitzia reginae*)

General characters: Erect evergreen perennial herb 4–6′ high. Leaves oblong-lance-shaped, pointed, long and long-stalked, bright green above. Flowers several in axil of sheath-like bract at top of tall erect stem. Sepals 3, free, lance-shaped, 3–4″ long, orange-yellow, 2 standing erect. Petals 3, dark blue, 2 lower converging to form arrow-

shaped blade with central channel in which stamens and style are placed, the third smaller. Stamens 5. Ovary inferior, 3-celled, ovules numerous. Style long, with 3 narrow branches 1″ long.

Habitat: Moist places, often on river-banks.

Pollination: By sun-birds probing for nectar.

Fruit: An oblong capsule.

Seeds: With endosperm. Few. Black, with bright orange woolly aril.

Range: S. Africa.

Uses: No information.

Family *ZINGIBERACEAE*

GINGER (*Zingiber officinale*)

General characters: Perennial aromatic herb with slender stems up to 3′ high. Leaves oblong, pointed, up to 6″ long, in 2 rows, with open sheath at base. Flowers pale yellow, arranged with greenish-yellow bracts in cylindrical cone-like spike at top of shoot which is often leaf-less. Perianth of 6 segments in 2 series, outer short and united into a narrow tube, inner forming a 3-lobed tube whose upper lobe is hooded. Stamen 1. Central staminode (infertile stamen) petal-like.

Ovary inferior, 3-celled, with several ovules. Style slender, held between the 2 anthers of fertile stamen.

Habitat: Warm moist shady places.

Fruit: A 3-valved capsule.

Seeds: With endosperm. Small, angled, black. Apparently seeds are rarely produced.

Vegetative reproduction: By branching rhizomes.

Range: Cultivated in China, India, Malaya, West Africa, West Indies.

Uses: Rhizomes yield the Ginger of commerce, which is used in sweets, cakes, beverages, perfumes and medicine (aromatic and pungent qualities of rhizome due to presence of oils and resins).

Family *CANNACEAE*

QUEENSLAND ARROWROOT (*Canna edulis*)

General characters: Perennial herb 3–6′ high. Stems erect, fleshy, purplish. Leaves alternate, large, broad, pointed, with distinct thick midrib, up to 2′ long and 1′ broad, with long winged stalks whose lower part clasps stem. Flowers red, large and showy, usually in pairs with bracts in loose branched or unbranched inflorescence at top stem. Sepals 3, small, green, free. Petals 3, narrow, joined at base and united to staminal column. Stamen 1, filament petal-like. Staminodes 5, large, petal-like. Ovary inferior, 3-celled, with numerous ovules.

Habitat: Grown in deep fertile soil.

Fruit: A capsule.

Seeds: With hard endosperm. Numerous, rounded, hard.

Vegetative reproduction: By rhizomes which produce abundant suckers.

Range: West Indies. Australia. Pacific Islands. Asia.

Uses: Leaves and rhizomes fed to dairy cattle. Young rhizomes cooked and eaten. Rhizomes yield starch that, being easily digested, is given to infants and invalids (starch called Queensland or Purple Arrowroot).

Family *MARANTACEAE*

ARROWROOT (*Maranta arundinacea*)

General characters: Perennial herb up to 3' high. Stems numerous, thin, branched. Leaves lance-shaped, pointed, large, in 2 rows along stem, on long stalks with open sheath at base. Flowers white, each with a deciduous bract, few in panicle with slender branches. Perianth of 6 segments in 2 series. Calyx of 3 free lobes. Corolla tubular, consisting of united inner perianth segments. Stamen 1. Staminodes 4–5, outer 2 large and petal-like. Ovary inferior, 1-celled, with solitary ovule. Style simple, short.

Habitat: Moist warm places, often near the sea.

Fruit: Small, round.

Seeds: With abundant endosperm. Small, rounded. Rarely produced in cultivation as flowers are removed.

Vegetative reproduction: By rhizomes.

Range: Tropics (most arrowroot starch of commerce is produced in West Indies).

Uses: Rhizomes contain 80% starch which is easily digestible and used to make biscuits and foods for invalids and babies.

Division **COROLLIFERAE**

Flowers with 2 similar whorls of perianth segments.

Order **LILIALES**

Family *LILIACEAE*

BOG ASPHODEL (*Narthecium ossifragum*)

General characters: Perennial herb up to 1½' high. Basal leaves narrow, up to 1' long, pointed, ribbed lengthwise, sometimes curved, sheathing at base. Stem-leaves 2–3, not more than 1½" long. Flowers yellow, fragrant, stalked (each stalk bearing a small pointed bract), with narrow bracts in racemes at top of erect stems. Perianth segments 6, narrowly lance-shaped, spreading in flower. Stamens 6, filaments densely hairy. Ovary superior, 3-celled, ovules numerous. Style 1, simple.

Habitat: Wet acid soils, bogs, moors, mountains.

Pollination: Cross-pollination by insects.

Fruit: A capsule.

Seeds: With copious endosperm. Numerous, small, with long tail at each end. Average weight: 0·0001005 gm. Wind-dispersed.

Vegetative reproduction: By creeping rhizome.

Range: Europe (including Britain).

Uses: No information.

Special comments: Said to be poisonous to cows.

LILY-OF-THE-VALLEY (*Convallaria majalis*)

General characters: Perennial herb. Leaves elliptic, up to 6" long, with sheathing bases, usually a pair of leaves with scale leaves at its base. Flowers white, very fragrant, nodding, stalked (with small pointed bract at base of stalk), in 1-sided racemes at top of slender leafless stalks. Perianth small, bell-shaped, 6-lobed. Stamens 6, inserted at base of perianth. Ovary superior, 3-celled, with several ovules in each cell. Style simple.

Habitat: Woods.

Pollination: By insects. Also self-pollinated.

Fruit: A globose red berry.

Seeds: With endosperm. Average weight: 0·0151 gm. Seed production often poor.

Vegetative reproduction: By much-branched creeping rhizome.

Range: Europe (including Britain). Temperate Asia. Cultivated in other parts of world and sometimes escaping.

Uses: Whole plant used medicinally as heart tonic.

Special comments: Poisonous to certain animals.

Asparagus (*Asparagus officinalis*)

General characters: Perennial herb with erect branched annual stems 4–10′ high. Leaves reduced to small dry whitish scales, with clusters of slender green cladodes (modified branchlets) in their axils. Flowers small, yellow or yellowish-green, stalked, solitary or in pairs from branch-axils, unisexual with sexes on different plants (rarely bisexual). Perianth bell-shaped, of 6 free segments. Stamens 6. Ovary 3-celled, with 2 ovules in each cell. Style 1.

Habitat: Often grown in light well-drained soil.

Pollination: By insects.

Fruit: A small red globose berry.

Seeds: With endosperm. Dispersed by birds which eat the fruit.

Vegetative reproduction: By creeping rhizome.

Range: Widely cultivated in temperate zones of world.

Uses: Young shoots eaten (contain vitamins A, B_1, B_2 and C, calcium, phosphorus, iron, protein). Seeds have been used as coffee-substitute.

Special comments: Above refers to Garden Asparagus, Ssp. *officinalis*. Wild Asparagus, European plant of maritime sands and sea-cliffs, is Ssp. *prostratus*.

Turk's-cap Lily (*Lilium martagon*)

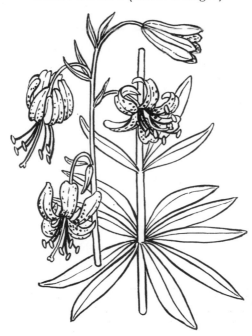

General characters: Perennial herb up to 6' high. Leaves lance-shaped, up to 8″ long, upper ones alternate, lower in whorls of 5–15. Flowers purple, rarely white, large, each on a nodding stalk up to 3″ long, up to 20 flowers in a loose raceme at top of erect stem. Perianth of 6 free oblong segments which are spotted and bent back from about the middle. Stamens 6. Ovary 3-celled, oblong. Style slender, curved, split into 3 at apex.

Habitat: Grassy places, woods, copses. Widely cultivated and sometimes escaping.

Pollination: By insects (Lepidoptera). Also self-pollinated.

Fruit: A 6-angled capsule about 1″ long.

Seeds: With endosperm. Flat.

Vegetative reproduction: By bulbs.

Range: Europe (including Britain). Asia.

Uses: Bulbs eaten by people in Mongolia and Siberia.

Family *TRILLIACEAE*

HERB PARIS (*Paris quadrifolia*)

General characters: Perennial herb up to 1½' high. Leaves reverse-egg-shaped, pointed, up to 4½″ long, usually in a single whorl of 4 at top of erect unbranched stem. Flower stalked, solitary, arising from centre of whorl of leaves. Perianth of 8 (rarely 10) free segments, 4 outer sepal-like and green, 4 inner petal-like and yellowish-green. Stamens 8 (rarely 10). Ovary superior, 4–5-celled, with numerous ovules. Styles 4–5, free.

Habitat: Damp woods.

Pollination: By flies. Also self-pollinated.

Fruit: A fleshy black globose capsule. Poisonous to people and poultry.

Seeds: With endosperm. Average weight: 0·00454 gm. Dispersed by ants and certain birds.

Vegetative reproduction: By rhizomes.

Range: Europe (including Britain).

Uses: No information.

PAINTED WAKE-ROBIN (*Trillium undulatum*)

General characters: Erect unbranched herb up to 2' high. Leaves egg-shaped, long-pointed, stalked, up to 8″ long and 5″ wide, in a whorl of 3 towards top of stem. Flowers stalked, solitary at top of stem. Sepals 3, green, spreading and persistent. Petals 3, white marked with red or purplish at base, margins wavy. Stamens 6. Ovary 3-celled, ovules numerous. Styles 3, slender.

Habitat: Mountain woods.
Pollination: Cross-pollination by insects. Failing this, self-pollination.
Fruit: A many-seeded egg-shaped berry. Bright red, shining.
Seeds: With endosperm.
Range: N. America.
Uses: No information. (*Trillium grandiflorum* and certain other species recommended as emergency food-plants.)

Order ALSTROEMERIALES

Family *ALSTROEMERIACEAE*

PERUVIAN LILY (*Alstroemeria aurantiaca*)

General characters: Erect perennial herb up to 4′ high. Leaves alternate, lance-shaped, up to 6″ long, short-stalked, lower surface facing upwards (leaf-stalk twisted through 180°). Flowers large and showy, in clusters at top of rather weak stems. Perianth of 6 free segments 1–1½″ long, 3 outer orange or yellow, 3 inner narrower and longer with reddish marks on 2 upper. Stamens 6. Ovary inferior, 3-celled, with numerous ovules. Style slender, shortly 3-lobed.

Habitat: Open places on light sandy soils.
Pollination: By insects.
Fruit: A 3-celled capsule which explodes suddenly when ripe, scattering seeds several feet (13′ in one *Alstroemeria* species).

Seeds: With copious endosperm. Numerous, globose, small.

Vegetative reproduction: By fragments of fleshy roots.

Range: Native of S. America, but grown in other parts of world and sometimes becoming a weed.

Uses: No information. (Edible starch obtained from roots of several other *Alstroemeria* species in Chile.)

Family *PHILESIACEAE*

WOMBAT BERRY (*Eustrephus latifolius*)

General characters: Climbing plant. Leaves alternate, stalkless, egg-shaped, glossy, $2\frac{1}{2}''$ long and up to $\frac{3}{4}''$ broad. Flowers small, white, pale pink or purplish, in clusters of 2–10 in leaf-axils. Perianth segments 6, spreading, inner ones fringed. Stamens 6, filaments joined. Ovary superior, 3-celled, with single style, small stigma.

Habitat: Climbing in trees.

Fruit: A 3-celled orange berry about $\frac{1}{2}''$ across. With 3–12 seeds. Called Black-fellow's Orange.

Seeds: With endosperm. Black.

Range: Australia.

Uses: Small tubers are sweet and edible.

Order **ARALES**

Family *ARACEAE*

SWEET FLAG (*Acorus calamus*)

General characters: Perennial herb up to 3′ high. Leaves narrow, up to 3′ long, pointed, erect, sheathing at base, strongly aromatic when bruised. Flowers yellowish-green, small, densely and spirally arranged on a cylindrical spadix (spike with fleshy axis) which projects from side of an erect leaf-like stem. Perianth of 6 free segments. Stamens 6.

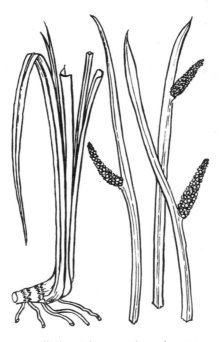

Ovary superior, 2–3-celled, with several ovules. Stigma minute. Style absent.

Habitat: Shallow slow rivers and streams, canals, ponds, marshes.

Pollination: Cross-pollination by insects.

Fruit: A red berry.

Seeds: Weight about 0·005 gm.

Vegetative reproduction: By rhizomes.

Range: Native of S.E. Asia. Europe (long naturalized). N. America.

Uses: Rhizome yields essential oil (Calamus oil) used in perfumery. Rhizomes also used medicinally as aromatic bitter in tonics.

LORDS-AND-LADIES (*Arum maculatum*)

General characters: Erect perennial herb up to 1½' high. Leaves spear-shaped, long-stalked, shining, uniformly dark green or with dark markings (due to a purple anthocyanin), containing needle-shaped crystals of calcium oxalate (raphides). Flowers without perianth, unisexual, sexes arranged in separate clusters on lower part of long fleshy axis (spadix) whose club-shaped top is purplish (rarely yellowish) and without flowers. Spadix enclosed in green (sometimes spotted) hood-like spathe whose edges overlap at base to form a chamber containing the flowers, to enter which insects must pass through a ring of stiff bristles. Male flower consists of 1 stamen, female of a single 1-celled ovary.

Habitat: Deciduous woodlands, hedgerows, gardens.

Pollination: Cross-pollination by midges which are not released from floral chamber until the ring of bristles shrivels.

Fruit: A small red berry. Poisonous to man.

Seeds: Globose. Marked with a network. Average weight: 0·04536 gm.

Vegetative reproduction: By "daughter" tubers from the mature tuber.

Range: Europe (including Britain).

Uses: Roasted or boiled tubers have been used as emergency food, but caution is needed as plant has poisonous properties.

BOG ARUM (*Calla palustris*)

General characters: Creeping perennial herb. Leaves broadly heart-shaped, pointed, stalked, the stalk with a long sheath. Flowers small, without perianth, covering upper part of stout spadix which is not enclosed by persistent white spathe.

Habitat: Rich muddy soil, swamps, moist places near ponds, lakes and streams.

Fruit: A red berry.

Seeds: Small, oblong, light grey. Float for 12 months.

Vegetative reproduction: By rhizome.

Range: Europe. N. America. Temperate Asia.

Uses: No information.

Family *LEMNACEAE*

GREAT DUCKWEED (*Lemna polyrhiza*)

General characters: Tiny herb floating on surface of still water, the plant-body being an almost rounded flat thallus with several roots.

Thallus up to 0·4″ across, but often smaller. Flowers rare in many parts of plant's range, minute, without perianth, unisexual, both sexes on margin of same plant. Male flower consists of 1–2 stamens, female of a single 1-celled ovary containing 1 or a few ovules.

Habitat: On ponds, ditches, and other still waters.

Seeds: Rarely produced.

Vegetative reproduction: By small turions ("winter buds"), which lie dormant in mud throughout winter.

Range: Cosmopolitan.

Uses: No information.

Special comments: Duckweed plants are dispersed by adhesion to water-birds and other creatures, and also by movement of water during flooding.

Wolffia arrhiza

General characters: Rootless floating herb consisting of minute egg-shaped thallus up to 1 mm. in diameter. Flowers rare, minute, without perianth, unisexual, sexes borne on surface of same plant. Male flower consists simply of 1 stamen, female of a 1-celled ovary.

Habitat: On ponds and stagnant water.

Vegetative reproduction: By "daughter" plants produced by budding.

Range: Cosmopolitan.

Uses: No information.

Special comments: The smallest flowering plant. Dispersed by adhesion to water-birds, frogs, toads and other creatures.

Order **TYPHALES**

Family *SPARGANIACEAE*

FLOATING BUR-REED (*Sparganium angustifolium*)

General characters: Perennial herb. Stems long, usually floating. Leaves long, narrow, flat, sheathing at base, floating. Flowers unisexual, arranged in many-flowered globose heads, 1–2 male heads at top of flowering stem and below them 2–4 female heads (lower ones stalked). Perianth of 3–6 pale thin segments. Male flower with 3 or more stamens, female with a 1-celled 1-ovuled ovary.

Habitat: Peaty pools (often in mountains).
Pollination: Wind-pollinated.
Fruit: Drupe-like. With spongy exocarp. Floats for several months.
Seeds: With mealy endosperm. Smooth, with thin seed-coat.
Range: Europe (including Britain). N. America.
Uses: No information.

Family *TYPHACEAE*

CAT'S-TAIL (*Typha latifolia*)

General characters: Erect perennial herb up to 8′ high. Leaves erect, long and narrow, up to ¾″ wide, sheathing at base. Flowers very small,

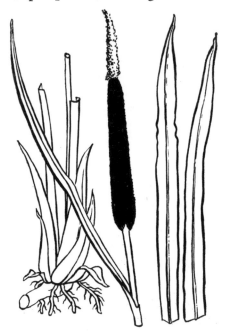

unisexual, mixed with soft hairs and densely crowded in a long cylindrical spike at top stem, males in upper part, females below them. Male flower with 2–5 stamens, female with a stalked 1-celled 1-ovuled ovary.

Habitat: Swampy margins of ponds, lakes, canals.

Pollination: Wind-pollinated.

Fruit: A minute achene whose plume of long hairs assists wind-dispersal.

Seeds: With mealy endosperm.

Vegetative reproduction: By dispersal of fragments of creeping rhizomes.

Range: Europe (including Britain). N.&S. America. N. Africa. N. Asia.

Uses: Leaves made into mats, chair-bottoms, baskets. (Rhizomes of some other *Typha* species have been eaten as emergency foods.)

Order **AMARYLLIDALES**

Family *AMARYLLIDACEAE*

SNOWDROP (*Galanthus nivalis*)

General characters: Bulbous herb, up to 9″ high. Leaves 2–3 from base, narrow. Flowers white, nodding, solitary at top of leafless stem,

enclosed at first by thin dry spathe. Perianth of 6 petal-like segments, 3 outer white and spreading, 3 inner much smaller and marked with green. Stamens 6, anthers finely pointed. Ovary inferior, 3-celled, with numerous ovules. Style simple, awl-shaped.

Habitat: Woods and damp shady places.
Pollination: By bees.
Fruit: An egg-shaped capsule containing 12–18 seeds.
Seeds: With fleshy endosperm. Dispersed by ants.
Vegetative reproduction: By bulbs.
Range: Europe (including Britain). Asia.
Uses: Flowers are useful source of early pollen for honey bees.

LODDON LILY (*Leucojum aestivum*)

General characters: Bulbous herb up to 2' high. Leaves all from base, long and narrow (up to $\frac{1}{2}''$ wide), sheathing at base. Flowers white, nodding, stalked, 2–7 together from a spathe at top of stout leafless stem. Perianth bell-shaped, of 6 equal petal-like segments, each tipped with a green spot. Stamens 6. Ovary inferior, 3-celled, with numerous ovules. Style simple.

Habitat: Wet meadows, wet places among willows.
Pollination: By bees.
Fruit: A capsule about 1" long.
Seeds: With fleshy endosperm. Often dispersed by water. Average weight: 0·05 gm.
Vegetative reproduction: By bulbs.
Range: Europe (including Britain). Asia.
Uses: No information.

BELLADONNA LILY (*Amaryllis belladonna*)

General characters: Perennial herb up to $2\frac{1}{2}'$ high. Rootstock bulbous. Leaves 6–10, arising from crown of bulb, strap-shaped, up to 2' long and $1\frac{1}{2}''$ broad, in S. Africa appearing after flowers. Flowers rose-pink, up to 4" long, stalked, in umbels at top stout leafless stems. Perianth with short tube, the 6 segments (2 whorls) cohering for most of their length, their pointed tips bent back. Stamens 6. Ovary inferior, 3-celled. Style slender, with a small 3-lobed stigma.

Habitat: Lower slopes of hills and mountains.
Fruit: A capsule containing few seeds.
Seeds: With fleshy endosperm. Large, rounded, fleshy.
Vegetative reproduction: By bulbs.
Range: S. Africa.
Uses: No information.
Special comments: In S. Africa flowers very freely after fires.

WILD DAFFODIL (*Narcissus pseudonarcissus*)

General characters: Bulbous herb up to 1' high. Leaves 2–4 from base, narrow (up to $\frac{1}{2}''$ wide), bluish-green, erect at first. Flower yellow, drooping, solitary from thin dry spathe at top of erect stem. Perianth with tube about 1" long and 6 pale yellow segments inside which is deep yellow trumpet-shaped corona. Stamens 6. Ovary inferior, 3-celled, with numerous ovules. Style simple.

Habitat: Damp woods and copses, pastures, river-banks.

Pollination: By humble-bees (*Bombus* species).

Fruit: A capsule up to 1" long. Opens by 3 valves.

Seeds: With fleshy endosperm. Seed-coat black, shiny. Often wind-dispersed.

Vegetative reproduction: By "daughter" bulbs produced in axils of foliage leaves.

Range: Europe (including Britain).

Uses: No information.

Special comments: Contains alkaloid narcissine which causes death in mammals (cattle, goats and pigs have been poisoned by the plant).

Order IRIDALES

Family IRIDACEAE

BLUE-EYED GRASS (*Sisyrinchium bermudiana*)

General characters: Erect perennial herb up to $1\frac{1}{2}'$ high. Leaves from base of plant, narrow, grass-like, sheathing at base. Flowers blue, about $\frac{3}{4}''$ across, stalked, 2–4 together in cluster at top winged and flattened stem, with 2 pointed bracts at their base. Perianth with very short tube and 6 spreading petal-like segments. Stamens 3, filaments united for most of their length. Ovary inferior, 3-celled, with numerous ovules. Style 3-lobed, the branches undivided.

Habitat: Moist meadows, woods, open grassy places.

Pollination: Cross-pollination by insects. Failing this, self-pollination takes place.

Fruit: A small capsule.

Seeds: With copious endosperm. Rounded, blackish, wrinkled.

Vegetative reproduction: By rhizome.

Range: Europe (including Britain). Eastern N. America.

Uses: No information.

GLADDON (*Iris foetidissima*)

General characters: Perennial herb up to $2\frac{1}{2}'$ high. Leaves narrow, flattened, evergreen. Flowers purplish or yellowish, about 3" across,

2–3 arising from spathe at top of stout unbranched stem. Perianth with short tube, divided above into 6 segments, 3 outer narrowly egg-shaped and bent downwards, 3 inner shorter, narrower, erect. Stamens 3, attached to base of outer segments. Ovary inferior, 3-celled, with numerous ovules. Style 3-lobed, the petal-like branches paddle-shaped and 2-lobed at tip.

Habitat: Woodlands on basic soils, hedgebanks, calcareous dunes.

Pollination: Cross-pollination by humble-bees.

Fruit: A club-shaped capsule containing about 30 seeds. Opens from top into 3 valves.

Seeds: With copious endosperm. Spherical. Orange-red. Average weight: 0·048 gm. Dispersed by birds.

Range: Europe (including Britain). N. Africa.

Uses: No information.

Special comments: An irritant poison.

PURPLE CROCUS (*Crocus purpureus*)

General characters: Perennial herb. Leaves in small tuft, narrow. Flowers showy, purple or white, solitary within the leaves, nearly stalkless on the corm. Perianth with long slender tube, bell-shaped above, with 6 nearly equal segments. Stamens 3. Ovary inferior, subterranean, 3-celled, with numerous ovules. Style 3-lobed, the orange branches shortly toothed.

Habitat: Meadows.

Pollination: Cross-pollination by insects.

Fruit: A long-stalked capsule.

Seeds: With copious endosperm.

Vegetative reproduction: By corms.

Range: Europe.

Uses: No information.

GLADIOLUS (*Gladiolus illyricus*)

General characters: Erect perennial herb up to 3' high. Leaves pointed, up to 1' long and $\frac{1}{2}$" wide. Flowers red, showy, stalkless, each between 2 pointed bracts, 3–8 in a 1-sided spike at top of unbranched stem. Perianth $1\frac{1}{2}$" long, with short curved tube and 6 long-clawed segments. Stamens 3, with large anthers. Ovary inferior, 3-celled, with numerous ovules. Style 3-lobed, branches undivided but suddenly expanded and egg-shaped at tips.

Habitat: Heaths, woods.

Pollination: Cross-pollination by insects.

Fruit: A 3-lobed capsule about $\frac{3}{4}$" long. Splits slowly from top.

Seeds: With copious endosperm. Flattened, winged. Wind-dispersed.

Vegetative reproduction: By offsets produced from corm.

Range: Europe (including Britain).

Uses: No information. (Corms of several other *Gladiolus* species used as food.)

Order DIOSCOREALES

Family *DIOSCOREACEAE*

WILD YAM (*Dioscorea villosa*)

General characters: Twining vine with slender stem 6–15' long. Leaves alternate, lower ones often opposite or whorled, broadly egg-shaped, gradually tapering to apex, up to 6" long and 4" wide, on long slender stalks. Flowers greenish-yellow, small, inconspicuous, unisexual, males in drooping panicles, females in drooping racemes. Perianth 6-lobed. Stamens 6 or 3. Ovary 3-celled, each cell with 2 ovules. Styles 3.

Habitat: Moist thickets.

Fruit: A yellowish-green 3-valved, 3-winged capsule.

Seeds: With endosperm. Flat. Thin-winged.

Range: N. America.

Uses: Dried rhizome used medicinally (expectorant and diaphoretic).

Special comments: Yams, including *Dioscorea alata*, White Yam, and *D. rotundata*, White Guinea Yam, are cultivated in wetter parts of tropics, their tubers, important sources of starch, being cooked as vegetable.

BLACK BRYONY (*Tamus communis*)

General characters: Perennial herb. Stems annual, twining, angled, up to 12′ long. Leaves alternate, heart-shaped, finely pointed, dark green and glossy, stalked. Flowers small, yellowish-green, unisexual, sexes on different plants, in racemes from leaf-axils. Perianth bell-shaped, with short tube and 6 narrow spreading lobes. Male flower with 6 stamens. Female flower with inferior, 3-celled ovary, with 2 ovules in each cell. Style 1, divided above into 3 two-lobed stigmas.

Habitat: Hedges, scrub, woodland margin.

Pollination: By insects.

Fruit: A globose red berry containing 1–6 seeds.

Seeds: With endosperm. Globose, pale yellow, wrinkled. Average weight: 0·016 gm. Dispersed by birds which eat the fruits.

Vegetative reproduction: By production of buds by fragments of tuber.

Range: Europe (including Britain). N. Africa. Asia Minor.

Uses: No information.

Order **AGAVALES**

Family *AGAVACEAE*

SOAPWEED (*Yucca glauca*)

General characters: Evergreen shrub with very short woody stem. Leaves all basal, stiff, sharp-pointed, narrow but up to 3′ long, with numerous thread-like fibres on margin. Flowers white, large (up to 3″ broad), nodding, in a raceme up to about 4′ long. Perianth bell-shaped, of 6 egg-shaped segments. Stamens 6. Ovary superior, 3-celled, ovules numerous. Style short, slender.

Habitat: Dry soil of deserts.

Pollination: Yucca flowers pollinated by the moth *Pronuba* which lays eggs in ovary, and then presses a ball of pollen into stigma. *Pronuba* caterpillars feed on young Yucca seeds, but plenty are left to mature and reproduce the plant.

Fruit: An oblong capsule 2–3″ long.
Seeds: With fleshy endosperm. Numerous, flattened.
Range: Western U.S.A. Mexico.
Uses: Fruits cooked and eaten by Indians. Leaves made into brooms. (From other Yuccas Indians have obtained leaf-fibres for rope, matting, and coarse cloth; buds and fruit for food; roots for making "soap.")

New Zealand Flax (*Phormium tenax*)

General characters: Perennial herb up to 15′ high. Leaves all arising from short rhizome, up to 9′ long and 5″ broad, sword-shaped, tough and leathery, dark green above, margins and midrib usually bordered with a coloured line (tint varies, but is often reddish or orange), tip sometimes bent back and split. Flowers often dull red (colour varies), 1–2″ long, on jointed stems, arranged on branches of a many-flowered panicle at top of tall leafless stem. Perianth tubular, of 6 segments joined at base, 3 outer erect and pointed, 3 inner longer and sometimes curved at tip. Stamens 6, inserted at base of perianth segments. Ovary superior, 3-celled, with numerous ovules. Style simple, slender.
Habitat: Lowland swamps (in New Zealand).
Pollination: Cross-pollination by nectar-feeding birds (tui, bellbird). Visited by honey bees in Britain.
Fruit: A 3-valved capsule 2–4″ long.
Seeds: With fleshy endosperm. Numerous, oblong, flattened, with shining black seed-coat.
Vegetative reproduction: Propagated by bulbils.
Range: New Zealand. Cultivated in tropics and elsewhere.
Uses: Leaves yield strong fibres used for sheeting, sacking, nets.

Century Plant (*Agave deserti*)

General characters: Densely tufted stemless perennial up to 15′ or more high. Leaves in basal rosette, fleshy, persistent, grey-green, tri-angular-lance-shaped, up to 1½′ long, edged with short pale prickles, with dark spine at apex. Flowers numerous, fleshy, yellow, up to 2″ long, in panicle at top of tall leafless stem arising from centre of basal rosette. Perianth of 6 narrow petal-like segments partially united into short tube. Stamens 6. Ovary inferior, 3-celled, ovules numerous (axile). Style 1, awl-shaped. Stigma 3-lobed.
Habitat: Rocky slopes and other dry places in deserts.
Fruit: An oblong capsule up to 2″ long.
Seeds: With fleshy endosperm. Numerous, black, thin, flat.
Vegetative reproduction: By numerous suckers (forms large colonies).
Range: S.W. United States. Mexico.
Uses: Base of leaves were roasted and eaten by Indians.

Order **PALMALES**

Family *PALMAE*

Coconut Palm (*Cocos nucifera*)

General characters: Slender tree 60–100' high with trunk often gradually curved from base. Leaves forming a cluster or crown at top of trunk, very large, up to 20' long, pinnate with many long narrow lance-shaped leaflets. Flowers small, unisexual, both sexes on same tree, arranged along numerous branches of inflorescence 5–6' long which is at first enclosed in sheathing spathe that eventually splits open. Perianth double (3 sepals, 3 petals). Female flowers usually solitary at base of branches of inflorescence, with superior 3-celled ovary (each cell with 1 ovule). Male flowers numerous, on upper part of inflorescence branches, with 6 stamens.

Habitat: Sandy soils of coastal regions and islands. Also cultivated inland.

Pollination: Cross-pollination by insects and wind. Apparently self-pollination is also sometimes possible in certain varieties.

Fruit: A large drupe containing 1 seed surrounded by hard woody endocarp ("shell"), a thick fibrous mesocarp, and thin tough outer

skin (epicarp). Distributed by the sea, in which it floats for great distances without injury, outer skin being impervious to salt-water.

Seeds: Large. Consists of very thin seed-coat, thick layer of white endosperm, very small embryo and "coconut milk," the milky fluid or sap found in the cavity of the endosperm.

Range: Wet tropics and subtropics.

Uses: Copra (dried endosperm) yields up to 60-65% coconut oil, which is used in production of soap, margarine, cooking fats, chocolate and cosmetics. Cake, residue after extraction of oil, is fed to animals. Coir, brownish fibres of mesocarp, made into mats, matting and ropes. Endocarp or "shell" burnt to produce charcoal. In tropics great use is made of coconuts for food and drink. Sugar and intoxicating drink are produced from sap of unopened flowering spathe. Leaves and trunks provide building materials for houses.

Special comments: Coconut palm starts to bear fruit when 5–7 years old (about 10 coconuts), produces 60–80 "nuts" at full growth (30 years), and has a useful life of 60–80 years.

DATE PALM (*Phoenix dactylifera*)

General characters: Slender tree up to 100′ high. Leaves forming a crown at top of main stem, 10–20′ long, pinnate with numerous rigid blue-green lance-shaped leaflets which are reduced to sharp spines at base of leaf-stalk. Leaf-stalk stout, rigid, fibrous, with expanded base sheathing stem. Flowers unisexual, sexes on different trees, in much-branched panicles that are enclosed at first in sheathing spathes. Male flowers fragrant, small, with cup-shaped calyx (3 outer perianth segments), 3 thick and leathery inner perianth segments and 6 stamens. Female flowers with small cup-shaped calyx (3 outer perianth segments), 3 small circular inner perianth segments and an ovary of 3 free carpels, each with short hooked stigma.

Habitat: Semi-arid desert areas.

Pollination: Growers assist pollination by placing a piece of male inflorescence among female flowers.

Fruit: A 1-seeded berry 1–3″ long. Colour (reddish-brown, yellow), shape, flavour, sugar content (60–70%) and consistency (soft, semi-soft, dry) vary according to variety (thousands of varieties occur). Besides sugar, fruit contains vitamins A, B_1, and B_2, calcium, phosphorus, iron and potassium.

Seeds: With hard endosperm. Seed-coat papery. Cylindrical, narrow, up to 1″ long.

Vegetative reproduction: By suckers which develop at base of tree.

Range: Dry arid tropics and subtropics.

Uses: Fruit are important food in hot dry regions of world. Elsewhere they are used in cooking or as dessert fruit. Leaves and stems used as building materials and fuel. Leaves and leaf-fibres made into ropes, mats and baskets. Intoxicating drink prepared from sap of flowering spathes.

Special comments: Cultivated for a very long time.

OIL PALM (*Elaeis guineensis*)

General characters: Erect tree up to 60' high, those grown in plantations being much shorter. Trunk stout, rough, leafless. Leaves large, forming a crown at top of stem, pinnate with many long narrow leaflets. Leaf-stalk strong, flattened, often with spines at base, clasping stem at base. Flowers unisexual, both sexes on same plant, arranged in inflorescences protected by leaf-bases, males in axils of upper leaves, females in axils of lower leaves. Male inflorescence (spadix) enclosed at first in sheathing spathe which opens to reveal male flowers embedded in tissue of the numerous branches. Male flower grey, with 6 separate oblong perianth segments and 6 stamens whose filaments are united at base. Female inflorescence much-branched, compact, somewhat rounded. Female flower subtended by a long-pointed yellowish-green bract and with 6 thin perianth segments and a 1-celled 1-ovuled superior ovary.

Habitat: In the wild state in tropical rain forests. Cultivated in plantations.

Fruit: A drupe 1–2" long. Oval with pointed apex. A thin leathery coloured (yellow, brown, reddish, varying according to variety) outer skin (epicarp) surrounds thick fibrous mesocarp which encloses the hard layer (endocarp) protecting seed. Mesocarp contains 50–65% palm oil, one of the world's principal vegetable oils. Fruit develop in large heavy bunches.

Seeds: With endosperm. Seeds contain 44–53% palm kernel oil.

Range: Native of tropical West Africa, but now extensively cultivated in Africa, S.E. Asia, Brazil.

Uses: Palm oil, an important foodstuff in Africa, now widely used in manufacture of soap and edible fats and in tin-plating. Palm kernel oil used mainly as edible fat.

Special comments: Many varieties cultivated.

Order **PANDANALES**

Family *PANDANACEAE*

KIE-KIE (*Freycinetia banksii*)

General characters: Climbing or scrambling shrub. Stems long, with numerous branches and aerial roots. Leaves long and narrow (up to 3' long and 1" broad), tapering to a fine point, sheathing at base,

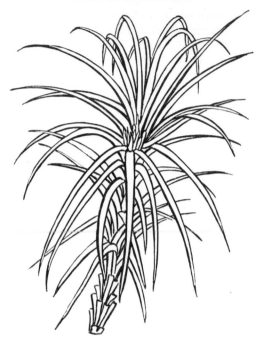

leathery, keeled, with small spines on margins and midrib, crowded towards tips of shoots. Flowers minute, without perianth, unisexual, with sexes on different plants, crowded in cylindrical spadices which are enclosed within leafy bracts and arranged in small clusters at tips of branches. Male flower with several stamens and rudimentary ovary. Female flower with a small 1-celled ovary surrounded by minute infertile stamens (staminodes), ovaries densely arranged on fleshy axis of spadix.

Habitat: Forests.

Fruit: The somewhat fleshy berries occur in an oblong mass (syncarp).

Seeds: With fleshy endosperm. Minute. Numerous.

Range: New Zealand.

Uses: Leaves plaited into baskets by Maoris. Leaf-fibres have been made into clothing and mats. Sweet fleshy bracts surrounding spadices are eaten.

Order **CYCLANTHALES**

Perennials, climbers, palm-like herbs or small shrubs growing mainly in tropical America. Flowers small, unisexual, densely arranged on the fleshy axis of a spadix. Perianth often absent. Stamens numerous. Ovary 1-celled, with numerous ovules. Multiple fruit fleshy, consisting of many berries. Seeds with endosperm.

Uses: Leaves of several *Carludovica* species used for thatching. Other species yield fibres or are made into brooms. Young leaves of *C. palmata* made into Panama hats.

Order **HAEMODORALES**

Family *HAEMODORACEAE*

GOLD-CREST (*Lophiola aurea*)

General characters: Perennial herb up to $2\frac{1}{2}'$ high. Leaves alternate, narrow. Flowers in cymes at top of stems. Perianth persistent, yellow within, shortly hairy outside, the 6 lobes much longer than perianth-tube. Stamens 6. Ovary superior (sometimes $\frac{1}{2}$-inferior), 3-celled.

Habitat: Moist pinelands and acid bogs.

Fruit: A long-beaked 3-valved capsule.

Seeds: With abundant endosperm.

Range: S.E. United States.

Uses: No information.

Order BURMANNIALES

Annual or perennial herbs, including many saprophytes with leaves reduced to scales. Perianth tubular, often 3- or 6-lobed. Stamens 3 or 6. Ovary inferior, 1- or 3-celled, with numerous ovules. Fruit a capsule. Seeds with scanty or no endosperm, minute, numerous.

Uses: No information.

Order ORCHIDALES

Family *ORCHIDACEAE*

LADY'S SLIPPER (*Cypripedium calceolus*)

General characters: Erect perennial herb up to $1\frac{1}{2}'$ high. Leaves broadly egg-shaped, pointed, sheathing, up to 5 on the stem. Flowers large (about 2″ across), nodding, solitary (rarely 2) at top of unbranched stem. Sepals 3, brownish-purple, egg- to lance-shaped upper sepal opposite the lip, other sepals joined nearly to tip and directed downwards behind the lip. Petals 3, the lip ("slipper") yellow and bag-like, 2 side petals brownish-purple, narrow, often spirally twisted. Fertile stamens 2. Pollen-grains granular, separate. Ovary inferior, 1-celled, with numerous ovules. Fertile stigmas 3.

Habitat: Woods and thickets on calcareous soil and rocky limestone slopes.

Pollination: Cross-pollination by small bees (*Andrena* species).

Fruit: A capsule which splits lengthwise.

Seeds: Without endosperm. Very numerous. Very minute.

Vegetative reproduction: By growth from separated branches of the rhizome.

Range: Europe (including Britain). N. Asia.

Uses: No information. (Dried rhizomes of 2 N. American *Cypripedium* species used medicinally as nerve stimulant and antispasmodic.)

Special comments: Lady's Slipper has suffered badly from activities of plant collectors and gardeners. In certain parts of Europe plant now protected by law.

EARLY PURPLE ORCHID (*Orchis mascula*)

General characters: Erect perennial herb up to 2′ high. Leaves 4–8, broad and blunt, spotted or unspotted, sheathing. Flowers purplish to pinkish (sometimes white) with coloured bracts in a loose spike 2–10″ long. Upper sepal and 2 side petals forming a hood. 2 side sepals bent back. Lip shortly 3-lobed, with a long cylindrical spur behind. Stamen 1, with 2 club-shaped pollinia (pollen masses), each attached to 1 of the 2 viscidia (viscid bodies). Fertile stigmas 2.

Habitat: Chalk downs, sea-cliffs, rock ledges, sand-dunes, oakwoods.
Pollination: Cross-pollination by bees and humble-bees.
Fruit: An erect capsule.
Seeds: Without endosperm. Minute.
Range: Europe (including Britain). N. Africa. N. & W. Asia.
Uses: Tubers are source of Salep, fine powder used as food and medicine.

DROOPING LADY'S TRESSES (*Spiranthes romanzoffiana*)

General characters: Erect perennial herb up to 2' high. Leaves narrow, pointed, erect, lower ones up to 4" long but upper ones on flowering stem short. Flowers white or creamy white, fragrant, the 3 spirally twisted rows forming a dense flower-spike. Upper sepal and 2 petals joined, forming the upper half of the perianth-tube, whose lower part consists of the trough-shaped lip. 2 side sepals joined below and sheathing base of lip. Fertile stamen 1. Pollinia 2, each consisting of 2 thin "leaves" of pollen-grains. Fertile stigmas 2.

Habitat: Wet boggy places, grassy meadows, hard wet peat, stony lake shores.

Pollination: Cross-pollination by insects (bees and humble-bees in Canada).

Fruit: A capsule covered with glandular hairs.

Vegetative reproduction: By separation from parent plant of small plants developed from lateral buds.

Range: Europe (found only in Ireland, Devon, and a few of the Scottish western isles). N. America.

Uses: No information.

VANILLA ORCHID (*Vanilla planifolia*)

General characters: Perennial herb climbing by means of adventitious roots. Stems green, succulent, brittle, reaching a great height (in cultivation they are trained over supports). Leaves alternate, thick, fleshy, stalkless, oblong, pointed, up to 9″ long and 2″ broad. Flowers greenish-yellow, stalked, each with a small pointed bract, in dense inflorescences 3–4″ long. Outer perianth segments ("sepals") 3, narrow, pointed, 2″ long. Inner perianth segments ("petals") 3, the 2 lateral segments narrow and pointed, lower segment rolled into a trumpet-shaped lip. Stamen 1.

Habitat: Tropical rain forests and islands.

Pollination: Cross-pollination by bees and humming-birds in Mexico. Elsewhere growers have to pollinate flowers by hand.

Fruit: A capsule 6–9″ long which splits open into 2 valves.

Seeds: Numerous, minute, black, embedded in dark oily material.

Vegetative reproduction: Propagated by stem cuttings.

Range: Central America. Java. Madagascar. Other parts of tropics.

Uses: Vanilla, which is used to flavour sweets, ice cream, and cakes and employed in perfumery, is prepared by fermenting unripe fruits ("vanilla beans").

FEN ORCHID (*Liparis loeselii*)

General characters: Erect perennial herb up to 9″ high. Leaves 2, broadly lance-shaped, pointed (broader and blunt in variety *ovata*), shining, sheathing at base. Flowers small, dull yellowish-green, 4–12 (sometimes more) in a loose raceme. Sepals and petals narrow, spreading. Lip broad, pointing upwards. Fertile stamen 1, lid-like, forming a lid on top of column, soon falling. Pollinia with waxy pollen.

Habitat: Fens, edges of lakes and pools, damp hollows of coastal sand-dunes.

Pollination: Authorities differ on this, some stating that self-pollination is usual, others that cross-pollination is brought about by insects.

Fruit: An erect spindle-shaped capsule.

Vegetative reproduction: By separation of new plants developed from pseudobulbs.

Range: Europe (including Britain). N. America.

Uses: No information.

Division GLUMIFLORAE

Perianth much reduced or represented by minute scales.

Order JUNCALES

Family *JUNCACEAE*

SOFT RUSH (*Juncus effusus*)

General characters: Erect perennial herb growing in tufts up to 4′ high. Leaves (often referred to as "stems") long, narrow, cylindrical. Flowers in cymes clustered at the top of an erect stem which continues above as a bract. Fresh flowering stems smooth, glossy, with numerous fine striations and containing continuous soft pith. Individual flower with 2 pointed bracts at base and consisting of 6 sharply pointed perianth segments in 2 whorls, 3 stamens, and an egg-shaped ovary with 3 styles.

Habitat: Wet meadows, damp woods, margins of ponds and streams, bogs.

Pollination: Wind-pollinated. Also said to be pollinated by insects. Self-pollination occurs in Germany, sometimes in closed flowers.

Fruit: A glossy capsule containing numerous seeds.

Seeds: With starchy endosperm. Small, yellowish. Become sticky when wet. Dispersed by animals and wind. Average weight: 0·000013 gm.

Vegetative reproduction: By radial growth of tufts.

Range: North Temperate Zone. Asia. S. America. Africa. Australia. New Zealand.

Uses: Stems made into mats and matting. Pith used for wicks.

HAIRY WOODRUSH (*Luzula pilosa*)

General characters: Erect tufted perennial herb up to 1′ high. Leaves mostly from base, grass-like, narrow, fringed with long white hairs. Flowers shining brown, single or in pairs in loose cymes. Perianth of 6 pointed segments. Stamens 6. Ovary 1-celled with 3 ovules. Stigmas 3.

Habitat: Woods. Hedges.

Pollination: Wind-pollinated.

Fruit: A 1-celled capsule containing 2–3 seeds.

Seeds: With starchy endosperm. Smooth, shiny, with a hooked appendage. Dispersed by ants.

Vegetative reproduction: By stolons.

Range: Europe (including Britain). N. America.

Uses: No information.

Hairy Woodrush (*Luzula pilosa*)

Order **CYPERALES**

Family *CYPERACEAE*

Sedge (*Cladium mariscus*)

General characters: Coarse perennial herb up to 6' high. Leaves ever-green but often with withered tips, long and narrow, somewhat bluish, hard, with rough toothed margins and keel. Flowers without perianth, each in the axil of a small bract (glume) and usually consisting of 2 stamens and a 1-celled 1-ovuled ovary with 3 stigmas. Flowers grouped in brown spikelets which are themselves arranged in branched inflorescences at top of tall hollow stems.

Habitat: Lakes and ponds (shallow water). Fens.

Pollination: Wind-pollinated.

Fruit: A 1-seeded nut with thick outer covering. Floats for 15 months or more. Also dispersed by adhesion to feet of birds.

Seeds: With endosperm.

Vegetative reproduction: By creeping rhizome.

Range: Widely distributed in temperate and some tropical regions.

Uses: Leaves used for thatching.

SEDGE (*Cladium mariscus*)

BOG-RUSH (*Schoenus nigricans*)

General characters: Tufted perennial herb up to 2′ high. Leaves narrow, stiff, mostly arising near base of plant. Each flower in axil of a bract (glume) and comprising a perianth of several bristles, 3 stamens, and a 1-celled 1-ovuled ovary (3 stigmas). Flowers in small spikelets which are grouped at top of stiff stems in dark brown or blackish heads each of which has 2 broad bracts at its base.

Habitat: Bogs and other damp places, especially near the sea.

Pollination: Wind-pollinated.

Fruit: A small shiny nut. Floats for 2 days.

Seeds: With endosperm.

Range: Northern hemisphere.

Uses: No information.

SEA CLUB-RUSH (*Scirpus maritimus*)

General characters: Perennial herb up to 5′ high. Leaves long, narrow, pointed. Flowers in axils of bracts (glumes), each with a perianth of 1 or a few bristles, 3 stamens and a 1-celled 1-ovuled ovary (3 stigmas).

Flowers in reddish-brown spikelets which are clustered in branched inflorescences at top of triangular stems with leafy bracts at their base.

Habitat: Margins of tidal waters, muddy shores, in salt lakes and brackish ponds near sea.

Pollination: Wind-pollinated.

Fruit: A small shiny nut. Floats for at least 1 month. Also dispersed by birds (in mud on feet).

Seeds: With endosperm.

Vegetative reproduction: By runners produced from rhizome.

Range: Almost cosmopolitan.

Uses: No information.

COTTON GRASS (*Eriophorum angustifolium*)

General characters: Perennial herb up to 2′ high. Leaves narrow, mostly from base. Flower in axil of bract (glume) with perianth of numerous fine bristles (which grow long and cotton-like in fruit), 3 stamens and a 1-celled 1-ovuled ovary (3 stigmas). Flowers grouped in somewhat nodding spikes, one or several of which occur at top of stem.

Habitat: Wet peat, bogs, bog pools, fens.

Pollination: Wind-pollinated.

Fruit: A small blackish-brown nut. Wind-dispersed.

Seeds: With endosperm.

Vegetative reproduction: By rhizomes.

Range: Europe (including Britain). N. America.

Uses: No information.

WOOD SEDGE (*Carex sylvatica*)

General characters: Tufted perennial herb up to 2′ high. Leaves long and narrow, sheathing at base. Flowers unisexual, sexes on same plant. Spike at top of slender stem contains numerous male flowers, each with a glume and 2–3 stamens. Arising from axils of bracts below male spike are long-stalked spikes containing female flowers, each with a glume, and a 1-celled 1-ovuled ovary enclosed within a sac (perigynium). Style 3-lobed (stigmas 3).

Habitat: Woods.

Pollination: Wind-pollinated.

Fruit: A small 3-sided nut.

Seeds: With endosperm.

Range: Europe (including Britain). N. America. N. Africa. Temperate Asia.

Uses: No information.

WOOD SEDGE (*Carex sylvatica*)

Order **GRAMINALES**

Family *GRAMINEAE*

MEADOW FESCUE (*Festuca pratensis*)

General characters: Erect perennial herb up to $3\frac{1}{2}'$ high. Leaves alternate. Leaf-blades narrow, tapering, pointed, hairless, with 2 narrow projections (auricles) at base. Leaf-sheaths sheathing stem, smooth. Flap at junction of sheath and blade (ligule) small, thin and dry. Individual flower comprising 2 minute pointed scales (lodicules), 3 stamens and a 1-celled 1-ovuled ovary (2 short styles with feathery stigmas). Floret consists of flower enclosed between 2 bracts (lemma and palea). Spikelet formed from 5–14 florets with bracts (glumes) at base. Flower-head at top of stem a loose panicle whose solitary or paired branches bear 1, 2 or several spikelets.

Habitat: Moist fertile loamy or heavy soils, water-meadows, pastures, roadsides.

Pollination: Wind-pollinated.

Fruit: A caryopsis. Enclosed in bracts (lemma and palea).

Seeds: With starchy endosperm. Average weight: 0·0017 gm.

Range: Europe (including Britain). N. America. S.W. Asia.

Uses: A valuable grass for grazing and hay-making.

Meadow Fescue (*Festuca pratensis*)

Meadow Barley (*Hordeum secalinum*)

General characters: Erect perennial herb up to 1½' high. Leaf-blades narrow, tapering to fine points, with short auricles at base. Lower leaf-sheaths hairy, others smooth. Ligules minute. Spikelets each of 1 floret, arranged in groups of 3 (middle one bisexual, others male or sterile) in dense spikes at top of slender stem. Lodicules 2, margins fringed. Glumes and lemma with bristle-like projections (awned).

Habitat: Meadows and pastures, often on moist heavy soils.

Pollination: Wind-pollinated.

Fruit: A caryopsis. Enclosed in bracts.

Seeds: With endosperm.

Range: Europe (including Britain). N. America. N. & S. Africa. Asia Minor.

Uses: No information. (Several important cereals, including barley, belong to genus *Hordeum*.)

REED (*Phragmites communis*)

General characters: Erect perennial herb up to 9' high. Leaf-blades long and narrow, flat, tough, with long fine points. Leaf-sheaths loose, overlapping. Ligule a ring of short hairs. Spikelets of 2–6 florets (lowest male, others bisexual and with long white silky hairs at base). Spikelets in large much-branched purplish panicle at top of stout stem. Lodicules 2, roughly oblong.

Habitat: Swamps, fen, shallow water of rivers, lakes.

Pollination: Wind-pollinated.

Fruit: A caryopsis. Contains compound starch grains. Wind-dispersed.

Seeds: With endosperm.

Vegetative reproduction: By creeping rhizomes and stolons.

Range: Almost cosmopolitan.

Uses: Stems used for thatching and also made into mats. Rhizomes eaten by American Indians. Stems and leaves sometimes used as stable litter.

CORD-GRASS (*Spartina townsendii*)

General characters: Stout erect perennial herb up to 4' high. Leaf-blades long and narrow, tapering and pointed, stiff. Leaf-sheaths smooth, overlapping. Ligule a ring of short hairs. Spikelets 1-flowered, arranged in stiff erect spikes, several of which form a panicle at top of stout stem. Lodicules absent.

Habitat: Coastal mud-flats.

Pollination: Wind-pollinated.

Fruit: With compound starch grains.

Seeds: With endosperm.

Vegetative reproduction: By rhizomes, portions of which are dispersed by the sea.

Range: Europe. N. & S. America. S. Africa. Australasia.

Uses: A valuable mud-binder used in land reclamation and for protecting foreshores from erosion.

Special comments: Known also as Rice-grass, *Spartina townsendii* is a hybrid between *S. alterniflora*, a N. American species, and *S. maritima*, a European plant. It was first noticed on mud-flats in Southampton Water in 1870.

CANARY GRASS (*Phalaris canariensis*)

General characters: Annual herb up to $3\frac{1}{2}'$ high. Leaf-blades long and narrow, rough, pointed. Upper leaf-sheaths inflated. Ligule thin, dry. Spikelets of 3 florets (lower 2 barren), arranged in erect egg-shaped panicle at top of stiff stem. Fertile floret with 2 pointed lodicules, ovary and 3 stamens.

Habitat: Cultivated and waste land.

Pollination: Wind-pollinated.

Fruit: With compound starch grains. Weight about 0·009 gm. Dispersed by birds.

Seeds: With endosperm.

Range: Native of western Mediterranean region. Now cultivated in Old and New World.

Uses: Fruits used as food for cage-birds.

SUGAR CANE (*Saccharum officinarum*)

General characters: Herb with thick erect (sometimes somewhat creeping) stems ("canes") 1–2″ in diameter and 8–15′ high. Leaf-blades long and pointed, often with sharp toothed edges. Flowers numerous, arranged in a woolly much-branched panicle (the "arrow") 1–2′ long. Spikelets surrounded by long silky hairs, arranged on secondary branches in pairs, 1 of each pair stalkless, the other borne on a stalk. Each spikelet with a pair of glumes (bracts) at its base, 2-flowered, lower floret barren (consisting simply of a sterile lemma or bract), upper floret bisexual, with a palea or bract, 1-celled ovary with triangular scales (lodicules) at its base, 2 styles with red feathery stigmas, and 3 stamens.

Habitat: Moist fertile soil.
Pollination: Wind-pollinated.
Fruit: A caryopsis.
Seeds: With starchy endosperm. Viable seed rarely produced. Minute, egg-shaped, yellowish-brown.
Vegetative reproduction: Propagated from stem cuttings ("sets").
Range: Cultivated in tropics and subtropics.
Uses: Stems yield sugar. Some sugar cane varieties used for forage.
Special comments: Many varieties in cultivation.

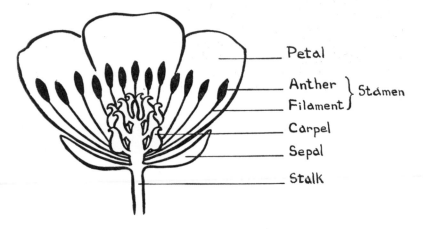

BUTTERCUP (*Ranunculus*): Half of flower.

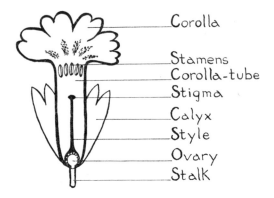

PRIMROSE (*Primula vulgaris*): Half of flower.

GLOSSARY

Achene: Small dry fruit not opening to release its single seed.

Alternate leaves: Not opposite one another.

Annual: Lasting one year or season.

Anther: Portion of stamen containing pollen.

Awned: With bristle-like projection.

Axil: Angle made by one part with another part (e.g. angle between leaf and stem).

Axile placentation: Ovules attached to central axis of ovary.

Beaked: Terminated by long pointed projection.

Berry: Succulent fruit with seeds immersed in pulp.

Biennial: Lasting two years or seasons.

Bisexual: With male and female parts present.

Bract: Modified leaf (leaf sometimes reduced to scale).

Bracteole: Small bract.

Bulb: Underground organ consisting of fleshy swollen leaf-bases and bud.

Bulbil: Small aerial bulb growing in a leaf-axil.

Bulbous: Growing from a bulb.

Calyx: Outermost whorl of a flower, composed of free or united sepals.

Capsule: Dry fruit which opens to release seeds.

Carpel: One of the units of which the female part of flower is composed.

Catkin: A crowded spike of flowers.

Chlorophyll: Green colouring matter.

Clawed: With narrowed base.

Corm: Short swollen underground stem.

Corolla: The second whorl of a flower (within the calyx), composed of free or united petals.

Cotyledon: Seed leaf.

Cross-pollination: Transference of pollen from one flower to the stigma of a different flower.

Cutting: Small portion of a shoot.

Cyme: A repeatedly branched inflorescence.

Deciduous tree or shrub: One that loses its leaves in autumn.

Dormancy: Resting condition.

Dormant: Resting.

Drupe: Fleshy fruit with seed or seeds surrounded by a hard stony layer.

Druplet: Small drupe.

Elliptic: Shaped like an ellipse.

Embryo: Rudiment of plant contained in the seed.

Endosperm: Nutritive tissue in the seed.

Epicalyx: "Extra calyx" surrounding the true calyx.

Epigeal germination: When cotyledons are pushed above the soil.

Epiphytic: Growing or supported on another plant.

Filament: Stalk of a stamen.

Follicle: A dry fruit opening along one side.

Free: Separate to the base.
Fruit: The mature ovary and ripe seeds contained in it.
Germinate: To begin to grow.
Gland: A small secreting organ.
Glandular: Provided with glands.
Grafting: The insertion of the base of a shoot into an incision in the stem of a rooted "stock" in order that union may take place.
Hybrid: A plant resulting from a cross between two different species.
Hybridize: To cross.
Hypogeal germination: When cotyledons remain under the soil.
Inferior ovary: With perianth inserted round the top of ovary.
Inflorescence: A cluster of flowers.
Involucre: A whorl of bracts surrounding or beneath a flower (or several flowers).
Latex: Milky juice.
Layering: Fixing branches (stolons) to the soil to encourage production of roots at the nodes.
Leaf-axil: Angle between leaf and stem.
Leaflet: Unit of a compound leaf.
Limb: Flattened expanded part of a corolla.
Lipped: Divided into lips or parts.
Mycorrhiza: An association of roots with a fungus ("fungus roots").
Nectar: Sweet sugary juice.
Nectary: Nectar-secreting organ.
Node: Point of insertion on the stem of leaf or leaves.
Nut: A hard fruit which does not open to release its single seed.
Nutlet: A little nut.
Opposite leaves: Paired at the same level on opposite sides of the stem.
Ovary: Female part of the flower enclosing the ovule or ovules.
Ovoid: Egg-shaped.
Ovule: The organ which develops into a seed after fertilization.
Palmate leaf: A compound leaf with more than three leaflets arising from the same point.
Panicle: A branched raceme.
Parasite: A plant which is attached to, and extracts food from, another plant (the host).
Parietal placentation: Ovules attached to walls of ovary.
Perennial: Living for more than two years.
Perianth: The calyx and corolla (especially when they cannot be distinguished).
Petal: One of the individual parts of the corolla.
Pinnate leaf: A leaf with leaflets arranged in two rows along a common stalk.
Pith: Soft tissue forming a central column in a stem.
Placentation: The arrangement of the ovules in the ovary.
Pollen: The fertilizing (male) grains in the anther.
Pollination: The transference of pollen from stamen to stigma.
Propagate: To multiply or increase.

Raceme: Unbranched inflorescence with stalked individual flowers.

Rhizome: An underground stem lasting more than one season.

Runner: Creeping stem rooting at the end and forming a new plant.

Samara: A winged fruit that does not open to release the seed.

Saprophyte: A plant which derives its food from decaying plant and animal remains.

Self-pollination: Transference of pollen from stamen to stigma in the same flower.

Sepal: One of the individual parts of the calyx.

Spathe: A large sheathing bract.

Spike: Unbranched inflorescence bearing flowers without stalks.

Stamen: Male organ of the flower (produces pollen).

Staminode: An infertile stamen.

Stigma: Tip of the style (surface which receives pollen).

Stipule: Outgrowth at base of leaf or leaf-stalk.

Stolon: Stem which touches soil and roots.

Style: A support frequently existing between ovary and stigma.

Subspecies (Ssp.): A subdivision of a species.

Sucker: A shoot arising from a root.

Superior ovary: With the perianth inserted round the base of the ovary.

Tendril: A thread-like climbing organ.

Terminal: At the tip or end.

Tuber: Swollen fleshy underground part of stem or root.

Umbel: An umbrella-shaped inflorescence.

Umbellate: Borne in umbels.

Umbellule: One of the small umbels of a compound umbel.

Unisexual: With one sex only.

Valve: Portion of a fruit which opens to release its seeds.

Variety: A subdivision of a species.

Vegetative reproduction: Formation of new plants from purely vegetative parts or organs.

Viable: Able to germinate.

Wind-pollination: Transference of pollen from stamen to stigma by wind.

INDEX